Lincolnshire
COUNTY COUNCIL

discover libraries

**This book should be returned on or before
the last date shown below.** SC1

Sᶜⁱ 01|14

27|02|15

24|02|16

To renew or order library books please telephone 01522 782010
or visit www.lincolnshire.gov.uk

You will require a Personal Identification Number.
Ask any member of staff for this.

D0552860

Belonging and Permanence:
Outcomes in long-term foster care and adoption

Nina Biehal, Sarah Ellison,
Claire Baker and Ian Sinclair

Published by British Association
for Adoption & Fostering
(BAAF)
Saffron House
3rd Floor, 6–10 Kirby Street
London EC1N 8TS
www.baaf.org.uk

Charity registration 275689 (England and Wales)
and SC039337 (Scotland)

British Library Cataloguing in Publication Data
A catalogue record for this book is available
from the British Library

ISBN 978 1 907585 01 2

Editorial project management by Shaila Shah, BAAF Publications
Designed by Helen Joubert Designs
Typeset by Avon DataSet Ltd, Bidford on Avon
Printed in Great Britain by TJ International
Trade distribution by Turnaround Publisher Services,
Unit 3, Olympia Trading Estate, Coburg Road,
London N22 6TZ

BAAF is the leading UK-wide membership
organisation for all those concerned with
adoption, fostering and child care issues.

Contents

List of tables

List of figures

Acknowledgements

In completing this study, the research team has benefited from the help and advice of many people. We would like to thank the Department for Children, Schools and Families for sponsoring this study and, in particular, Dr Caroline Thomas for her unfailing support throughout. We are also very grateful to our research advisory group for their advice throughout the course of the study. Thanks are due to Elaine Dibben, Julia Feast, Jenny Gwilt, Maureen Phillips, Professor Gillian Schofield, Dr Julie Selwyn and Namita Singh, and to Isabella Craig and her policy colleagues at the DCSF. Other academic and local authority colleagues also gave us valuable advice and support at different stages of the study, including Professor David Quinton, Professor John Triseliotis, Dr Beth Neil and Michael Upsall.

We would also like to thank academic colleagues at the Social Policy Research Unit and elsewhere who assisted with aspects of the initial analysis, including Dr Shalhevet Attar-Schwartz, Stefanie Buechner, Dr Ian Gibbs and Andrew Richards. Thanks, too, to Sally Baker, Jaqui Dally, Sam Silverman and Alison Vanes, who provided valuable help with interviewing or other data collection. Special thanks go to Dawn Rowley, who painstakingly edited the final manuscript.

We are very grateful to the many people in the local authorities that took part in this study who found time to give us their advice and assistance. We would particularly like to thank the managers and practitioners who took part in our focus groups and the social workers who completed our survey questionnaires.

Thanks are also due to those who helped us design our recruitment materials and questionnaires, including the looked after children's group with whom we spent an enjoyable afternoon and who gave us valuable advice on the design of our recruitment leaflets. Thanks, too, to Leeds Children's Rights Service, who were extremely helpful in facilitating this meeting with the children and to Andy Edwards Design, who designed the leaflets. Our thanks are also due to the foster carers and adoptive parents in our focus groups and reference groups, who helped us with the development of our research questions and the design of our survey questionnaires.

Above all, we would like to thank the children, foster carers and adoptive parents who took part in this study. We are very grateful to those who took part in our interviews and also to the carers and parents who completed our questionnaires. Without their willingness to share their experiences with us, this report could not have been written.

Notes about the authors

Nina Biehal is a professor at the Social Policy Research Unit (SPRU) at the University of York, where she directs SPRU's programme of research on social work with children and young people. She previously worked as a social worker and as a researcher at the universities of Leeds and Bradford. Her research focuses principally on children in foster and residential care, adolescents on the edge of care and on young offenders. She has completed studies of treatment foster care, outcomes for maltreated children who enter care, family support services for adolescents on the edge of care, leaving care and runaways from care, as well as research reviews on the reunification of looked after children and on allegations of abuse in foster care.

Ian Sinclair is a Professor Emeritus at the University of York. After a first degree in philosophy and ancient history, he worked in teaching, probation, social services, counselling and industrial and social research. He has a PhD from the London School of Economics and has done work on delinquency, elderly people and adult relationships. He was Director of research at the National Institute of Social Work and then Professor of Social Work and co-director of the Social Work Research and Development Unit at the University of York. His recent work has been on residential care and foster care for children.

Dr Claire Baker is Senior Policy Manager for the National Care Advisory Service (NCAS), part of young people's charity Catch22. Prior to this, she worked as a Research Fellow at the Social Work Research and Development Unit at the University of York, concentrating on children in and leaving care (particularly disabled children), children in foster care, and stability and permanence issues. She is co-author of a number of titles in this field, including *The Pursuit of Permanence: A study of the English child care system.*

Sarah Ellison has been a Senior Research Fellow at SPRU and previously at the Social Work Research and Development Unit, where she worked on the national evaluation of Sure Start. Her research has focused on foster care, youth justice and family support services. Her previous studies include evaluations of the Intensive Fostering pilot programme, family support services for adolescents on the edge of care and preventive services for young offenders.

The Adoption Research Initiative

This series brings together the research studies in the Adoption Research Initiative (ARI), a programme of research on adoption funded by the former Department for Children, Schools and Families (DCSF). It is designed to evaluate the impact of the Labour Government's adoption project, including the Adoption and Children Act 2002 and various related policy initiatives. The research initiative is examining how these objectives are being translated into local policies, procedures and practice.

There are seven studies within the Adoption Research Initiative. They address four broad themes: permanency planning and professional decision-making; linking and matching; adoption support; and the costs of adoption. They also complement other recently reported and current research on the full range of placements for looked after children, including kinship care, foster care, residential care, private fostering and return home.

More information on the Adoption Research Initiative is available at www.adoptionresearchinitiative.org.uk.

Published by BAAF:
- *Enhancing Adoptive Parenting: A test of effectiveness*, Alan Rushton and Elizabeth Monck, 2009
- *Linking and Matching: A survey of adoption agency practice in England and Wales*, Cherilyn Dance, Danielle Ouwejan, Jennifer Beecham and Elaine Farmer, 2010
- *Pathways to Permanence for Black, Asian and Mixed Ethnicity Children*, Julie Selwyn, David Quinton, Perlita Harris, Dinithi Wijedasa, Shameem Nawaz and Marsha Wood, 2010
- Special Guardianship

Executive summary

Aims of the study

This study addresses the key question of how best to meet the needs of children who cannot safely be reunited with their parents. It aims to answer two questions that follow from this:

- How successful are adoption and long-term foster care in providing security and permanence, and in promoting positive outcomes for children?
- How do children perceive the emotional and legal security and sense of permanence offered by different types of permanent placement?

To answer these questions, the study compared three types of permanent placement: adoption by strangers, adoption by carers and long-term foster care.

Study design

The study had five components:

- focus groups and interviews with managers, staff and foster carers in seven local authorities;
- a census of local authority administrative data on 374 children (the census sample);
- a postal survey of the carers/adoptive parrents and social workers of 196 children (the survey sample). All of these children had been in foster care in 1998/99 and, three years later, had still been living in the same foster placements (their "index" placements) or had been adopted by strangers or their foster carers;
- analysis of historical data on a sub-sample of 90 children in the survey sample. This group had been surveyed in the York studies of foster care five and eight years earlier;
- interviews with 37 children and their foster carers or adoptive parents.

Pathways through care

Our analysis of administrative data on the 374 children in our census sample showed that seven or more years after they entered their index foster placements:

- 45 per cent of the children in the study had left the care system through adoption (36 per cent), reunification with birth parents (less than five per cent) or residence orders (less than five per cent);
- 32 per cent were still settled in their long-term foster placement (our "stable foster care" group);
- 23 per cent had left their index foster placements after periods of three or more years (our "unstable care" group).

Our postal survey of carers/adoptive parents and social workers of the 196 children in our survey sample provided more comprehensive information about children's pathways.

- Twenty-two per cent of the children were fostered by relatives or looked after by them on residence orders.
- Over one-third of those who had left the care system by the time of our survey remained with their former foster carers, who had obtained adoption or residence orders for them. In total, therefore, 72 per cent of our survey sample had been settled with the same carers for seven or more years, either in stable, long-term foster placements or under a new legal order.
- One-quarter of the children in the survey sample were disabled; half of them had learning difficulties. Most were in stable foster placements or had been adopted by their former foster carers. Overall, there was no difference in the proportion of children who were disabled among those who were adopted and those in stable foster care (29 per cent of each group).

The pathways taken by children were associated with their age at last entry to care. Children adopted by strangers had last entered care significantly younger (mean age 1.5 years) than those adopted by carers (mean age 3.1 years), in stable foster care (mean age 3.9 years) or in the "unstable care" group (mean age 5.3 years).

What influenced decisions about adoption?

Children were more likely to be adopted if they had last entered care at a young age and lived in certain local authority areas. Nearly two-thirds of those adopted by strangers last entered care before they were one year old, as had half of those adopted by carers. Adoption was more likely if children had never been placed with relatives and if their face-to-face contact with birth parents had been discontinued.

The nature of any continuing relationships with birth families and a child's own wishes are important factors in determining whether or not adoption is in the child's best interests. The research also showed that some foster carers were reluctant to adopt the children they cared for due to fears that they might lose support. However, decisions about adoption may also be influenced by local policy, resources and practice cultures. It was clear from our focus groups that views varied as to which children would benefit from adoption.

Comparing emotional and behavioural difficulties

Just over one-third of the children who were adopted or in stable foster care had clinically significant total scores for emotional and behavioural difficulties. There was no significant difference in this respect between children in long-term foster care and those who had been adopted. In one sense this was a positive finding, as those children in our sample who were in stable foster care (all of whom had lived with their current carers for seven years or more) were doing no worse than those who were adopted. The corollary of this, however, is that the emotional and behavioural difficulties among the adopted children in our sample were such that a number of them were likely to have support needs similar to those of children in stable foster care. Children in our "unstable care" group had worse scores for emotional and behavioural difficulty on the Strengths and Difficulties Questionnaire (SDQ) than those in permanent placements.

For the sub-sample of 90 children on whom we had collected these measures five and eight years earlier, we found that, on average, scores on the SDQ showed little change over time. The severity of children's emotional and behavioural difficulties may therefore be determined largely by pre-placement adversities and the length of children's exposure to them.

Educational participation and progress

On a composite measure of participation and progress in education, the children in stable foster care were doing as well as those who were adopted. However, the "unstable care" group was doing significantly worse in terms of participation and progress in education. This issue is complex, as educational progress and participation were associated both with the severity of children's emotional and behavioural difficulties and with whether or not they were disabled. The key predictor of participation and progress in education was the severity of children's emotional and behavioural difficulties (as measured by the SDQ).

Comparing the stability of long-term foster care and adoption

Long-term foster care is intended to be permanent, but for many children it is not. Disruption rates for children in foster care compared unfavourably with those for children adopted. Just 13 per cent of the children who had been placed for adoption or adopted at any point in their lives had experienced the breakdown of an adoption/placement for adoption. Among the children in our survey sample who had not left the care system (or who had remained with their former foster carers on a new legal order), 28 per cent had left their index foster carers after placements lasting three or more years.

When comparing the stability of adoption and long-term foster care, it is difficult to compare like with like. Children in long-term foster placements generally enter these placements at a significantly older age than children enter adoptive placements. Previous research on both adoption and foster care has found a strong relationship between age at placement and the risk of disruption, so differences in disruption rates need to be interpreted in the light of differences in age at placement.

The children in our study who were adopted by strangers were significantly younger at the time of our survey than those in our long-term foster care and "unstable care" groups. Placements of older children are known to be more vulnerable to disruption, so this too makes it difficult for us to be sure that in comparing disruption rates we are comparing like with like.

What influenced placement stability?

Age at placement was also a key predictor of placement stability. Children in stable foster placements had entered their index foster placements at a mean age of 4.1 years, whereas those in the unstable care group had only begun their final episode of care at an average age of 5.3 years.

The severity of the children's emotional and behavioural problems also appeared to increase the risk of placement disruption. For a sub-sample of 90 children, we had collected data five and eight years before our survey. Comparing scores on measures completed by foster carers earlier in the children's lives, we found that the small group of children in our unstable care group already had significantly worse scores on our measure of emotional and behavioural difficulties (the SDQ) eight years earlier, compared to children who went on to experience stable foster care or be adopted.

There may also be carer-related reasons for placement disruption, although they may not be the sole reason. There may be an interaction between children's emotional and behavioural difficulties and carers' parenting style, which may increase the risk of placement breakdown. However, our qualitative data showed that those foster carers who persisted in caring for children despite their behavioural difficulties often felt a genuine love and a powerful commitment to them.

In a small number of cases, events in carers' lives, such as marital breakdown or bereavement, also contributed to placement disruption. Worryingly, for five of the children in our unstable care group, their previous long-term foster placements had ended when evidence of carer abuse or neglect had come to light. Among the sample as a whole, five per cent (10) of children were reported to have experienced abuse or neglect by former foster carers. Clearly, placement quality is as important as placement stability.

A large part of the difference found in stability rates is likely to be due to the fact that children who are adopted (by strangers) often enter care before they are one year old, thus reducing the length of their exposure to pre-care adversity. Long-term foster care is often, though not always, used for children who enter care at a later age and for whom placement outside the care system has not been planned or, if planned, has not been achieved.

Perceptions of belonging and permanence

Our interviews with children and their adoptive parents or foster carers explored perceptions of belonging and permanence. Many of the children adopted by strangers had been placed as infants and their primary identification was often with their adoptive families. Birth parents were psychologically present for the children, to varying degrees, but none of them had any direct contact with birth parents, although some were inquisitive about their birth relatives. These children appeared to feel emotionally secure in their adoptive families.

Children adopted by carers indicated a strong sense of belonging to their adoptive families. Although a few wondered about their birth parents, there was no apparent sense of divided loyalties at this stage in their lives. The fact that carer–child relationships were already strong before the adoption application was made contributed to the success of these carer adoptions.

Most of the cildren settled in long-term foster homes viewed their carers as parental figures and felt a strong sense of belonging to their foster families. The exclusive nature of some foster placements, where the severity of parental abuse or rejection meant there was no direct contact with birth parents, appeared to facilitate the children's sense of emotional security and belonging.

For another group of children, foster care was inclusive as they had relatively unproblematic face-to-face contact with birth parents. These children appeared able to reconcile the fact that they, in different senses, belonged to both a birth family and a substitute family. Although there was some ambivalence and anxiety on the part of some children or carers, the children appeared able to manage attachments to two families without too much inner conflict and generally seemed to feel a reasonable sense of emotional security, despite lacking the legal security afforded by adoption.

A third group of children in stable foster care were more obviously troubled by feelings of ambivalence, hurt and anger towards their birth parents. Although settled in their foster placements, complex feelings about their birth parents led them to feel a more qualified sense of belonging to their long-term foster families.

Implications for policy and practice

- This study shows that the experience of long-term, stable foster care may be very positive. Although it cannot give legal security, long-term foster care may provide emotional security and a sense of permanence to children. The problem remains, however, that although long-term foster care can offer permanence, in practice it may fail to do so. However, placement quality is as important as placement stability.

- Timely decision making and timely planning for permanence are essential to enable children to enter their permanent placements as early as possible. This may enhance both the likelihood of placement stability and, where it is in children's best interests, the chance of adoption. This has implications both for children's services and the courts.

- Carer adoption gives later-placed children a chance of adoption. It is important, where it is appropriate for the child, for carers to be encouraged and supported to obtain a legal order, for example, residence, special guardianship or adoption.

- It is encouraging that, in many respects, children in stable, long-term foster placements may do as well as those who are adopted. This is important, as adoption will not be appropriate for all children and not all children wish to be adopted. At the same time, it is discouraging that adopted children in the study were no less likely to have serious emotional and behavioural difficulties than those in stable foster care.

- For the children in our unstable care group, whose previous long-term foster placements had disrupted after three or more years, emotional and behavioural difficulties were particularly serious and had contributed both to placement instability and to poor integration and progress at school. In these circumstances, even high-quality substitute parenting may not easily produce substantial change, and support to children and carers is likely to be needed.

- Even if permanent adoptive or foster homes are found in which children experience loving and stable care, many children (and their carers or adoptive parents) are likely to need substantial ongoing support if they are to have a chance of realising their full potential.
- The age at which children are taken into care is a crucial determinant of their subsequent pathways. The likelihood of adoption may be influenced by local differences in policy and practice and some authorities may be more effective in planning for other permanent placements and in supporting these arrangements.
- Local policy makers and senior managers can help to shape practice through mechanisms set up to ensure effective decision making and planning for permanence. Policy decisions about the resources devoted to increasing and supporting adoption, or to supporting children and foster carers, clearly contribute to shaping the pathways of individual children. Other reasons for local variation in the use of permanent placements include the actions of local courts and local practice cultures, which may be harder to address.
- Children's needs may not be the only driver of decisions about looking after children, as local policy and practice in relation to thresholds for taking children into care may also play a part in shaping children's care pathways. Local thresholds may, in turn, be influenced not only by concern about resources but by the bleak view of the care system evident in much public and professional debate. Although there is clearly much that can be improved in relation to placement stability and outcomes, our findings show that these concerns about the quality of care may not necessarily apply to many children who settle in long-term foster care.
- A lack of confidence in the quality of care may lead to a philosophy of "last resortism" within children's services and the courts, which may leave some children unprotected or delay their inevitable entry to care. In these circumstances, delaying difficult decisions about entry to care, or delaying decisions about permanency, may mean that children lose their chance of adoption or, if adoption is not appropriate, of stable foster care.

1 Background to the study

Increasing the number of children adopted from care became a key policy aim early in the life of the 1997 Labour Government and culminated in the passing of the Adoption and Children Act 2002. However, it is unlikely that a single type of permanent placement – adoption – will be appropriate, or achievable, for all looked after children who cannot return to live with their families. Older children may be particularly hard to place and children from minority ethnic groups are under-represented among those adopted from care (see Thoburn *et al*, 2000; Frazer and Selwyn, 2005 for a summary). Equally, some children do not wish to be adopted. For the foreseeable future, other forms of permanent placement will need to be found for those children who cannot be, or do not wish to be, adopted by strangers.

This chapter provides a brief overview of the existing research on permanent placements and then outlines the aims of this study. The study provides important new information on the outcomes of adoption and long-term foster care, focusing not only on placement stability but also on a wider range of outcomes, including child mental health and participation in education. It compares patterns of birth family contact, perceptions of permanence, and agency support. These issues may not only be associated with outcomes but may also have some bearing on the readiness of carers or strangers to adopt children or, indeed, on the readiness of children to consider adoption.

Permanency planning and the use of adoption

During the 1970s, researchers highlighted the problem of children who "drifted" in long-term care due to a lack of attention to planning (Rowe and Lambert, 1973). During the same period, concern was expressed about the possible consequences of long-term care for the psychosocial development of children (Goldstein *et al*, 1973). In response to these concerns, the permanency planning movement emerged in the USA in the early 1970s and rapidly gained support in the UK. The permanency planning approach encouraged a focus on finding permanent homes for children who could not live with their birth families. In the USA, rehabilitation with families was the placement of choice but failing that, adoption was recommended (Maluccio and Fein, 1983). However, in the UK, the focus of the permanence movement was principally on adoption. Increasing interest in placing children who were older or who had special needs coincided with a decline, from the late 1960s onwards, in the number of babies available for adoption. The study, *Children Who Wait* (Rowe and Lambert, 1973), was hugely influential in the UK and had a major impact on the development of the Children Act 1975, which facilitated the adoption of children from care, both by strangers and by carers (Sellick and Thoburn, 1996). The practice of active planning for children in care began to take root in the 1980s, but British studies during this period nevertheless revealed that children continued to drift in care for lengthy periods of time without proper planning for their future (Department of Health and Social Security, 1985; Rowlands and Statham, 2009).

These concerns about drift have formed one element of the continuing conflict between protagonists representing two value positions in child care: the "state as parent" model and the "kinship defenders" (Fox Harding, 1991). Drift in care was of concern to protagonists in both camps and was used to lend weight to arguments both for more rapid decision making regarding permanent placement and also for greater attention to prevention and rehabilitation. As the 1970s progressed, public inquiries into child abuse scandals in the UK helped to tip the balance towards greater state intervention to remove children from families and the number of children in care rose until they reached a peak in 1980. However, with the passing of the Children Act 1989 there came a renewed emphasis on support for families to prevent the need for children to become looked after. In the years that followed, this emphasis was reinforced by an influential overview of research on child protection, which recommended a refocusing of social work services on support to families (Department of Health, 1995). Although attention continued to be devoted to child protection, the balance shifted somewhat from "child saving" to the defence of the birth family.

This shift had implications for the use of adoption, which was no longer high on the policy agenda during the 1980s and was not specifically dealt with by the Children Act 1989 (Lewis, 2004). However, by the early 1990s, concern about placement instability and poor outcomes for looked after children, together with scandals about abuse in care, contributed to renewed government interest in adoption. By this time, cumulative policy changes had led to changes in the nature of the care population, which now included a higher proportion of children with serious difficulties who were unlikely to be reunified with their parents. As a result, the proportion of children in care who stayed long term began to rise, leading to increased pressure on resources (Biehal, 2006). At the same time, there were growing concerns about a shortage of foster carers. Together, these developments contributed to the new policy emphasis, from the late 1990s, on adoption for looked after children. It is significant that, while acknowledging that it would not be appropriate for all children, adoption was referred to in *The Prime Minister's Review of Adoption* as the option that could provide "real permanence" for children (Performance and Innovation Unit (PIU), 2000).

Who is adopted?

It is well established that the likelihood of adoption decreases with age. Although the potential for placing older children has improved, finding adoptive placements for children over the age of five or six has remained problematic (Lowe *et al*, 2002; Thoburn, 2002; Sinclair *et al*, 2007). Influences on the likelihood of adoption may include the child's age, their age at entry into care and the seriousness of their emotional and behavioural difficulties (Lowe *et al*, 2002; Selwyn *et al*, 2006; Sinclair *et al*, 2007). As we shall see, professional views as to who is adoptable may also play a part. Young people from minority ethnic backgrounds are under-represented among those placed for adoption and appear harder to place (Lowe *et al*, 2002; Thoburn, 2002; Sinclair *et al*, 2007). While adults from minority ethnic communities may wish to provide care, some may find, for cultural reasons, that adoption is a step too far (Department for Education and Skills, 2005). Furthermore, the population has become so diverse that it has become increasingly difficult to provide "same race" placements, unless very broad ethnic categories are used (Selwyn and Wijedasa, 2009). Children with disabilities are also less likely to be placed for adoption, although they may be more likely to be adopted by their foster carers (Lowe *et al*, 2002; Sinclair *et al*, 2005c, 2007). Children's relationships and levels of contact with their birth families have also been identified as crucial factors influencing agency decisions about adoption (Lowe *et al*, 2002; Sinclair *et al*, 2005c).

Evidence from a study of children for whom adoption was recommended (Selwyn *et al*, 2006) suggests that the chance of adoption is also strongly influenced by avoidable delay. The researchers suggested that the chance of adoption may be missed either through the activities of the courts, or, more commonly, because social workers persist with plans for rehabilitation even after it has become apparent that these are not working.

Carer adoption

It has always been possible for foster carers to adopt children they have fostered (Thoburn *et al*, 1986). However, it is difficult to trace the extent to which adoption by carers has been used in practice and it is possible that the use of carer adoption, like other forms of permanent placement, may have varied over time. The professionalisation of foster care from the mid-1970s involved, among other things, a discouragement of "fostering with a view to adoption" and an emphasis on the different nature, and requirements, of foster and adoptive parenting. Nevertheless, foster carers have continued to adopt children whom they have fostered long term. But carer adoption appears to be a little-used form of permanence. A survey in the late 1990s found that foster carers accounted for just 13 per cent of all local authority adoptions, while government statistics for 2002/03 indicated that only 15 per cent of all looked after children adopted in England and Wales were adopted by their foster carers (Ivaldi, 2000; Department for Education and Skills, 2003).

Relatively little is known about the use and outcomes of carer adoption, which may offer a chance of adoption to children who are hard to place because of their age or other difficulties (Triseliotis, 2002). In keeping with this, the York foster care study found that carer adoption was almost the only likely route to adoption for children over six years old at placement. In that study, children adopted by carers were more likely to have a disability of some kind or to have learning, communication or behavioural problems. As a result, there had often been difficulties in getting the child adopted and, during the lengthy placement, carers and children had bonded (Sinclair *et al*, 2005c). Children adopted in this way tend to be older, with an average age at adoption of six years eight months compared to three years ten months for other children adopted from care (Department for Education and Skills, 2003).

A study of permanency planning found that policy as to whether foster carers should be allowed to adopt varied between local authorities. Overall, attachment to foster carers was one of the most frequently cited reasons for *not* considering adoption, so it is clear that adoption by foster carers was rarely considered (Lowe *et al*, 2002).

Where foster carers have been reluctant to pursue adoption or residence orders for children in their care, disincentives have tended to centre on the emotional and behavioural problems of children, the perceived need for ongoing social work support, the financial implications of this transition and, in relation to residence orders, the difficulties that may arise through sharing parental responsibility with birth parents (Schofield *et al*, 2000; Sinclair *et al*, 2005c).

There is little evidence on the outcomes of carer adoption. In the York outcome study (Sinclair *et al*, 2005c), children adopted by their foster carers had better scores on measures of attachment status than those adopted by strangers. There is also some evidence from the USA that carer adoptions have a better chance of success than stranger adoptions (Barth and Berry, 1988). This is likely to be because such adoptions only take place after placements have stabilised. The available English evidence is not conclusive, partly because the degree of benefit may depend on the point at which outcomes are measured. The Bristol study found that the benefits of carer adoption were more evident early on and that disruptions occurred later, but the number of carer adoptions in this sample was small (Selwyn *et al*, 2006).

Long-term foster care

Long-term foster care was the model on which the foster care service originated, and the one which predominated for most of the 20th century. Although the Children Act 1948 required social workers to work towards rehabilitating children with their birth families, in practice many remained in foster care long term (Schofield et al, 2000). The emergence during the 1970s of concerns about drift in care led to a questioning of the value of long-term care. From the late 1970s onwards, short-term task-centred fostering schemes began to develop and foster care became increasingly viewed as a short- to medium-term service, the aim of which was to return children to their birth families or prepare them for adoption. The drive to professionalise foster care involved a rejection of models of fostering in which carers took on a quasi-parental role that was exclusive of the birth family (George, 1970; Holman, 1975). By the 1980s, foster carers were being discouraged from claiming children as part of their families and excluding birth parents from children's lives, hence the change of nomenclature from foster parent to foster carer (Schofield et al, 2000).

However, reunification is not safe for all children and adoption may not be appropriate or feasible for all children either. Long-term foster care has continued to offer an alternative form of long-term care, albeit to less than a quarter of the population of looked after children at any point in time. One of its strengths may be its therapeutic role and its ability to offer children "normal" family life (Schofield, 2009). Nevertheless, studies have consistently pointed to the challenge of providing stability and continuity for looked after children in foster settings, and there have been concerns that children in long-term foster care may feel insecure and have a troubled sense of identity and belonging (Rowe et al, 1984; Packman and Hall, 1998; Shaw, 1998; Jackson, 2002).

A recent study has highlighted the contribution that long-term foster care may make to the progress of children with emotional, behavioural and relationship difficulties. The study followed up 52 children who were newly placed in long-term foster families, although some were in former short-term placements that had evolved into long-term ones and so were already well established in these families. One to four years after these long-term placements began, 60 per cent of the children were found to have made good progress in most aspects of their lives. Behavioural difficulties had diminished for some children, self-esteem was generally good and all were thought to have a sense of permanence within their foster families (Beek and Schofield, 2004). However, the York study of foster care was more cautious about the ability of long-term foster care to provide permanence, as less than one in six children remained with their original carers. Nevertheless, those whose placements had remained stable tended to view their foster homes as their family base. Some of these children and carers showed a strong mutual commitment, but other children felt somewhat ambivalent, troubled by an unfulfilled yearning for their birth families. The problem, the authors observed, was that although foster care can offer permanence, it is apparent from the statistics on placement stability that it often fails to do so (Sinclair *et al*, 2005c).

Comparing outcomes of adoption and foster care

A number of studies have compared the outcomes of adoption and foster care, but caution is needed in making such comparisons to ensure that we are comparing like with like. Much of the research evidence on outcomes for children who have been adopted comes from studies of children adopted in infancy, whereas children in long-term foster placements have generally arrived in these placements at an older age (Howe, 1998). Rushton's review of research on adoption identified only a dozen studies of the outcomes of adoptive placements for later-placed children (Rushton, 2004).

Numerous studies have noted high levels of placement disruption for children in long-term foster care (Parker, 1966; George, 1970; Berridge and Cleaver, 1987). Adoptive placements have generally been found to be less vulnerable to disruption than long-term foster placements (Triseliotis, 2002; Rushton, 2004). However, in relation to older children, the evidence on the outcomes of adoption as against fostering is somewhat equivocal. In part this is because of a lack of baseline measures. Most studies of the outcomes of adoption as against the fostering of older children have taken placement disruption as their key outcome measure. Although some studies have used a wider range of outcome measures, researchers have not always been in a position to administer baseline measures (for example, Gibbons *et al*, 1995). The few studies that have looked at measures at two points in time (Rushton *et al*, 1988; Quinton *et al*, 1998) have included very few fostered children.

In relation to both adoption and foster care, the evidence points to a strong relationship between age at placement and the risk of disruption, so it is important to compare outcomes for children placed at similar ages (Berridge and Cleaver, 1987; Triseliotis *et al*, 1997; Thoburn *et al*, 2000; Rushton, 2004). Some adoption studies have focused on infant adoptions, often defined as adoptions taking place before the child is six months old, although in practice many of the children studied joined their families at the age of two to three months. Others have focused on late adoptions, defined in some studies as adoptions occurring before the child is six months old and in others before the child reaches the age of 12 months old. Research in the field of developmental psychology has indicated that outcomes for children in permanent placements of any kind, especially for those who enter these placements after the age of six months, are likely to be shaped by the interaction of the current placement environment with the effects of their genetic inheritance and their early adverse environment, although the child's temperament is also thought to play a part (Rutter, 2000).

It is also important to take account of length of follow-up when making comparisons between studies. Children with emotional and behavioural difficulties at placement or with a history of maltreatment are also more likely to experience placement breakdown (Barth and Berry, 1988; Rushton *et al*, 1988; Fratter *et al*, 1991; Gibbons *et al*, 1995; Quinton *et al*, 1998). Rates of disruption may be lower in samples that include higher proportions of children adopted by carers, as in the study by Barth and Berry. Disruption rates for children adopted by strangers when past infancy range from 10–50 per cent and average out at around 20 per cent, while for children who are fostered, they range from 17–50 per cent, again depending on age at placement and length of follow-up.

It has been argued that, once age at placement is held constant, breakdown rates for adoption and long-term foster care are not dissimilar (Sellick and Thoburn, 1996; Thoburn, 2005). However, these claims are based on the findings of a study of permanent placements for 1,100 children which were made by voluntary agencies (Fratter *et al*, 1991). The placements were all planned as permanent from the start, the children were matched with their carers and high-quality, permanence-focused social work support was provided. The findings on the similarity of stability rates may therefore apply in such conditions but not necessarily to the full range of long-term foster placements made by local authorities.

Selwyn and colleagues compared disruption rates for children in adoptive placements with others in intended long-term foster placements (but for whom the original plan had been adoption). The fostered children in this study had been older at entry to care and more likely to have learning disabilities and health problems. Forty-six per cent of the intended long-term foster placements disrupted, compared to 17 per cent of the adoptive placements (Selwyn *et al*, 2006). The disruption rate of 27 per cent at three-year follow-up in Beek and Schofield's study of 58 planned long-term foster placements was not dissimilar to a disruption rate of 29 per cent for adoptive placements in Rushton and Dance's analysis of 133 adoptive placements (Beek and Schofield, 2004; Dance and Rushton, 2005). However, this study of foster care measured outcomes after one to four years, whereas the adoption study followed up children at the age of 16, much later than the fostering study. This illustrates the difficulty of drawing firm conclusions from such comparisons.

It is similarly difficult to come to firm conclusions when comparing studies that have used measures of psychosocial outcomes. Children's pre-placement histories have been found to be predictive of future psycho-social adjustment, even for children placed as infants (Brodzinsky, 1993; Selwyn *et al*, 2006). For example, a study that compared a group of six- to seven-year-old children placed for adoption at a mean age of 3.2 months with a matched group of non-adopted children found that, despite the early age at entry to the adoptive placement, psychosocial outcomes for the adopted children were worse than for non-adopted children. The adopted boys were more likely to manifest behaviour problems and also did worse on a measure of social competence than the non-adopted boys. Adopted girls did worse than the non-adopted children in relation to both externalising and internalising behaviours (Brodzinsky *et al*, 1984a).

Adversity that continues beyond the age of six months is known to

increase the risk of developmental disturbance, so late entry to a permanent placement may make developmental recovery harder to achieve
(Howe, 1998; Rutter, 2000). The fact that children in long-term foster care
typically enter their long-term placements well beyond the age of six
months makes comparisons of the outcomes for early adoption and foster
care problematic. Furthermore, some studies of disturbance in adopted
children do not sample adoptions that have broken down and therefore
paint a rosier picture, as they only consider outcomes for children whose
adoptions survive (Howe, 1998). For example, one well-known study of
91 adolescents, who had been placed for adoption when five to 12 years
old, followed up only those adoptions that lasted for more than one year
(Kadushin, 1970).

Some follow-up studies have found the behaviour and adjustment
problems of children in long-term foster care to be worse than for adopted
children (Bohman and Sigvardsson, 1980; Rowe *et al*, 1989; Thoburn,
1990; Triseliotis, 1990), although in one such study numbers were
extremely small and the findings non-significant (Gibbons *et al*, 1995). A
Swedish study compared three groups of children who had been considered for adoption and found that psychosocial problems were
significantly worse for children who were placed with foster carers at an
average age of nine months (70 per cent of whom were adopted by the age
of seven years) than those for children adopted as infants or returned to
birth parents (Bohman and Sigvardsson, 1980). These findings are hard to
interpret, as the "fostered" group included many children who experienced late adoptions, and this group entered their permanent placements
later than those adopted in infancy. It is therefore difficult to disentangle
the effects of placement type and age at placement.

The recent York study of foster care suggested that on a number of
outcome measures there was, after allowing for initial status, little difference between adopted and other children, although such differences as
there were tended to favour adoption (Sinclair *et al*, 2005c). Selwyn and
colleagues' study similarly found little difference between fostered and
adopted children on measures of emotional and behavioural outcomes
(Selwyn *et al*, 2006). However, both of these studies found that adopted
children did better than fostered children on criteria related to attachment,

although it is possible that these findings may reflect differences between the children in each type of placement.

Children's perceptions of belonging and permanence

Another key issue concerns the meaning that children give to their status and experience. Some studies have suggested that adopted children generally have a greater sense of security and belonging than those who remain in long-term foster placements (Triseliotis, 2002; Rushton, 2004). Some children clearly attribute major significance to the status of adoption, variously seeing it as betokening real security or as a potential threat to their family identity (Sinclair, 2005c). An outcome study in the USA found that it was the perception of permanence by both child and carer rather than the child's status (as fostered or adopted) that was the key to improvement in child well-being (Lahti, 1982). These perceptions are intimately connected with issues of identity, attachment and family loyalty. Many studies have indicated that children who have experienced poor or disrupted early care are at risk of attachment problems (Howe, 1998). Research on looked after children has shown that placement stability may be undermined by children's persistent yearning for inconsistent or rejecting birth parents who may not necessarily want the child to return but may not want the child to settle either (Wade *et al*, 1998; Sinclair *et al*, 2005c).

Although a few studies have interviewed children (for example Thoburn, 1990; Owen, 1999; Thomas *et al*, 1999; Macaskill, 2002; Sinclair *et al*, 2005c), most studies of adopted children's sense of belonging and identity are based on samples of adults adopted long ago (Howe and Feast, 2000). This lack of research on children's perceptions of belonging and permanence means there is little available evidence about the process by which some children achieve at least a sufficient resolution of their complicated feelings about their birth families to enable them to abandon their fantasy of rejoining families who may reject or severely abuse them and to settle for permanence in another family. Some children appear to achieve a resolution that is satisfactory to them, for a time at least. Others do not. Why this is so is uncertain. We explore these issues in Chapter 13 and 14.

Aims of the study

This study aims to contribute to these debates on permanency planning, outcomes and the meanings of different types of permanent placements. In Chapter 2 we outline the policy developments on adoption, foster care and other permanent placements which form the context for these debates. The rest of the book presents findings from our follow-up study of a sample of children in long-term foster placements or adopted from care. The aims of the study are to:

- investigate local policy and practice in relation to three types of permanent placement: stranger adoption, carer adoption and long-term foster care;
- compare the characteristics, outcomes and meanings (to children and carers) of these three types of permanent placement.

2 Permanence in law and policy

Adoption

Adoption was first placed on a legal footing by the 1926 Adoption of Children Act. After the passing of this Act, the number of adoptions rose rapidly and eventually reached a peak in 1967. The wider social changes of the 1960s, including improved contraception, the legalisation of abortion, the availability of welfare benefits to single mothers and changing social mores led, by the 1970s, to a significant decline in the number of babies available for adoption. Throughout this period, however, only a very small proportion of adopted children were adopted from public care, although it is difficult to be sure of the exact numbers because relinquished babies were not included in the care statistics of the time.

The reform of adoption law embodied in the passing of the Adoption and Children Act 2002 was the culmination of a lengthy process of change that began in the 1970s. The Children Act 1975 gave social workers greater powers to provide permanent homes for "hard-to-place" children through adoption, so that by the 1980s, the population of adopted children had begun to include increasing numbers of children adopted from care, especially older children with challenging behaviour and children with disabilities. The 1975 Act also strengthened the position of foster carers considering adoption (Thoburn *et al*, 1986). However, the regulatory framework of the 1976 Adoption Act failed to recognise the needs of this changing population (Ball, 2005). By the late 1980s, it was already apparent that these children had very high levels of need, resulting in higher rates of disruption than for the infants placed in earlier decades (Thoburn, 1990).

Today, few babies born in the UK are placed for adoption and looked after children, often beyond infancy when placed for adoption, are the main group needing permanent placement.[1] Many have traumatic

---

[1] The introduction of placement orders by the Adoption and Children Act 2002 means that one placement move is always built in to the adoption process, so children are no longer available to be placed for adoption immediately after birth (unless they enter a concurrent planning placement).

histories of abuse or neglect and some have physical or learning disabilities. These changes have important implications for adoption policy and practice. For older children in need of adoption, delay in decision making and in placement is likely to have serious consequences for the formation of new attachments. It is also likely to be more difficult to recruit adopters willing to take older children with complex needs and, given the complex needs of many of the children, adoptive parents are more likely to require support. Furthermore, the previously exclusive model of adoption, in which all contact with birth families was severed following adoption, may not always be appropriate now that many children are adopted at an older age and may have developed relationships with members of their birth families.

By the time of the much-delayed implementation of the Adoption Act 1976, in 1988, adoption practice had changed to such an extent that the Act was already out of date. Only one year after the 1976 Adoption Act came into force, the Government therefore commissioned a review of adoption law, which subsequently reported to ministers in 1992. This review identified a range of reforms that were needed, including recognition that for some children a continuing role for birth families might be appropriate and, for some, a secure alternative to adoption would be desirable (Department of Health and Welsh Office, 1992). A White Paper followed in 1993 but did not result in legislative reform (Department of Health, 1993).

Shortly after New Labour came to power, government attention turned once again to adoption. In 1998, the Government issued new guidance to local authorities: *Adoption: Achieving the right balance (LAC 98 (20)* (Department of Health, 1998). This noted the lack of consistency in adoption practice that had been identified in Social Services Inspectorate reports and emphasised the benefits of adoption for children unable to return to their families. Although the Children Act 1989 requires local authorities to make all reasonable efforts to rehabilitate children with their families wherever possible, the Government view expressed here was that there was a common perception 'among too many in the field' that efforts at rehabilitation should be pursued no matter how long it might take. Arguing that 'time is not on the side of the child', the guidance aimed to redress the balance to ensure that timely decisions were made about whether children could return to their birth families and, if that were not possible, that decisions would be made about placing them with perm-anent families *'as a matter of priority'*. A key emphasis of the guidance was thus on timely decision making and on avoiding delay in placing children with permanent families. Delay was to be avoided because the longer children drifted in care, the less likely they were to be able to form secure, long-term relationships with new parents and as a result, they were at greater risk of subsequent placement disruption.

In 2000, the Performance Innovation Unit (PIU) was commissioned by the Prime Minister to undertake a thorough review of adoption policy. Later that year it published *The Prime Minister's Review of Adoption*, a consultation paper that discussed whether more use could be made of adoption for looked after children and whether the adoption process could be improved. It identified a number of barriers to the adoption of looked after children, including slow decision making, inconsistency in the use of adoption between authorities and a lack of support for adopters (PIU, 2000). These concerns underpinned the Government's decision to encourage the wider use of adoption and other permanency options. The PIU report also identified carer adoption as one means of increasing the number of adoptions.

Government plans to ensure permanent placement for a wider group of children were set out in the White Paper, *Adoption: a new approach*, which rapidly followed the PIU report and took forward many of its recommendations (Department of Health, 2000). The White Paper defined permanence in broad terms as 'a secure, stable and loving family to support children through childhood and beyond'. As well as adoption, it outlined a range of options that would offer permanence, including residence orders, long-term foster care and informal care with family or friends.

The White Paper was rapidly followed by publication of the Adoption and Children Bill and, while this Bill was still being debated, the National Adoption Standards for England were published in 2001. In the following year, the Adoption and Children Act 2002 was passed, although it was not fully implemented until December 2005. In recognition of the changes in adoption practice since the 1980s, the Act overhauled the Adoption Act 1976, amended some sections of the Children Act 1989, and reformed the legal framework for both domestic and intercountry adoption. In this radical reform of adoption law 'only the legal concept of adoption – the irrevocable transfer of a child from the birth to the adoptive family . . . remains unaltered' (Ball, 2005, p 6). However, despite the initially broad conceptualisation of permanency options in the White Paper, the Government's subsequent focus was principally on adoption. The 2002 Act set out the Government's expectation that more children should be adopted from care and presented a number of new provisions to increase the number of looked after children being adopted.

One of the main aims of the Act was to align adoption law with the Children Act 1989, incorporating the 1989 Act's welfare principle and welfare checklist into adoption law so that the child's welfare would be paramount in decisions about adoption. It also aimed to minimise delay for children in a variety of ways, including through its provisions to ensure that the consent of birth parents would be addressed at an earlier stage, either through a court-ordered placement order, which replaced the old provision of freeing for adoption, or through placement by consent. If the welfare of the child required it, the court could now dispense with the consent of a parent even if their objection was reasonable. The new requirement for local authorities to appoint Independent Reviewing Officers was also intended to minimise delay, as their role was to strengthen care planning and prevent drift in the implementation of care plans.

The Adoption and Children Act 2002 deals separately with two sets of circumstances in which contact between children and their birth families may occur: when a child is placed for adoption and following an adoption order. The Adoption and Children Act 2002, along with the National Adoption Standards 2001, recognised that for some children, maintaining links with their birth families or other significant people from their past may be helpful, although decisions about contact must be consistent with the welfare principle that is central to the Act. Under the 2002 Act, relatives other than birth parents are also allowed to apply for contact with a child.

The Act (and the Adoption Standards regulations implemented in 2003) included provisions to strengthen adoption support services (including financial support), extend the range of potential adopters and increase the number of adoptions by foster carers. It also set out clear timescales for permanency planning and for the different stages of the adoption process. It also included other important changes in relation to the making of adoptive placements, parental responsibility and contact after adoption and introduced a new provision for special guardianship.

Consistent with the emphasis on increasing the number of looked after children being adopted, a target was set in 2000 to increase by 40 per cent the number of children adopted or placed in other 'genuinely legally secure placements' by 2004–05 (Department of Health, 2000). In 2001 a further target was set, with a view to minimising delay in the adoption process. This target aimed to increase the percentage of looked after children placed for adoption within 12 months of a best interests decision being made from 81 per cent in 2001 to 95 per cent by 2005. From 2001, Performance Assessment Framework (PAF) indicators included indicator C23 (Adoptions of Children Looked After), which measured the number of children adopted as a percentage of children looked after for six months or more. This indicator is no longer included in the national indicators monitoring the performance of local authorities.

Long-term foster care

Due to a number of policy developments since the late 1980s, there has been a significant increase in the proportion of looked after children who are placed in foster care rather than residential care. Today, the majority (73 per cent in 2008/09) are placed in foster care. Until the end of the Second World War, the general assumption was that children placed in foster care would usually remain there long term. They were expected neither to keep in touch with their parents nor to return to them. This changed with the advent of the Children Act 1948 and the establishment of the new Children's Departments. These developments brought a gradual shift towards viewing foster care as a temporary service to families, one that aimed eventually to return children to their parents (Triseliotis, 1990). Nevertheless, until the 1980s it was not unusual for foster parents to bring up children as if they were their own, on a quasi-adoptive basis, with little or no contact with their birth families.

However, the development of specialist fostering from the late 1970s contributed to a gradual shift towards a more task-centred approach and to the professionalisation of foster care. The old, often exclusive, model of foster care has since been replaced by a more inclusive model, whereby foster carers are expected to work in partnership with parents, not replace them. Foster "parents" have become known as foster "carers", in accordance with the redefinition of their role in children's lives. Nevertheless, for the relatively small proportion of fostered children who are today in long-term foster care, some foster carers may still have a quasi-parental role in children's lives, as we shall see later in this report.

Developments since the late 1980s, including the passing of the Children Act 1989, have contributed to changes in the balance of the population of children who are looked after (Biehal, 2006; Rowlands and Statham, 2009). The period 1994–2004 saw a steady rise in the number of children looked after, followed by a slight fall from 2005–08. However, following the high-profile case of Baby Peter, numbers entering care rose in 2008/09 (Pemberton, 2010). The trend since the mid-1990s has been for children to enter care younger, increasingly for reasons of abuse and neglect, and to remain longer due to the seriousness of their difficulties (Department of Health, 2001a). In many cases, the severity of these difficulties are such that they may be unable to return to their parents and will therefore need permanent placements. Nevertheless, the proportion of children who are looked after long term remains small. Less than a quarter (24 per cent) of children who ceased to be looked after in 2005/06 (the year of our survey), had been looked after continuously for three or more years (Department for Education and Skills, 2007b).

The legislation and statutory guidance that govern foster care today, principally the Children Act 1989, do not distinguish between long-term foster care and other forms of care provision, as there is no legal status of "long-term" or "permanent" foster care (Schofield *et al*, 2008). For children who are looked after, the Children Act 1989 requires that parental responsibility is either retained by parents (for children accommodated voluntarily) or shared between birth parents and the local authority (for children looked after on a care order). This means that, even where foster carers have cared for children for most or all of their lives, those carers do not have legal parental responsibility, although in practice local authorities may allow long-term foster carers some discretion in day-to-day decision making. The Children Act 1989 also requires local authorities to work in partnership with parents. It imposed a new duty on local authorities to promote contact between children who are looked after and those who are connected with them. Local authorities are required to allow reasonable contact with the child's parents or any other guardian the child was living with before entering care. They also have a duty to conduct formal reviews of the children's well-being and progress every six months.

From the late 1990s, the Government began a radical overhaul of the public care system, within a broader programme of change in services for children. First, the Quality Protects and Choice Protects policy programmes brought renewed policy attention to services for looked after children, focusing on, among other things, placement stability, quality and choice. These were followed in 2004 by the Every Child Matters: Change for Children programme, which focused on improving outcomes for all children, including those in public care, and by the Children Act 2004, which aimed to bring about a reconfiguration of children's services in England. In 2006, the Government published its initial consultation paper *Care Matters: Transforming the lives of children and young people in care*, which included proposals for the reform of foster care, and in the following year published the White Paper *Care Matters: Time for change* (Department for Education and Skills, 2006, 2007a). As part of the implementation of the *Care Matters* White Paper and the Children and Young Persons Act 2008, in 2010 the Labour Government revised the guidance that accompanies the Children Act 1989, with the aim of improving the quality and consistency of care planning, placement and case review for looked after children (HM Government, 2010). The Care Matters programme and the Treasury's policy review on children and young people in 2007 have been characterised by two key concerns (Department for Education and Skills, 2006, 2007a; Treasury/DfES, 2007). There has been a focus on *prevention and early intervention* and, where this fails to prevent long-term separation, on *permanency*, which may be achieved through reunification, adoption, special guardianship or, if these are not possible, through long-term foster care.

The Government has also tried to regulate the quality of public care through the use of performance indicators. In 2008, its Performance Assessment Framework (PAF) was replaced by a new set of National Indicators (NIs). These build on earlier PAF indicators in monitoring local authority compliance with the policy of increasing placement stability for looked after children. NI62 monitors the percentage of children with three or more placements during a single year, while NI63 measures the percentage of children looked after continuously for at least two-and-a-half years who are currently in a foster placement where they had spent at least two years, or who have been placed for adoption. Fortunately, the Government acknowledges that, although most children are likely to benefit from placement stability, in some cases a change of placement may be in a child's best interests (HM Government/Communities and Local Government, 2008). Too rigid an adherence to such indicators may have perverse consequences, as it may encourage local authorities to keep children in placements that do not meet their needs. The foster placements of children under 11 rarely disrupt, so younger children in particular may remain unhappily in foster placements in situations where a move might be beneficial (Sinclair *et al*, 2007).

Foster care services and long-term foster carers therefore work within an extensive framework of law, policy and guidance, none of which was designed specifically to cover long-term foster care. As Schofield and colleagues have argued, fostering services are located in a bureaucratic system, within which they must meet the long-standing challenge of providing secure care for children in need of a permanent placement who can neither live with their birth families nor be adopted, while at the same time responding to new demands and pressures (Schofield *et al*, 2000).

Residence orders

Residence orders may still be made under s.11(7) of the Children Act 1989. These confer parental responsibility on carers who would not otherwise have that responsibility, but do not end the birth parents' parental responsibility. However, a person who has parental responsibility without a residence order cannot remove the child from the physical care of the holder of the residence order. Any person with whom a child has lived for three of the previous five years, or any person who has the consent of a local authority while a child is in its care, may apply for a residence order.

The residence order settles the question of who the child is to live with and may contain conditions or directions. It can remain in force until the child is 16 and, in exceptional circumstances, until the child is 18 (for example, if the child is disabled). The holder of a residence order can make all day-to-day decisions in the child's life including giving consent to medical treatment, taking the child abroad and deciding which school the child attends, and may be entitled to financial support from the local authority in the form of a residence allowance. Residence orders therefore provide a way for relatives or (ex-)foster carers to offer children a long-term home with degree of legal security outside the care system, and give holders a level of parental responsibility much closer to that of birth parents than is the case for foster carers.

Special guardianship

In *A Review of Adoption Law* (Department of Health and Welsh Office, 1992) it was recognised that adoption might be inappropriate for some older children in need of permanent placements. In circumstances where children live in permanent placements with relatives or foster carers, residence orders previously constituted the principal means of offering children legal security outside the care system. However, residence orders normally cease once the child reaches the age of 16 and offer only limited parental responsibility to carers. The concept of special guardianship was therefore introduced in the White Paper, *Adoption: A new approach*, to strengthen legal security for children in these circumstances and was intended to be a half-way house between a residence order and an adoption order (Department of Health, 2000).

Special guardianship orders are one of the most important amendments to the Children Act 1989 contained in the Adoption and Children Act 2002. They confer parental responsibility on the carer in the same way as a residence order but include the added safeguard that any application by a parent or child to vary or discharge the order requires the leave of the court. Thus, the order strengthens the parental responsibility of its holder and restricts the exercise of parental responsibility by the birth parents, although it does not remove this entirely. The order provides legal security for the child for a longer period of time than a residence order. However, unlike adoption orders, special guardianship orders cease once the child reaches the age of 18. Local authorities have duties to provide support to the holders of special guardianship orders. The use of special guardianship has been investigated in a companion study (Wade *et al*, 2010).

The use of permanent placements outside the care system

Among those children who cannot be reunified with their parents and who move to permanent placements outside the care system, the majority (13%) are adopted from care. Smaller proportions leave the care system via the use of residence orders (4%) or special guardianship orders (5%) (Department for Children, Schools and Families, 2009a). However, this change of legal status may not entail a move, as some children are adopted by their foster carers. Similarly, residence and special guardianship orders may be granted to the children's former foster carers. This was the case in relation to over half of the special guardianship orders made in 2009 (Department for Children, Schools and Families, 2009a). The use of adoption from care has shifted over time, as discussed below.

Changing patterns of adoption

After the passing of the Children Act 1975, there was a gradual decrease in the number of children adopted, mainly due to a decline in the use of adoption for children who were not in public care. The number of adoptions from care remained reasonably constant from the mid-1970s to the end of the 1990s, but after the new Labour Government turned its attention to adoption from care, numbers began to rise (Office for National Statistics, 2007). The number of children adopted from care increased from 2,100 in 1997/98 to a peak of 3,800 in 2004/05. However,

Table 2.1

Number of looked after children adopted: year ending 31 March 1998–2009

1998	1999	2000	2001	2002	2003	2004	2005	2006	2007	2008	2009
2,100	2,200	2,700	3,100	2,100	3,400	3,500	3,800	3,700	3,300	3,200	3,300

since this initial rise, the number adopted from care has fallen steadily, as shown in Table 2.1.

The Government's programme of adoption reform clearly had its greatest impact on increasing adoption from care in the five years *before* the implementation, in December 2005, of the Adoption and Children Act 2002. Since then, the flurry of national and local activity in relation to increasing adoption from care appears to have declined. The figure for the year ending 31 March 2009 represents a decrease of 13 per cent from the numbers in 2004/05. During the same period, there was an even greater decrease in the numbers placed for adoption, which fell by 28 per cent (Department for Children, Schools and Families, 2009a). Nevertheless, the most recent figures for adoption from care were still roughly 50 per cent higher in 2008/09 than they were ten years earlier, before the programme of adoption reform began.

Between the publication of new government guidance on adoption in 1998 (Department of Health, 1998), *The Prime Minister's Review of Adoption* in 2000, the White Paper which followed, the issuing of the National Adoption Standards in 2001 and the Adoption Support Regulations in 2003 and the passing of the Adoption and Children Act in 2002, the Labour Government spent over £66 million on improving adoption services. The reforms, targets and funding introduced during the period 1998–2005 undoubtedly contributed to the rise in the number of adoptions during this period, through its impact on local authority policy and practice. In Chapter 4, we focus on the early implementation of the adoption reform programme to explore its effects on local policy and practice in our seven study authorities.

The rise in adoptions from care was mainly due to an increase in the use of adoption for younger children. In the 1990s, children aged between five and nine were the most likely to be adopted, but from the late 1990s,

Table 2.2
Age at adoption: percentage of all looked after children adopted

Age (years)	2002 %	2003 %	2004 %	2005 %	2006 %	2007 %	2008 %	2009 %
Under 1	6	6	6	6	5	4	4	2
1–4	59	62	58	62	64	64	70	72
5–9	29	27	30	28	26	27	22	23
10–15	5	5	6	4	5	5	4	3
16+	1	0	0	0	0	0	1	<1

the highest number of adoptions were of children between one and four years old (Office for National Statistics, 2008). Children aged one to four years old accounted for 72 per cent of all children adopted in the year 2008/09, as shown in Table 2.2.

At the same time, there was also an increase in the proportion of adopted children who began their final period of care before they were one year old, which rose from 53 per cent in 2004 to 62 per cent in 2008. In 2008/09, only nine per cent of children adopted from care began their final episode of care at the age of four years or over (Department for Children, Schools and Families, 2009a). Adoption is increasingly being used for children who enter care as infants, who are then adopted while very young.

It is unclear why the initial impetus towards a greater use of adoption has not been sustained, as it is unlikely that the number of children who might benefit from adoption has fallen. There are a number of possible explanations. It may be the case that local authorities are no longer prioritising adoption in their permanency planning, or indeed that they are no longer focusing as sharply on proactive permanency planning at all. Equally, there may be problems in recruiting adopters.

It is also possible that, in relation to some children who might have been considered for adoption, social workers and courts may be making use of the new provision for special guardianship, which was implemented in December 2005. The decline in the use of adoption has corresponded with increasing take-up of special guardianship as a permanency option, although special guardianship orders are being used as an alternative to residence orders as well as to adoption (Wade *et al*, 2010).

While the introduction of the special guardianship provisions may have contributed to the decline in the use of adoption, we should not assume that is the sole reason for the decline in adoption from care since 2005. Other reforms or developments may also have had an impact on the use of different types of permanent placement, including adoption, such as the crisis in safeguarding following the Baby Peter case, the shortage of social workers and the negative media coverage of adoption. In Chapter 4 we focus on the seven local authorities that took part in the study to explore the range of factors which influenced local use of adoption as a permanent placement during the implementation of the adoption reform programme. Chapter 7 then takes this further by investigating permanency planning at the level of the individual, exploring the reasons for decisions on permanent placements of children who took part in our study.

3 Design and methods

This study took place in the seven authorities that participated in the University of York's longitudinal programme of foster care research (Sinclair *et al*, 2005b, 2005c). The authorities were diverse in nature – including three London boroughs, two shire counties, two unitary city authorities and one metropolitan district. They were also geographically spread, ranging from London and the Home Counties to the north of England.

Research design

Our comparison of different types of permanent placements had a comparative design with a longitudinal component. It had four stages:

1. *an exploratory study of policy and practice* based on documents, interviews with key informants and focus groups in our seven local authorities
2. *a survey* of 196 children adopted by strangers or carers or in long-term foster placements and studied through postal questionnaires sent to their adopters/foster carers and social workers
3. *a census* of administrative data available on 374 children who met the criteria for inclusion in our survey sample
4. *an intensive study* of 37 children drawn from the larger sample, based on qualitative interviews with the children and their foster carers/ adoptive parents.

1. Policy and practice study

The aim of this initial phase of the study was, first, to examine the impact of the renewed policy attention to adoption evident from 1998 onwards and, second, to explore the views of managers, practitioners, foster carers and adoptive parents on different types of permanent placement.

Key informant interviews were conducted with senior managers of children's services and the managers of local fostering and adoption services. These interviews took the form of semi-structured discussions with two or three senior staff in each of our seven local authorities. The focus of these interviews was the changing policy context and how policies on permanence had been developed and implemented in these authorities in recent years. These key informant interviews, together with the analysis of local policy documents, allowed us to explore both the process of policy change and variation between local authorities in policy and practice.

Seven focus groups were also held, one in each authority. Three were with fostering and adoption staff, two with social workers, one with foster carers and one with adoptive parents. In these focus groups we explored different stakeholders' views on the key themes of the study in relation to the differences between long-term foster care and adoption. These consultations with foster carers, adoptive parents and professionals were used not only as data in themselves but also to inform the development of our research instruments for the survey and the intensive study.

2. Postal survey

We undertook a postal survey of the carers and social workers of 196 children who, in 2001 or 2002, had either been living with the same foster carers for three years or been adopted from care. Ninety of these children (the *York sample*) had previously been surveyed in 1998 and 2001 by Sinclair and colleagues' in their studies of foster care (Sinclair *et al*, 2005b, 2005c).

Postal questionnaires were sent to the carers/adoptive parents (hereafter both referred to as carers for reasons of brevity) of the children in our survey sample. For children who had been adopted, we identified the social worker with the most recent knowledge of the child. Our strategy was to include a number of questions on key factual issues for both potential respondents, to ensure that we would have some key data even if only one respondent returned a questionnaire. Children were included in the survey sample if at least one respondent returned a questionnaire.

Sampling

Our survey sample comprised two groups of children: the *York sample* and the *booster sample*. The York sample for our survey was drawn from a sample of 596 children who were fostered in seven local authorities in January 1998 and who were previously studied by Sinclair and colleagues. With one exception, all of these children had been aged eight years or under at that time and their carers had previously agreed to take part in the research. Children who were fostered as part of an agreed series of short-term breaks were not included in that study (Sinclair *et al*, 2005b). This cross-sectional sample of children was then followed up in 2001 (Sinclair *et al*, 2005c).

We aimed to follow up a sub-sample of the original 596 children yet again, in order to compare experiences and outcomes for children in different types of permanent placements. This was a valuable opportunity to investigate the outcomes for children about whom, in most cases, we already had data collected at two earlier time-points. We aimed to follow up all of the 116 children within the larger sample who had been surveyed in 1998 and who, in January 2001, either:

- were still with the same foster carer, or
- had been adopted from care (either by a stranger or by their foster carer).

We succeeded in including 90 of these children in our survey, a response rate of 78 per cent. We also managed to obtain some limited information on placement outcomes for 22 (of the 26) children for whom no questionnaires were returned.

To boost the size of our survey sample so as to increase statistical power, we also identified an additional *booster sample* with broadly similar placement experiences to those in the *York sample*. Our *booster sample* was a cross-sectional sample of children from the same seven local authorities who had been in foster care in 1999 (one year later than the cross-sectional sample for the *York sample* was drawn) and who, in 2002, were still settled in the same foster placement or had been adopted. Our *booster sample* was drawn from a sampling frame of all children in each authority who were not in the original York cohort and who:

- had been in a foster placement on 31 March 1999, *and*
- were aged nine years or under on that date.

Children were included in the sampling frame for our *booster sample* if they met the above conditions and also in March 2002:

- were still fostered by the same carer as in 1999, *or*
- had been adopted by the carer who had fostered them in March 1999, *or*
- had been adopted by a stranger.

From their computerised administrative data, local authority IT staff attempted to identify all children who met the above criteria and sent us the client information numbers and current placement details of 270 children. A stratified random sample was drawn from this group to enable us to compare the circumstances of children in long-term foster care, adopted by carers or adopted by strangers. This sample was stratified according to the nature of the child's placement in 2006. Since the majority of children in the *York sample* had been adopted, we decided to oversample children in foster care in the *booster sample*. The *booster sample* therefore includes a higher proportion of children in foster care than the *York sample*.

The identification of an accurate sampling frame for the *booster sample*, as well as up-to-date contact data on the whole survey sample, depended crucially on the state of the database systems of the local authorities concerned. The last few years have generally been a time of rapid, and sometimes quite radical, development for local authority IT departments. Three of the authorities in our study, for example, were in the process of migrating their data to entirely new database systems. It was difficult to ascertain the precise nature of the various difficulties that were reported to us, but it was clear that the historical data upon which the identification of our booster sampling frame depended had not always been successfully transferred to new systems. We therefore cannot be sure that all children eligible for inclusion in our booster sampling frame were identified. However, although we were concerned that a few children might not have been included in the sampling frame, analysis of the varied problems with data extraction across the authorities suggested that there was unlikely to be any systematic exclusion of particular groups of children. We were therefore confident that the sampling frame for the *booster sample* was likely to be representative of the total group of children who met the criteria for inclusion within that sampling frame.

Questionnaires on 229 children were posted to carers/adopters and social workers. The potential size of the *York sample* was determined by the number of children who met the above criteria for inclusion in that sample (n = 116), while the potential size of the booster sample was determined by the need not to overburden social workers in adoption teams and looked after children's teams with too many questionnaires. Twelve of the 116 children eligible for inclusion in the *York sample* could not be surveyed because local authorities no longer had their contact details or, in a few cases, were unwilling to forward questionnaires because the placement was under stress at the time or, in one case, because the child had recently died. Questionnaires were therefore posted to the carers and the current/ last social workers of 104 of these children. Details of the methods used to recruit the survey sample are given in Appendix 1.

Response rate

Questionnaires were returned by adoptive parents/carers, social workers or both in relation to 196 children.

At least one questionnaire was received in relation to 86 per cent of the children surveyed. The proportion of cases in which questionnaires were returned by foster carers and by adoptive parents was similar (77–78 per cent respectively).

Table 3.1
Respondents

Data source	Number (%)
Current carer	46 (24)
Both carer and social worker	95 (49)
Social worker only	55 (28)
Total	**196 (101)**

For the *York sample*, sample attrition over the five-year period since they were last surveyed (in 2001) was just 13 per cent. If the 12 children in the *York sample* whose parents/carers could not be surveyed (because local authorities were unable or unwilling to forward questionnaires to them) are taken into account, the attrition rate for the *York sample* rises to 19 per cent. Sample attrition for the *York sample* is discussed in Appendix 2.

When questionnaires were returned, we discovered that some children identified by local IT teams as being in foster care at the time of the survey were in fact on residence orders or, in one case, a special guardianship order. Ten others were in residential care and four had returned to birth parents.

Similar proportions of children came from each county or unitary authority (15–19 per cent of the sample from each), but a smaller proportion came from each of our two London boroughs (6–10 per cent), largely due to the smaller populations of looked after children in London boroughs.

Data collection

The survey questionnaires included a mix of pre-coded and open-ended questions, so we were able to use them to collect qualitative as well as quantitative data. They were supplemented with administrative data from the local authorities' SSDA 903 annual returns to government on the children included in our survey (although these data were missing for three children). Survey questionnaires for carers were piloted with a reference group of adoptive parents and foster carers and the social worker questionnaires were piloted with individual social workers.

The survey questionnaires included a number of key variables that had previously been used in Sinclair and colleagues' earlier studies of the *York sample*.

The Strengths and Difficulties Questionnaire (SDQ) is a screening measure of children's emotional and behavioural difficulties. We scored this according to instructions in the original article (Goodman, 1997).

The carer's parenting measure. Social workers who had been in recent contact with carers or adoptive parents were asked to rate them on six four-point scales (caring, accepting, clear about what they wanted, not easily upset by child's failure to respond, sees things from the child's point of view, encouraging). We averaged the result to give a parenting score.

The Child Orientation Measure was developed by Marjorie Smith of the Thomas Coram Research Unit. It contains ten items that refer to activities which the parent might undertake with the child and which the child might be expected to like. The items were scored 1 (Never), 2 (Sometimes) or 3 (Always) and the carers were also allowed to put "not applicable" (for example, child too young). The items were added together.

The rejection measure (how child and carer were getting on). We asked foster carers whether they were fond of the child, were unsure that they could go on living with/putting up with the child, felt there was no point in telling the child why they did not like her or his misbehaviour, liked or disliked having the child there, were quite sure there was no 'point in asking the child why he or she misbehaves'. Each of these questions could be answered on a three-point scale (from "not at all true" to "true to a large extent") with the exception of the question about liking or disliking, which was a five-point scale. Carers were also allowed to indicate that the question was not applicable. The score was formed by addition.

The family integration measure was based on carer or adoptive parent responses to the following questions. How far would you say the child: feels part of your family, trusts you, feels you care about him or her, feels encouraged, talks to you about personal things, feels encouraged, fits in better than when he or she first came?

The exclusion measure asked similarly about the child feeling the odd one out, wanting to leave, or feeling picked on. The carers could answer each question "a great deal", "to some extent" or "not at all". We counted the number of times a carer answered "a great deal" for the integration score and "to some extent" or "not at all" for the exclusion measure.

The Expression of Feelings in Relationships (EFR) questionnaire was completed by carers in our 2006 survey. This measure has been developed by David Quinton of the University of Bristol. It consists of 30 items and asks carers to rate, on a three-point scale, the manner in which the children display their feelings. Using the EFR, we were able to calculate a total score for attachment difficulties as well as scores for "inhibited", "disinhibited" and "disregulated" behaviour in relationships. High scorers on the inhibited sub-scale were said by their carers to bottle up emotions, show little affection, hide fears and hide feelings of sadness. High scorers on the disinhibited sub-scale were said to seek attention by misbehaving, be more friendly with strangers than the carer would like, seek a lot of attention, and show affection like a younger child.

Eight items from an earlier version of the EFR (the *Expression of Feelings Questionnaire*, or *EFQ*, also developed by David Quinton) were included in questionnaires to carers when our original *York sample* was surveyed in 1998 and in 2001. These same items were used in both studies to calculate scores for inhibition in relationships (referred to as the "stoicism" score in the earlier surveys) and for disinhibition (referred to as the "childlike attachment" score in the earlier surveys). We are therefore able to compare scores for children whose carers had completed the EFQ in 1998 and 2001 with scores for the same eight items on the EFR in 2006.

3. The census study

In order to investigate placement pathways in a wider group of children than those included in the survey sample, we conducted a secondary analysis of computerised administrative data (SSDA 903 data) collected by our seven local authorities. The census date was 31 December 2006, the same as for our survey sample. Our census sample (n = 374) comprised the entire sampling frame (n = 270) from which the *booster sample* was drawn and 104 children from the original *York sample* (local authority data were not available on the remaining children in the original *York sample*). This sample included all but three of the 196 children in our survey sample, the children from the booster sampling frame not selected for inclusion in the survey, and 14 of the children from the *York sample* whom we were unable to include in our survey.

4. Intensive study

The carers who completed our anonymised questionnaires were asked at the end of the questionnaire whether they might consider participating in face-to-face interviews along with the child they cared for, for which each would receive a gift voucher. We invited them to provide their names and addresses if they were willing to receive further information which would explain what would be involved. Just under one-third of the carers (60) returned their names, addresses and telephone numbers to us.

Recruitment packs were posted to the 60 families who provided us with their names and addresses, of whom 37 agreed to be interviewed. The interview sample therefore constituted just under one-fifth of the total survey sample.

Ten adoptive parents/carers declined on behalf of their children. Seven did so because they felt that their children's special needs were too severe to participate in an interview, one felt their child was too young, one that their child was too unsettled, and one declined because their child was currently trying to sever his relationship with his birth parents. Two parents/carers declined due to illness, and four gave no reason. Two young people declined, one of whom indicated that she no longer wanted to consider herself adopted. Finally, one carer withdrew because their child had suddenly left home, having reached the age of 16. In the four remaining cases it proved impossible to arrange interviews with the families.

Children and carers were usually interviewed separately, although in a small number of cases carers of younger children remained in the room for some of the interview. Children and carers were assured that what they said would be treated as confidential, with the proviso that if they said something that indicated that the child was at risk of harm, we would need to discuss with them who should be told about this. Children were told that they did not have to answer questions if they did not want to and that they could stop the interview at any point.

A great deal of work was undertaken to maximise the size of the intensive sample and to facilitate the full participation of the children who agreed to take part. The recruitment and interview methods employed are described in Appendix 1.

The interview sample

The ages of the children in the interview sample ranged from eight to 17 years and just over half (20) were male. Although those who responded were a self-selected rather than representative group, they were remarkably similar to the full survey sample in most respects. Tables 3.2, 3.3 and 3.4 compare the composition of the interview sample to that of the survey sample.

Table 3.2
Child characteristics: interview and survey samples – % (n)

	Interview sample (n = 37)		Survey sample (n = 196)	
	%	n	%	n
Age 7–9 years	24	(9)	20	(39)
Age 10–12 years	22	(8)	26	(51)
Age 13+ years	54	(20)	54	(106)
Male	54	(20)	55	(88)
Black or minority ethnic origin	22	(8)	18	(28)
Disabled	27	(10)	25	(40)

Table 3.3
Placement type: interview and survey samples – % (n)

	Interview sample (n = 37)		Survey sample (n = 196)	
	%	n	%	n
Carer adoption	24	(9)	16	(31)
Stranger adoption	22	(8)	22	(43)
Long-term foster care	32	(12)	32	(63)
Moved from 2001 placement	19	(7)	19	(37)
Residence order/special guardianship	3	(1)	8	(16)
Other	0		3	(6)

Table 3.4
Time in current placement: interview and survey samples – % (n)

	Interview sample (n = 37)		Survey sample (n = 196)	
	%	n	%	n
<2years	8	(3)	12	(23)
2–4 years	11	(4)	10	(20)
5–7 years	22	(8)	28	(55)
8 years or over	59	(22)	50	(98)

The main differences between the two samples were that the interview sample included a smaller proportion of children with disabilities, a higher proportion adopted by carers, and a higher proportion who had entered care as infants. Further comparisons of the interview and survey sample are presented in Appendix 1.

Data analysis

Analysis of quantitative data

First, we analysed the secondary data collected from our seven local authorities, namely the administrative data on our *census sample*. As these data covered children's entire care pathways from their first entry to care to their exit from the care system, if they had left it, we used it to undertake a prospective analysis of their placement histories. We used this data to compare pathways and placement outcomes for children who were fostered long term or adopted.

Second, we focused on the 196 children in our survey sample to compare the care pathways, circumstances and outcomes for children adopted by strangers, adopted by carers, in stable foster care, or with experience of unstable care. In our analysis of patterns of placement stability and change for the *survey sample*, we also drew on the administrative data collected from local authorities for the census study.

Administrative data on our *census sample* and the answers to pre-coded questions on our survey questionnaires were analysed using the computer program SPSS-15. Where both carers and social workers answered the same factual questions, composite variables were derived from the data. Where answers conflicted, decision rules were made on the basis of which respondent was likely to have the most accurate knowledge of the issue in question. Non-parametric tests were used to analyse nominal variables. Parametric tests were used where dependent variables were in the form of interval data and were normally distributed. Details of tests and results for each analysis are given in footnotes.

Analysis of qualitative data

The interviews with children and carers and the focus groups and key informant interviews conducted for the policy study were tape recorded and transcribed. Together with written comments from carers and social workers in response to open-ended questions on our survey question-naires, these data were analysed using the software program Atlas–ti. We undertook a thematic analysis of our focus groups and key informant interviews and of the qualitative data from our survey questionnaires. The qualitative data from the survey questionnaires, together with data from our interviews with children and carers, were used to explore decisions about permanence and a range of other issues dealt with throughout this book.

The principal focus of our analysis of the interviews with children and carers was an exploration of the narratives used to describe and make sense of what had happened in the child's life. We also explored perceptions of belonging and permanence, views of contact with birth families and children's feelings about their birth families. Data were first coded using both descriptive (for example, "nature of contact") and conceptual (for example, "sense of belonging") thematic categories. The emerging themes were then examined in relation to the different types of permanent placement. Within these placement types, we aimed to identify patterns in perceptions of belonging and permanence through careful comparison of case studies of individual children. These case studies drew principally on the interviews with children and their carers, but also made use of factual data on the children's histories provided by social worker survey questionnaires, if these were available.

Pen pictures of the circumstances and histories of each of the young people in the interview sample were also composed, based on the data provided by all respondents in each case. One of the problems in analysing qualitative data in applied policy research lies in trying to grasp the complexity of each individual account while carrying out a cross-sectional analysis that can deliver useful insights across a range of subject areas. When data are first coded thematically and then analysed across cases, there is a danger that in the subsequent analysis these themes will become detached from the context in which the fragments of text were situated. In order to avoid losing sight of a holistic appreciation of each case while carrying out this cross-sectional analysis, data from particular interviewees were always considered in the context of the pen picture. The aim was to build a cross-sectional analysis of the data based on a holistic interpretation of the interview transcripts.

Limitations to the study

As the *York sample* was derived from a cross-sectional sample of children in foster care in a previous study and our *booster sample* was also cross-sectional, no baseline data on the children at the point of entry to care were available. This lack of baseline data collected prior to, or at the point of, entry to care represents limitation to this study. Unfortunately, prospective studies of looked after children are rare. Also, despite our efforts to include all eligible children in the sampling frame for the *booster sample*, the inaccuracies we discovered in the way children had been selected by some local authorities' IT staff made us concerned that we had not been told of all eligible children. It is possible that some children were wrongly omitted from the lists of case numbers that we were sent. However, the numbers omitted are likely to be small and we did not detect evidence of any systematic bias in the final sampling frame.

Summary

- The aim of the study was to compare pathways and outcomes of adoption by strangers, adoption by carers and long-term foster care. The study had a comparative, longitudinal design. It built on a previous follow-up study of children in foster care (Sinclair *et al*, 2005c) and was conducted in the same seven English local authorities which took part in that study.

- The study had four components: an exploratory study of policy and practice, a census of administrative data (n = 374), a postal survey of carers and social workers (n = 196 children) and qualitative interviews with 37 children and their carers/adoptive parents.
- The policy and practice study involved interviews with two or three key informants in each of the seven local authorities, focus groups (n = 7) of managers, professionals, foster carers and adoptive parents in these authorities and analysis of policy documents.
- The survey sample included 90 children who were previously surveyed in 1998 and 2001 in the York studies of foster care. Children and carers in the interview sample were drawn from the survey sample.

4   Adoption reform: the local impact

This chapter examines national and local patterns of adoption and then explores the local policies and practices that lie behind these figures. We describe local responses to the Government's programme of adoption reform and, more broadly, local attitudes to planning for permanence and supporting permanent placements, drawing on evidence from our key informant interviews with managers and our focus groups with managers, professionals, foster carers and adoptive parents in seven local authorities. The interviews were conducted in 2005, just before the implementation of the Adoption and Children Act 2002.

Local variation in adoption and long-term foster care

National statistics and research indicate considerable local variation in the use of both adoption and long-term foster care (Lowe *et al*, 2002; Sinclair *et al*, 2007; McSherry *et al*, 2008). In 2006, the year of our survey, the proportion of children adopted in our seven study authorities ranged from 5–10 per cent of those looked after for six months or more (Department for Education and Skills, 2007b). This variation was not related to the type or size of authority. The authorities with the lowest and the highest percentage adopted were both London boroughs, and there were no obvious differences in percentages for small unitary authorities and large counties, where the proportion was generally around six to seven per cent.

The proportion of all children looked after in long-term foster care is also very small. As we saw in Chapter 2, less than a quarter of children in public care are looked after for three years or more. In 2001, less than half (45 per cent) of those looked after for four years or more were in long-term foster placements, defined as placements lasting for two years or more. As for adoption, there is considerable local variation in this respect, as figures for the proportion of children looked after for four or more years who are in long-term foster care placements ranges from 20 per cent to 65 per cent, and one study of 24 local authorities found that the proportion ranged from 17–53 per cent (Department of Health, 2002; Schofield *et al*, 2008). In our seven study authorities, the proportion of children looked after for four or more years who had lived in the same foster placements for at least two years ranged from 43 per cent to 61 per cent (in 2004). Variations in the use of long-term foster care are likely to be linked to local policies on the use of alternative permanent placements, such as adoption, special guardianship and residence orders.

The local impact of the Adoption and Children Act 2002

Managers and staff in our seven study authorities broadly welcomed the adoption reform programme which began in 1998, feeling that it gave much-needed attention to the needs of children who are looked after long term. They felt that the Adoption and Children Act 2002 had given a welcome impetus to the use of adoption and, importantly, had provided new money to develop services:

> . . . the *Act really focused on adoption, which meant there was money to do things which we could not have done before.* (Manager)

Although the primary emphasis of the Act is on adoption, several authorities had been prompted by the preceding White Paper, *Adoption: A new approach*, to re-evaluate their policies on permanence more broadly. Some managers and staff commented that the 2002 Act had served as a catalyst for a cultural change and had inspired a determination to find adoptive placements for a broader group of children. Although managers expressed some anxiety about the financial implications of the new requirements for adoption support, they hoped that the increased availability of resources for adoption support might increase the number of potential adopters and hence the number of children who might be adopted. All agreed, though, that they were now placing 'older and more damaged children' who might not have been considered for adoption in the past, although as we have seen, this reported move to placing older children is not reflected in the national statistics on adoption. One manager explained:

I think there are quite a lot of children now that have, in the past, drifted on in the care system, that active plans are now considered for permanence through adoption. (Manager)

Managers also welcomed the way that adoption reform had 'forced the agenda' on planning for permanence. They felt that the initial White Paper and subsequently the 2002 Act had brought a cultural shift that led them to give increased attention to planning for all forms of permanence, including long-term foster care, residence orders and the new special guardianship orders. The National Adoption Standards, a key element of the programme of adoption reform, require a permanence plan to be made at the second statutory review, four months after the child becomes looked after. Such plans must consider rehabilitation but also set out contingency plans for those circumstances where rehabilitation is not possible (Department of Health, 2001b).

However, despite the Act's welcome emphasis on permanency planning at an early stage, several managers were worried that its focus on adoption as the principal route to permanence would lead to the devaluing of long-term foster care. One manager argued that adoption was now the 'dominant idea', a dominance enshrined in the national performance indicators. Another manager commented:

I think it's unfair. In one year we had 86 permanent placements and that doesn't show in any way on our performance figures, it doesn't show in the adoptions. They were residence orders, they were long-term fostering . . . (Manager)

Changes in local service delivery

The publication of *Adoption: Achieving the right balance* (LAC(98(20)) (Department of Health, 1998), *The Prime Minister's Review of Adoption*, the White Paper, the National Adoption Standards, the performance indicators and finally the 2002 Act not only provoked cultural change in local authorities but also prompted organisational change. All seven of the authorities were reorganising and often expanding their adoption and fostering services. Managers from one authority mentioned that the

Adoption and Permanence Taskforce had also given impetus to the local restructuring of services and decision-making forums. These developments took place in the context of a broader restructuring of children's services prompted by the Every Child Matters programme (Department for Education and Skills, 2004a), which argued for a greater integration of services.

Most of the authorities had either set up, or were in the process of setting up, permanence panels to replace former adoption panels, although in some authorities these changes had begun before the publication of the White Paper on adoption. For example, in Unitary (Midlands) the impetus to set up the permanence panel came from the emphasis on care planning in the Quality Protects initiative and was reinforced by the official guidance, *Adoption: Achieving the right balance* (Department of Health, 1998). The role of this panel is to scrutinise care planning for all children under the age of 10 years who have been looked after for one year or more.

Local systems for permanency planning were diverse and were linked to differences in the use of panels, as other research has found (Schofield *et al*, 2008). Although in some authorities the permanence panels focused solely on adoption, in others these panels considered all options for permanent placement and also took responsibility for scrutinising whether timescales were being kept to. In one authority, the intention was that the permanence panel would have responsibility for approving both adopters and matches. The permanence/adoption panels considered potential matches for children and adoptive families (and sometimes long-term foster carers), whereas fostering panels in these authorities focused on approving foster carers but did not attempt to match them with children.

Most authorities had expanded their adoption services and had split their adoption teams into family-finding and support teams. Some had also appointed new adoption support staff. Local managers explained that the restructuring of adoption services had been prompted by a number of factors: the development of new guidance, legislation and National Adoption Standards; the rise in demand created by the rise in the number of looked after children remaining in care long term; and a desire to perform well on the new performance indicators measuring placement stability and the use of adoption.

The arrangements tended to vary in relation to the size and geographical spread of the authorities. For example, one of the large counties had reorganised their adoption services into a single, centralised recruitment team alongside a number of local adoption support teams, which were also managed centrally. The foster care teams in this authority were similarly divided into teams for recruitment and support. In view of their small size, two of the unitary authorities instead formed consortia with neighbouring authorities for their adoption work. One of these, a city, had an arrangement whereby children from their city were often placed with adopters in the neighbouring county, to reduce the risk that birth parents and children would run into each other in the city centre, while the neighbouring county placed its children with adopters in the city.

Recruiting adoptive parents

The Adoption and Children Act 2002 sought to increase the pool of potential adopters by broadening the range of people who might be considered as adoptive parents. Managers and adoption staff in our seven authorities felt it was still too early to assess whether the Act would indeed make it easier to find adoptive parents but, given the adoption targets for local authorities, a great deal of effort was being spent on recruiting adopters. Strategies included using a specialist recruitment officer with a media background, translating recruitment literature into different languages and building links with local faith communities to recruit adopters from specific ethnic and religious backgrounds. The national Adoption Register was also used and had been found to be useful. Some authorities focused on recruiting adopters for specific children, while others also aimed to recruit a pool of adopters who could subsequently be matched with children.

Encouraging carer adoption

One way of raising the number of children adopted envisaged by the 2002 Act was through increasing adoption by foster carers. Carer adoptions constitute only a small proportion of all adoptions of children in care. In 2002/03 only 15 per cent of all children adopted from public care in England and Wales were adopted by their foster carers (Department for

Education and Skills, 2003). The York study of foster care discovered that around 10 per cent of foster carers wanted to adopt a child placed with them long term and around 10 per cent of children wanted to be adopted by their carers, although willing carers were not always matched by willing children (Sinclair *et al*, 2005b). Local variation in commitment to adoption by foster carers, where appropriate, may have some influence on local adoption rates. However, since carer adoption tends to constitute a relatively small proportion of all adoptions from care, this is unlikely to explain a great deal of the local variation in adoption figures.

The Adoption and Children Act 2002 allows carers to apply to adopt a child after s/he has lived with them for ten weeks (or after 12 months if their application is not supported by the local authority). The Adoption Support Services Regulations (2005) aimed to remove disincentives to adoption in these circumstances, easing the financial transition for foster carers by allowing local authorities to continue to pay allowances to carer adopters for the initial two years after adoption. Such payments may only continue beyond two years in exceptional circumstances, in order to avoid the development of a two-tier adoption system in which former foster carers are in a more advantageous financial position than other adopters.

There was general agreement in all our focus groups that carers' motivation to adopt children in their care derived from the development of a strong bond with that child and an emotional commitment to them. Sometimes, in circumstances where a strong bond has formed, the decision to adopt could be prompted by the child rather than the carer:

> . . . *there comes a point when the kids reach 10, 11, 12 and they say 'why haven't you adopted me?' And the foster carers will then adopt, because up to that point it hasn't made any difference to them because they are totally committed to the child* . . . (Fostering worker)

The extent to which foster carer adoption was encouraged varied between authorities but in two authorities managers appeared more equivocal, feeling that foster carers who applied to adopt might not always be the best people to meet that child's long-term needs. Managers and adoption workers in these authorities sometimes felt that the motivation to foster and to adopt were quite different and questioned whether carers would be good adoptive parents in the longer term:

> *It's a different motivation . . . 'Well I didn't really want to adopt these children but I feel a strong pull towards them' . . . But a lot of adopters, they want a child for life, they want to be a parent . . . the motivation is different.* (Manager)

Other authorities attached greater weight to the positive effects of carers' emotional commitment to a child they had bonded with and some local policy documents contained clear statements that carer adoption could provide continuity and stability for a child. Managers in authorities that appeared well disposed towards carer adoption were clear that it would be welcomed if it was thought to be in the child's best interests, even if this meant that the authority would lose a much-needed foster carer. However, at least two authorities had encountered problems when foster carers from independent fostering providers (IFPs) had adopted children. IFPs were unhappy with this because they could lose a foster carer, and managers reported that IFPs sometimes insisted that local authorities provided financial compensation.

A manager from one large county authority mentioned that there had been a huge increase in carer adoptions in that authority in the previous two years, which he felt was largely due to a change in the authority's attitude and an accompanying change in workers' responses to carers wishing to adopt. He felt that these changes had been prompted by the general focus on permanence in recent years, which had led to greater acceptance that carer adoption might be desirable. Some adoption staff, however, expressed concern that social workers occasionally pressurised foster carers into considering adoption in circumstances where the child was settled and no alternative long-term placement had been found.

Some managers and adoption staff mentioned concerns about matching. This, they felt, could be a particular problem where a foster placement initially intended to be short term had subsequently become long term, and so the question of matching had never been addressed. The ages of carers and of children were felt to be important too when deciding whether or not children were well matched to carers wishing to adopt them. Foster carers who wished to adopt young children were sometimes in late middle age and it was felt they were unlikely to meet the child's needs during adolescence. However, it was clear that occasions arose when, despite an initial feeling that carers were not the ideal match as adoptive parents, they were eventually allowed to adopt, not only because they loved the child but also because, as one manager put it, 'We can't find anyone else, there is no one else.'

Support for carer adoption

A few managers and fostering staff felt that the loss of financial or other support would not deter carers from adopting children, due to the strength of their commitment to them. The more widespread view, however, was that despite the Adoption and Children Act's provisions for transitional financial support for foster carers wishing to adopt, the time-limited nature of this support was likely to act as a disincentive to carer adoption. A foster carer's comments in one of our focus groups supported this view, explaining that she could not afford to adopt:

> *At the end of the day, I still need to have a wage . . . No, if we were millionaires we'd be adopting.* (Foster carer)

Some staff thought that the provision of only time-limited financial support was particularly likely to discourage adoption by carers of children with disabilities. These carers were often eligible for enhanced allowances, which they would continue to receive until the child was 18, after which they might continue to receive an allowance as the carer of an adult with a disability. Enhanced allowances of this kind were likely to be higher than adoption allowances, which in any case were time limited. One manager hypothesised that foster carers might instead opt for special guardianship, which could give entitlement to financial support until the child reached the age of 18. The loss of other forms of support was also thought to be a deterrent to carer adoption:

> *The foster carers I worked with always said that the reason they would want to foster is because they would want to have constant access to the social worker, constant access to services.* (Manager)

Again, the lack of support might be most likely to deter the carers of disabled children. One manager commented that foster carers might feel that disabled children in foster care might receive better support from health and education agencies than disabled children whose only advocate was an (adoptive) parent.

Long-term foster care

The managers and professionals who took part in our key informant interviews and focus groups also discussed the use of foster care as a permanent placement. Previous research has highlighted the diversity of systems and terminology for long-term and/or permanent foster care services among local authorities and IFPs in England and Wales (Schofield *et al*, 2008). In our study authorities, the terms long-term foster care and permanent foster care were used in a variety of ways. Some used the term long-term fostering to refer to all placements that were long lasting, irrespective of whether or not they were intended to be permanent. Others made a distinction between long-term fostering, defined by duration, and permanent fostering, where there was a clear plan that the child would remain into adulthood. Further distinctions related to the planning process: between long-term placements that were intended to be permanent from the start, short-term placements that had drifted, and placements that had become permanent because a decision had been made to convert a short-term placement to a long-term one. There was some overlap between the second and third of these groups, as sometimes placements became long term through drift but a plan was subsequently made that the carers would offer a permanent home to the child. We will return to these issues in Chapter 7.

The managers and professionals we spoke to generally viewed long-term foster care as appropriate for children considered too old to have any realistic chance of adoption and for those who identified strongly with their birth families, especially if they had ongoing contact with them. Children who enter care at an older age are more likely to have continuing relationships with birth families and it was felt this might make adoption less feasible. Even if children saw their birth families only infrequently, it was felt that some would not necessarily wish for 'that full-blooded commitment' from adoptive parents.

Our focus groups with professionals indicated that, in most cases, long-term foster placements began as short-term placements and were subsequently converted to long-term ones. The most common pattern was for local authorities to recruit short- and medium-term carers and assess how well they fulfilled this task before considering them as long-term carers. Our focus group with foster carers indicated that foster carers may hold similar views, as they may wish to see how well a child fits into their family before making a longer-term commitment:

> *They said, well, you have to have a child move in, knowing that you're going to keep that child long term and we said, but you need to know that child before you commit yourself to long term really because you could have a child just come and you might not hit it off together and that child has already been told that they're here long term.* (Foster carer)

Recruiting foster carers specifically to offer permanent placements appeared to be unusual, although a manager in one authority observed that this was something they felt they should move towards. A manager elsewhere commented that it was extremely difficult to recruit long-term carers for older children. There was some discussion among professionals about whether it was feasible to recruit a pool of long-term foster carers, who could be approved for a permanent placement subject to matching. One fostering social worker observed that it would be difficult to "protect" these placements for the purpose of long-term care, since placements were generally in such short supply that demands would inevitably be made to use this resource for other purposes. An alternative suggested by others was that carers should be recruited, when needed, to care for specific children who needed long-term foster placements, although it seems likely that this would lead to delay in the same way as the search for adopters may do.

However, one authority (Unitary East) was beginning to recruit permanent foster carers for specific children, often older children in residential units, who were normally aged eight to 14 years. The aim was to identify carers who would make a commitment to such children from the start and to plan for permanent placement, matching children to carers and devising appropriate support packages. Both new and established carers were invited to presentation evenings that aimed to recruit permanent carers for children with complex needs. For children who had spent several years in residential care and were thought to be institutionalised, periods of respite foster care were arranged. This served two purposes: to assess the children in a family setting and to re-introduce them gradually to family life, with a view to subsequently placing them in a permanent foster home.

Decisions about long-term foster care also have implications for support to carers. In at least two of our authorities, it was felt that long-term carers had historically received far less support from social services than short-term carers, as placements were more settled. If permanent foster care is to be successful for a wider group of children, more attention may need to be given to supporting these placements.

Local views on barriers to adoption

Despite their enthusiasm for improving permanency planning and increasing the use of adoption for children unable to return to their birth families, managers and staff raised a number of concerns about what they saw as potential barriers to increasing the rate of adoption from care.

Perceived limits to the pool of potential adopters

Some professionals felt that, despite their best efforts to recruit adoptive parents, prospective adopters were not necessarily willing to take on the older or more difficult children whom authorities wished to place. They were critical of the Government for not understanding the real difficulties involved in finding suitable adopters prepared to adopt children in public care. As one manager argued:

> *The dominant idea that kicked it all off was that we've got all these adopters who want children and all these children who want adopters and aren't local authorities stupid because they're not matching the two.* (Manager)

Despite the injection of additional resources to help authorities develop their adoption services, finance was nevertheless viewed as a significant barrier to recruiting adopters. For example, the adoption team in one authority had been told that it was prohibited from advertising nationally for adoptive parents because the budget was overspent. For reasons such as these, decisions about the use of adoption could be influenced by the availability of adopters, or by perceptions of their likely availability (Lowe *et al*, 2002).

Children considered "not adoptable"

There was variation between both individuals and local authorities in views as to which children were "adoptable". As other studies have found, decisions about the choice of adoption rather than long-term foster care were often strongly related to the age of the child and to the development of more challenging behaviour as children grew older (Lowe *et al*, 2002; Schofield *et al*, 2008). For example, in one county, staff were required to consider the possibility of adoption for all children aged nine or under, whereas in one London borough adoption was recommended for those under five years old. Some managers and adoption staff expressed the view that children who entered long-term care at the age of 10 or over were difficult to place for adoption. Often these children were looked after due to parental substance abuse and neglect and had experienced several failed attempts at rehabilitation. Unhelpful delay in decision making meant that, by the time decisions about permanence were finally made, the young people were felt to be too old, and might be displaying behaviour that was thought too challenging, to appeal to prospective adopters. Several managers and staff also mentioned that they did not consider children suitable for adoption if they had continuing relationships and contact with their birth parents and said it was hard to find adoptive homes for disabled children and sibling groups, as other research on care planning has also found (Lowe *et al*, 2002).

Other managers were more optimistic about the feasibility of finding adopters for older children and for sibling groups, and one insisted that, 'no child is not adoptable'. He felt that his authority's success in placing older children for adoption was due to the determination, creativity and drive of the adoption team manager. Another manager similarly felt that skilled, experienced adoption workers 'who know what they are looking for, who know what realistic criteria are for a family' could make all the difference, while yet another felt that being 'less cautious' about who might be considered for adoption could increase the numbers adopted.

Shortage of skilled staff

There was also some concern about the feasibility of recruiting sufficient staff with the necessary expertise. Managers in one authority felt that much of the drift and delay in their system was due to a shortage of skilled social workers, while in another authority there was concern about the difficulty of recruiting enough staff with experience of adoption work. Social workers' lack of training and expertise in adoption work was identified as a potential problem by the Performance and Innovation Unit's report in 2000, and this problem is likely to be compounded by the continuing problems that local authorities experience with the recruitment and retention of qualified social workers. In County (South), for example, staffing shortages in the county's adoption teams had reduced capacity for undertaking assessments.

Concern was also expressed in several authorities that field social workers had far too little experience of adoption to manage the process without significant assistance from specialist adoption teams. Social workers inexperienced in adoption work may be reluctant to plan for its use (PIU, 2000; Lowe et al, 2002). In one authority, adoption staff stated that social workers were not normally involved in permanency planning and lacked the experience and expertise that the adoption team had developed over the years. Social workers' lack of expertise in adoption meant that they needed help in thinking through and planning for the consequences of seeking to place a child for adoption, for example, in relation to the impact on siblings who are not adopted, for contact with the birth family and for ongoing support, and that they needed to give greater attention to avoiding delay in permanency planning.

Prioritisation of ethnic matching

Research has shown that children from black and minority ethnic groups are less likely to have a plan for adoption and less likely to be adopted than those who are white (Lowe *et al*, 2002; Sinclair *et al*, 2007). A desire to find an appropriate ethnic match, in the context of a shortage of prospective adopters, may create delay and eventually reduce the chance of a child being adopted (Social Services Inspectorate, 2000; Allen, 2003). A review of research on transracial adoption recommended that children should be placed in "same race" placements wherever possible, but if these could not be found this should not preclude adoption (Rushton and Minnis, 1997). From 1998, government exhortations to widen the pool of potential adopters included calls for greater efforts to be made to recruit adopters from minority ethnic groups. However, managers and adoption staff in two authorities believed that local demographics made it particularly difficult for them to increase the numbers adopted, as they took the view that children should be very precisely matched with families of the same ethnicity. Such attempts to find very specific ethnic matches may lead to delay in finding or approving permanent placements for children (Frazer and Selwyn, 2005).

Adoption staff in our study authorities mentioned how a failure to find long-term placements that were matched on ethnic criteria could mean that young children remained for longer than originally anticipated in "transracial" placements. If their foster carers then applied to adopt them, they were reluctant to allow this if they were not well matched on ethnicity, even if the child and carers had formed a close attachment and no other placement had been found despite a lengthy period of searching. Such children were apparently left in a perpetual state of impermanence. The comments of one adoption worker indicate the kind of prioritisation of an "ideal" ethnic match over all other criteria that was evident among staff in at least two authorities:

> *It's probably controversial, but we have a black child with white foster carers who are wanting to adopt him. She wanted to adopt him quite early on but we said, 'No, please let's find a black carer'. But we couldn't. So about 18 months down the line we are assessing her and she does have a black partner and she does have black children, the children are of mixed parentage, so all I am saying is let's try to find someone who is of Nigerian ethnicity.* (Adoption worker)

These attitudes run counter to the requirements of the 1998 government circular, *Adoption: Achieving the right balance*, and in the subsequently published National Adoption Standards, which state that children should be matched with families who can best meet their needs, but that they should not be kept waiting for a "perfect match" for a lengthy period of time (Department of Health, 1998, 2001b). While agencies should undoubtedly make strenuous efforts to recruit and support an ethnically diverse pool of adopters, research has shown that, for children from some minority ethnic groups, demographic factors may set limits to the size of that pool. The number of adults potentially available as adopters may be limited for children of mixed parentage, Bangladeshi or Pakistani origin or from Muslim and Sikh communities, due to the very young age profiles of these communities. Other cultural and religious factors may also influence the availability of black, Asian and mixed relationship adopters (Frazer and Selwyn, 2005).

The foster carers who took part in our focus group in one authority were highly critical of the way ethnic matching was prioritised over emotional attachment. One couple explained that in their experience local authorities would accept "transracial" foster placements but placed far greater emphasis on matching on ethnic or religious grounds when making adoptive placements. They spoke of their distress at seeing advertisements attempting to recruit adopters of the same ethnic origin for a child they had fostered for several years and had themselves wished to adopt.

Variation in thresholds for looking after children

It is well known that thresholds for looking after children may vary between local authorities (Oliver *et al*, 2001; Ward and Skuse, 2001; Biehal, 2005; Dickens *et al*, 2007). Managers from two of our authorities expressed the view that their local authorities' strong commitment to family support resulted in high thresholds for admission to care and this, they felt, meant that decisions to place for adoption were less readily made. However, we might anticipate that authorities with a particularly strong commitment to family support might have a looked after population in which *more* children might require permanent placements outside their birth families, not less. In authorities with higher thresholds for admission, children who do eventually become looked after are more likely to be those with very serious difficulties (Schofield *et al*, 2007). In such authorities, adoption might instead be the most appropriate option for a *higher* proportion of children who become looked after, compared to authorities with lower admission thresholds. Nevertheless, for some children in these authorities, entry to care may be delayed rather than prevented, with the result that children are older by the time permanence plans are made. Their older age may reduce the chance that adoption is chosen, or achieved, as a permanent placement.

Influence of the courts and children's guardians

Managers and staff felt that care proceedings had become increasingly complex and subject to an unprecedented level of scrutiny, which often led to delay in placing children in permanent placements. The recommendations of children's guardians and the decisions of the courts clearly influence local use of both adoption and alternative permanent placements. Some local courts and some children's guardians may be more likely than others to insist on the further assessment of birth parents or relatives and on further attempts at rehabilitation. Indeed, some social workers may feel that the views of children's guardians carry more weight with courts than their own recommendations (Lowe *et al*, 2002; Ward *et al*, 2006). The low status accorded to social work as a profession and perceptions of their lack of expertise by the courts may lead to considerable delay in permanency planning (Munro and Ward, 2008). As one manager explained, the local courts' reluctance to make care orders without repeated attempts to re-assess parents and relatives and "try" the children at home sometimes had serious consequences for the well-being of children and could delay matters so much that they became less likely to be adopted:

> . . . *I think that stems from the Human Rights Act, the courts are not willing to make any more care orders . . . without every stone being turned for these children to live with their birth family, or a significant other attached to their birth family . . . So I think the time of care proceedings is a lot, lot longer, which makes the children a lot, lot older and they have been through more in their lives.*

Where unsuccessful attempts at rehabilitation are made, children may not only lose their chance of being adopted due to delay in identifying the optimum route to permanence for them, they may also be re-exposed to abuse, as the limited evidence available on the outcomes of rehabilitation suggests (see Biehal, 2006). For example, a manager in Unitary (East) commented:

> *Adoption is very scrutinised. But I don't think (family support) is just tried, I think a lot of it has been exhausted as well. And that is leading children into experiencing different forms of abuse that haven't been able to be resolved.* (Manager)

Managers from two of our authorities argued that much of the reason for delay arose from local courts' interpretations of the Human Rights Act, which was implemented in October 2000. In their local courts, barristers were sometimes advising birth parents to use the Human Rights Act 1998 to make legal challenges to local authorities' plans for adoption, a practice that has also been identified by other studies (Lowe *et al*, 2002; Ward *et al*, 2006). They considered that courts had become more likely to allow specialist assessments and less likely to make a final care order unless all aspects of the care plan were assured. Adoption hearings were being delayed when, for example, children's guardians were not entirely satisfied about contact arrangements. Lengthy delay due to repeated attempts at rehabilitation with parents may result in children losing their chance of adoption, given that they will be older once plans for permanence outside their birth families are made. Children's repeated moves in and out of care and prolonged exposure to adversity may also increase the severity of any emotional and behavioural difficulties, and will also make them harder to place.

Legislation in different policy areas may therefore have contradictory effects. On the one hand, the Children Act 1989 and the Adoption and Children Act 2002, both underpinned by the welfare principle, implicitly prioritise the rights of children (to protection from significant harm and to the promotion of their proper development). Consistent with this, the 2002 Act emphasises the need for timely planning for permanence in order to meet children's needs for emotional and legal security early in their lives. On the other hand, it appears that the Human Rights Act has influenced some local courts to prioritise the rights of parents to family life, resulting in significant delay in decision making for children in need of permanent placements. Yet, as Williams points out, the right of a child to have a family life under Article 8 of the Human Rights Act 1998 'may, in an abusive family, be in direct conflict with the state's positive duty to protect her, or him, from inhuman or degrading treatment' (Williams, 2004, p 44). There may be a tension between parents' claims to the right to family life and the principle expressed in the United Nations Convention on the Rights of the Child that the best interests of children should be the main consideration.

On the limited evidence on this issue available to this study, tensions appear to exist between different policies and different professionals, and between attempts to prioritise the needs of children for safe and permanent care and parents' rights to retain parental responsibility or remain in contact with their children. This reflects the long-standing conflict between proponents of the "state as parent" and the "kinship defenders". A tension between state paternalism and the defence of the birth family has been in evidence at least since the Children Act 1948 (Fox Harding, 1991; Packman and Jordan, 1991).

Financial disincentives to adoption

Managers felt that inconsistencies in the level and duration of financial and practical support to the carers of children in different types of permanent placement not only raised issues of equity but also posed financial disincentives to existing carers wishing to offer permanent placements to children. Some managers feared that concerns about financial support might discourage some people from adopting, as previous research has indicated (Lowe et al, 2002). For example, one manager mentioned two sets of foster carers who wished to adopt sibling groups but who were trying to negotiate long-term allowances that would increase with the age of the children before making a final decision about adoption.

In two authorities, the same allowances were being paid to adopters, long-term foster carers and holders of residence orders to ensure equity across all types of permanent placement. Managers were wrestling with the difficulty of drafting clear policies on the exceptional circumstances in which allowances might be paid, particularly since any decisions on exceptional payments nevertheless had to be consistent with the various regulations.

The case of kinship care was a good example of these difficulties over equity and of the consequent disincentives to carers to move to arrangements that might give a greater sense of legal security to children. Mr Justice Munby's judicial review of Manchester City Council's financial support to kinship carers was felt to have complicated matters. The implications of that judgment were that local authorities could not pay a lower rate to kinship foster carers than they did to non-kinship carers. This raised the thorny issue of whether kinship carers should be paid a fee as well as a maintenance allowance. One manager feared that if fees were paid they would no longer be able to establish kinship care arrangements outside the looked after system and was worried that, 'we'll just suck children into the system'. She felt that relatives wishing for a higher level of financial support were unlikely to apply for residence orders, as financial support packages are means tested. She also mentioned that some lawyers were advising relatives against applying for them as they would be better supported if they cared for children as kinship foster carers.

Summary and conclusion

Consistent with national statistics and previous research, we found variation in the use of adoption and long-term foster care between authorities that were apparently similar in terms of structure, size or demographics. Evidence from our key informant interviews and focus groups suggests that these local variations in the use of different types of permanent placement are related to variations in local policy and practice.

The Government's adoption reform programme, which began in 1998, had clearly led to significant changes in culture, policy and practice within our study authorities by 2005. In all these authorities, the programme had led to a much sharper focus on the use of adoption and also, more broadly, on planning for permanence.

Despite this general enthusiasm for increasing the use of adoption,

significant cultural differences between authorities nevertheless remained. Some were clearly more, or less, willing to consider older children for adoption. Sometimes a readiness to seek out adoptive placements
for older children derived from specific local policy recommendations
and sometimes from the enthusiasm, commitment and skill of particular
adoption managers and staff. Similarly, although staff from all authorities
stated that adoption by carers was an acceptable route to permanence,
there was evidence that some individuals were less enthusiastic about
supporting plans for carer adoption. There was also some variation in how
positively long-tem foster care was viewed, and whether such placements
were planned and were intended to be permanent from the start.

The question of matching could also be viewed differently in different
authorities. Two authorities were particularly rigid in prioritising matching
on ethnic criteria over all others, even though this could ultimately
preclude the finding of a permanent placement. This practice runs counter
to specific guidance on this issue in the Government circular *LAC
(98(20))* (Department of Health, 1998).

Other cultural differences may also be influential; for example, some
authorities may focus more on rescuing children than on planning for
them, whereas others may be more mindful of the need to plan for
permanence at an early stage. A failure to plan in a timely and effective
manner or to properly support the placements of more challenging
children may lead to drift in care or to placement instability. Such
approaches may change as leadership and management change over time.

Another possible reason for variation in the use of permanent placements is related to the different ways managers developed local policies
in response to the complexity of regulations on financial support for
different types of permanent placement. These complexities raised problems of equity and could also result in perverse incentives *not* to adopt.
The different solutions to these anomalies developed by different local
policy makers and managers could potentially lead to greater incentives
or disincentives to adoption, particularly for kinship carers and other
foster carers. Local responses to complex financial regulations on support
for different placements are also influenced by wider local decisions on
policy and resources for children's services.

Finally, the actions of courts and children's guardians could also have an impact on the permanency plans for children, and these are likely to vary from one local court to another. Their decisions or recommendations sometimes caused extensive delay, as repeated attempts at rehabilitation were tried or a number of potential kin carers were assessed sequentially. A balance between children's and parents' rights is difficult to strike in the complex situations that courts have to deal with, but it should be recognised that extended attempts to repeatedly try rehabilitating children at home or find relative carers for them may implicitly give greater weight to parents' rights. The lengthy prolongation of attempts to find a solution within the birth family may cause such lengthy delay that it may eventually become much more difficult to place children for adoption.

All of these factors are likely to interact to produce the local variations evident in national statistics. Changes in national policy and the introduction of new performance indicators set new requirements for local authorities, which may be interpreted and implemented differently by different local authorities. Local cultures vary and may also change over time as a result of wider changes in local policy or as managers come and go, and these developments are likely to contribute to variations in the use made of different permanent placements too. Local decisions on permanency may also be influenced by the perception that applications for certain types of permanent placement will be subject to less scrutiny by the courts, or involve a lesser degree of assessment, than others. However, whatever the local context, decisions on the appropriate permanency plan should always be based on a holistic assessment of the best way to meet the child's long-term needs for emotional and legal security.

5   Adoption, stability and change: care careers of the census sample

This chapter explores pathways through care for a large sample of children who had been in the same foster placement for a minimum of three years or had been adopted from care. It presents a prospective analysis of the placement careers of our census sample of 374 children, drawing on data from the administrative databases of our seven local authorities (their SSDA903 data). We compare the characteristics and care histories of children taking different pathways but, as our census sample is unlikely to be truly representative of all children in long-term placements, we do not aim to predict precisely how many children in long-tem placements might take any specific pathway.[2]

Characteristics of the census sample

Age at census

At the time of our census in 2006, the ages of all but one of the children ranged from seven to 18 years.[3] At this point, just under half were under 13 years old and just over half were adolescents, as shown in Table 5.1.

Since the children in this sample had been placed away from home for seven or more years by the time of our census, the sample included a higher proportion of older children than is the case for the general population of children in care.

---

[2]   Administrative data from local authorities were carefully checked for accuracy but we cannot be sure that we were informed of all eligible cases in each authority. It is therefore possible that the drawing of incomplete samples in some authorities may have resulted in some systematic sample bias. However, local problems with data extraction varied across the seven authorities, so it may be that possible sampling bias in one authority may have been offset by a different type of bias in another.

[3]   One child from the original York sample was now 24 years old and therefore excluded from some of our analyses.

Table 5.1
Age of census sample at survey (n = 374)

Age (years)	%	Number
7–9	17	64
10–12	30	113
13–15	35	133
16–18	17	63
24	<1	1

Changes in legal status from 1998–2006

All of the children had been in foster care in 1998/99. By 2001/02, just over three-quarters of them had been continuously looked after in the same foster placement for a minimum of three years and just under a quarter had been adopted (or freed for adoption). Four to five years later, by the time of our 2006 census, many more children had left the care system. Over one-third had been adopted and a small number were now cared for on residence orders or had been reunited with their parents, as shown in Table 5.2.

The proportion adopted is much higher in this sample than is the case nationally. Just over five per cent of English children who spend six months or more in the care system are subsequently adopted. This difference is due to the way our sample was selected, since one of the

Table 5.2
Legal status 1998/99–2006 (n = 374)

	1998/99		2001/02		2006	
	%	(n)	%	(n)	%	(n)
Looked after	100	(374)	77	(287)	51	(189)
Freed for adoption/adopted			23	(87)	36	(136)
Residence order				–	5	(17)
Discharged to parents				–	5	(20)
Ceased to be looked after (other)				–	3	(12)
Total		**374**		**374**		**374**

criteria for selecting this sample (in 2001/02) was that a child had either remained in the same foster placement for at least three years or had been adopted from care during that time.

Patterns of stability and change

Although we cannot predict whether intended permanent placements would indeed endure into adulthood, seven or more years after they had entered their index foster placements, three-quarters (76%) of the children were living in placements that were *apparently* permanent. These fell into two groups. The first comprised all those who had lived continuously with the same foster carers since 1998/99 (32%) and the second included those who had left care either through adoption, the granting of a residence order or a single return home that had apparently endured (45%). How-ever, the remaining 23 per cent had experienced unstable care careers, as shown in Figure 5.1.

Figure 5.1
Stability groups % (n = 374)

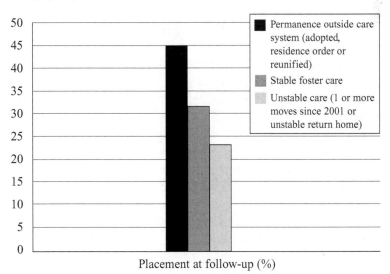

Placement at follow-up (%)

Legend:
- Permanence outside care system (adopted, residence order or reunified)
- Stable foster care
- Unstable care (1 or more moves since 2001 or unstable return home)

Nearly one-third of the total sample appeared to have achieved stability within the care system through a single placement in foster care lasting for a minimum of seven years. We use this as our definition of long-term foster care, rather than the definition embodied in the national indicator for placement stability (noted in Chapter 2). In this study, long-term foster care is defined by duration and not according to whether the placements were originally planned as permanent. Nine of these children had left the care system before our census date in December 2006, but the majority (106) were still looked after by their index foster carers at that point.

The group whose care careers we defined as "unstable" included both children who had moved one or more times since 2001/02 (that is, after a minimum of three years in a settled foster placement) and those who had returned home and then re-entered care. In nearly one-quarter of all apparently stable cases, long-term foster placements had ended and children had gone on to experience one or more changes of placement. In some cases, placement moves may be beneficial to children, even after three years or more, if they are in poor-quality placements. It is also possible that in a few cases it may have taken three years to explore options such as reunification or alternative forms of permanence, to obtain court approval for adoption and then fail to find an adoptive placement and, if the current carers were unable to offer long-term care, to find an alternative permanent placement. In such cases, the index placement could not be said to have disrupted. Nevertheless, if such a series of events extended over a lengthy period of time and then resulted in children moving on from foster placements in which they had been settled for three or more years, the effect would be to create instability in the children's lives. Children in such situations effectively experienced unstable care, even if their index placements had not ended as a result of disruption and the move had been a positive one. Details of the children's current placements in 2006 are shown in Table 5.3.

The administrative data cannot tell us whether the adopted children had remained with their adoptive parents. However, it is likely that this data would indicate whether any children had returned to care after the making of a residence order or discharge home (unless they had moved to

Table 5.3
Placement in 2006 (n = 374)

	%	Number
Permanence outside care system	**45**	**170**
• Adopted	36	136
• Residence order	5	17
• Single return home without re-entry to care	5	17
Stable foster care	**32**	**118**
• Remained in same foster placement since 1998/99	29	109
• Stable until discharge (current residence unknown)	2	9
Unstable care (moved 1+ times since 2001/02)	**23**	**86**
• Foster care	14	53
• Residential care	5	18
• With birth parents (eight placed with parents on care order)	3	11
• Not known	1	4
Total	**100**	**374**

Note: Percentages do not add up to 100 due to rounding.

another authority), so we can be reasonably confident that these groups of children had not moved again.

Only eight per cent were known to have returned to their birth parents by this point. It is unsurprising that so few children had been reunited with their parents. All of the children not adopted had been in foster care for a minimum of three years and, as the evidence from many other studies indicates, the likelihood of reunion with birth families decreases with the passage of time, for a variety of reasons (Biehal, 2006; Sinclair *et al*, 2007).

In our sample, the proportion adopted is far higher than the proportion nationally (5.4% in 2008/09). This is due to the nature of sample selection for this study, which included only children in long-term foster care or adopted from care. Since all of the children who remained in the care system had spent at least three years in a single foster placement, the proportions in the "stable" and "unstable" groups are also likely to differ from the proportions that might be found in a sample that included all looked after children. Furthermore, as this was not a truly representative sample, the proportion within each stability group might be somewhat different in another sample (of children in long-term foster care or adopted from care). Given local variations in the use of different types of permanent placements discussed earlier, it might also vary across authorities. We therefore compare the characteristics and care histories of children in the different stability groups, but do not aim to predict precisely how many children in long-tem foster placements might eventually find themselves in any specific group.[4]

Comparing care careers

Placement moves

Less than one-fifth of the children had remained in the same placement throughout their time in care. This is not unusual, as children often move at least once from an initial placement made for assessment, or in an emergency, to a planned placement. However, 62 per cent moved two or more times during the total time they were looked after and 29 per cent had between four and 19 placement moves.

The average number of placement moves was significantly higher or lower in particular local authorities. The average number of placement moves was lower (0.7) for the children in our Inner London Borough and higher (6) for those in Unitary (North).[5] These local differences could not be explained by the age profile of the children, nor by the extent to which residential care was used by these authorities. This local variation is therefore likely to be influenced, at least to some extent, by variations in local policy and practice.

---

[4] When the same analysis was done for the booster sampling frame alone n = 269 (excluding data on those eligible for the York sample), the proportion who left the care system was 36%, of whom 26% had been adopted; 38% remained in stable foster care and 26% experienced unstable care, as defined above.

[5] One-way Anova. Tukey test significant at p = .05 for total placement moves by local authority: mean placement moves in the other five authorities ranged from 2.1 to 3.2.

Most placement moves had occurred at a relatively early stage in the children's care careers, before they settled in their index foster placement or were adopted. However, among the children still looked after in 2006, 43 per cent had moved one or more times after spending three or more years in their index placements (by 2001/02).

Table 5.4
Looked after children: moves after 3 years in index placement (n = 189)

Number of moves since 2001/02	%	Number
0	56	106
1	15	28
2–3	14	27
4–6	7	14
7–19	7	14

Note: Percentages do not add up to 100 due to rounding.

The 18 children who were in residential care by the time of our census had experienced the highest total number of placement moves – an average of 7.6 since the start of their care careers. Unlike those who moved to adoptive homes, to new foster placements or back home to their parents, most of the movement experienced by the children who were in residential care by 2006 had occurred *after* they left their index placement, not before. The residential care group had moved an average of five times after leaving their index foster placements, compared to 1.25 moves for those in new foster placements and 1.5 moves for those who eventually returned home.[6]

Duration of final care episode
Children who had left the care system had, on average, done so within four years of entering it. Those who were adopted spent the least time in

---

[6]   Tukey test significant at p = .05 for residential care compared to a homogeneous sub-set of all other placement types in 2006 (for which mean moves ranged from 2.5–3.9).

care, an average of 3.2 years. Nearly one-quarter had been adopted within two years of last entering care and two-thirds had been adopted within four years.

Children cared for on residence orders tended to spend longer in the care system, while those discharged home to their parents had spent longer still, as shown in Table 5.5.

Table 5.5
Duration of last care episode (years)

	Still in care (n = 189)	Left care (n = 185)	Adopted (n = 137)	Residence order (n = 17)	Discharged home (n = 21)
Mean	9.4	3.8	3.2	4.7	5.5
Range	2–14	0–11	0–11	0–10	1–9
SD	2.02	2.4	2.18	2.6	2.08

Compared to those adopted, children on residence orders had spent 1.5 years longer in care, while those who were discharged home had been looked after 2.3 years longer, on average.[7]

Duration of last placement

Children in stable foster placements had lived there for an average of 8.1 years, for periods ranging from four years (for some who had returned home before our census) to 12 years. However, for children in other circumstances, their latest or final placement in care had been much shorter. The average duration of the children's latest or final care placement varied according to the nature of the placement, as shown in Table 5.6.

---

[7]   One-way Anova significant at <.001. Tukey test comparing adoption with other exit types significant at p = <.001 for discharged home and p = .024 for discharge via residence order.

Table 5.6
Duration of last placement by placement status in 2006 (n = 361)[8]

	Mean duration years (SD)
Adopted	1.15 (1.68)
Residence order	4.29 (2.64)
Stable foster care	8.42 (1.74)
New foster placement	1.35 (1.27)
With birth parent	1.75 (1.69)
Residential care	1.88 (1.77)

Some of those with shorter placements had been adopted after a relatively short period of care, while others had had unstable care careers and had moved only recently. The majority (78%) of those who were living at home in 2006 had been in their last placement for less than three years because they had returned home relatively recently.

Children still looked after at the time of the census

Only half (51%, 189) of the children were still looked after at the time of our census. Well over half (58%) of those who were still looked after remained in stable foster care, still living in their index foster placements. Two-thirds (67%) of those in the unstable care group had moved to new foster placements and most of the remainder (23%) were in residential care.

Those in the stable foster care group had lived continuously with the same foster carers for seven years or more and 43 per cent of them had been settled for nine to 12 years. Nearly one-third (30%) of those in the unstable care group had lived in their current placement for less than one year, but one-fifth of them had moved to another placement that had lasted for three years or more. For half of this small group, their second long-term placement was in residential care. It may be that many of the children in long-term residential care were those with disabilities since, as

---

[8]   One–way Anova significant at p = <.001.

we shall see in Chapter 6, nearly half of the children in our survey sample who were in residential care were reported to be disabled.

Summary

- We conducted a prospective analysis of administrative data on place-ment pathways and outcomes for our census sample of 374 children, seven or more years after they had entered their index foster placements.
- Seven or more years after they entered their index foster placement only half of the children continued to be looked after. Over one-third (36%) had been adopted, five per cent were cared for on residence orders and five per cent had been formally discharged.
- By this stage, 45 per cent had moved to permanent placements outside the care system, 32 per cent were in apparently permanent, long-term foster placements (which had endured for seven or more years) and 23 per cent had experienced unstable care careers. Children were significantly older at the time of our census than those adopted or in stable foster placements.
- After three or more years in their index foster placements, 28 per cent of the children had moved two or more times (and 14% moved between four and 19 times).
- Half of the children were still looked after at the time of our census. Over half of them (58%) were still in their index foster placements but 42 per cent had less stable care careers, having moved to new place-ments. A small number had settled in a second long-term placement that had lasted for three or more years.

6 Children and placements: the survey sample

The previous chapter described the pathways, characteristics and care histories of the children in our census sample, drawing solely on administrative data. Administrative databases can provide information on patterns for a large number of children, but on a limited range of variables. The rest of this study focuses on the 196 children in our *survey sample*, on whom we have much richer data provided by carers and social workers to supplement the information available from local authority databases. In this chapter we describe the children in our survey sample and their placements at the time of our survey, and compare the characteristics and care histories of those with different pathways through care. In the chapters that follow, we go on to compare histories, circumstances, outcomes and perceptions of permanence for children who were adopted, in stable foster care or who had unstable care histories.

Stability and placements

By the time of our survey, seven or more years after the children last entered care, just under half of them had moved to permanent placements outside the care system and nearly one-third were in long-term, stable foster placements. Just under one-fifth had experienced unstable care careers. The proportion in permanent placements outside the care system was slightly higher and the proportion with unstable care careers slightly lower than for our census sample, but the proportions in stable foster care were virtually identical, as shown in Table 6.1.

If we consider only those children who were still looked after at the time of our survey (n = 100), we find that 63 per cent were in stable foster care and so appeared to have achieved permanence within the care system. As noted in the previous chapter, not all of the children in our unstable care group may have left their index placement as a result of disruption. It is also important to note that placement stability should not

Table 6.1
Stability groups in 2006 (n = 196)

	Survey sample %	Survey sample (n)	Census sample %
Permanence outside care system	**49**	**(96)**	**45**
• Adopted	39	(77)	36
• Residence order/special guardianship	8	(16)	5
• Single return home without re-entry to care	2	(3)	5
Stable foster care	**32**	**(63)**	**32**
• Remained in same foster placement since 1998/99	32	(63)	32
Unstable care (moved 1+ times since 2001/02)	**19**	**(37)**	**23**
• Foster care	13	(26)	14
• Residential care	5	(10)	5
• With birth parents	<1	(1)	3
Total	**100**	**(196)**	**100 (374)**

be the only consideration, as placement quality is of equal importance, an issue we shall return to in Chapter 15. Some children may therefore have moved from their index foster placement for good reason. Nevertheless, whatever the reason for the change of placement, such a move built instability into their lives after a period of settled care, so they are included in our unstable care group. As the above table shows, most of the children with unstable care careers had moved to new foster placements, but a small group had moved to residential placements, as shown in Table 6.2.

Among the children who had been adopted, 57 per cent were adopted by strangers and 39 per cent had been adopted by their former foster carers. The proportion of children adopted by their foster carers is higher than that likely to be found among all children adopted from care, which was just 15 per cent in 2002/03 (Department for Education and Skills,

Table 6.2
Placement in 2006 (n = 196)

Type of placement	%	(n)
Foster care	45	(89)
Adopted, of which:	39	(77)
adoption by foster carer	15	(30)
adoption by stranger	22	(44)
adoption by aunt and uncle (1) or unknown	1	(3)
Residence order/special guardianship	8	(16)
Residential unit	5	(10)
With birth parents	2	(4)

Note: Percentages do not add up to 100 due to rounding.

2003). This is due to the way our survey sample was selected.[9] As mentioned in the previous chapter, this study aims to compare histories and outcomes for children in different types of permanent placement but does not attempt to estimate the proportions likely to take different pathways through care.

All but one of the young people in residential care were adolescents. Although nearly half (four) had moved to their current placement in the past year, an equal number had been there for two or more years. One 14-year-old boy who had a disability and health problems was placed in a residential school but the others were living in ordinary residential units. Half of this group had a disability, health problem, or both.

Fifteen of the children were on residence orders and one nine-year-old, who had been cared for by his grandparents since he was a baby, was now on a special guardianship order. Many of the children on residence orders were cared for by relatives, in most cases grandparents. Over one-quarter

---

[9] Cross-sectional samples of looked after children normally include a higher proportion of children in long-term care, as these accumulate over time and so are more likely to be in placement on the census date. As we shall see, children in care for longer periods of time were more likely to be adopted by carers than by strangers. Children (often very young) who stayed less than three years in care before being adopted (by strangers) would have a lower chance of being included in a cross-sectional sample like this one.

of the children who were still looked after were placed with kinship foster carers, as shown in Table 6.3.

Table 6.3
Children with kinship carers per cent in each group (n) (n = 190)

Kinship carers	Carer adoption (n = 30)		Stranger adoption (n = 44)		Stable foster care (n = 63)		Unstable care (n = 37)		Residence/special guardianship orders (n = 16)	
	%	n	%	n	%	n	%	n	%	n
Yes		0		0	33	(21)	16	(6)	69	(11)
No	100	(30)	100	(44)	67	(42)	84	(31)	31	(5)

In total, over one-fifth of the children were living with relatives, including one adopted by his aunt and uncle. In nearly one-fifth of all cases, former foster carers had offered permanence outside the care system either by adopting the children or, in five cases, by caring for them on residence orders.

Table 6.4
Carer's relationship to child (n = 196)

Type of placement	Total sample	
	%	n
Birth relatives, of which:	22	(43)
grandparent (foster care or residence order)	11	(22)
aunt/uncle (foster care, residence order, adopted)	7	(14)
birth parent (placed with parents or discharged)	2	(4)
other relative (foster care)	2	(3)
Adoptive parent (stranger)	22	(44)
Former foster carers (adopted/residence order)	18	(35)
With non-relatives/not adopted	38	(74)

Legal status

As might be expected in a predominantly long-stay group of children, the majority of those who were still looked after were placed on care orders, as shown in Table 6.5.

Table 6.5
Legal status (n = 196)

	%	*Number*
Adopted	39	77
Care order	46	90
Accommodated	5	10
Residence order	8	15
Special guardianship	<1	1
No legal order	2	3
Total	**100**	**196**

Of the ten children who were accommodated, seven were in long-term foster placements and three were in residential placements. The three children who were not under any legal order were all living with their birth parents at the time of the survey.

The children

Age and sex

Many of the children were teenagers by the time of our 2006 survey. Their ages ranged from seven to 18 years, although one child from the original York sample was now 24 years old (and was therefore excluded from many of our analyses). Adopted children in our sample tended to be younger than those still looked after. Among those still looked after, children with unstable care careers were more likely to be aged 13 years or over than those in stable foster placements.

Table 6.6
Age at survey by placement group per cent (n = 190)

Age in years	Carer adoption (n = 30)	Stranger adoption (n = 44)	Stable foster care (n = 63)	Unstable care (n = 37)	Residence/ special guardianship order (n = 16)	Total sample (n = 190)
7–9	17	55	6	0	19	20
10–12	47	25	26	11	38	26
13–15	20	13	52	57	38	38
16–18	13	7	16	32	6	16
24	3	-	-	-	-	<1
Total	**100**	**100**	**100**	**100**	**100**	**100**

Note: Percentages do not add up to 100 due to rounding.

Children adopted by strangers were two years younger, on average, than those adopted by carers. The key differences in age lay between children adopted by strangers, whose mean age was significantly lower than that of the children in all other groups, and between children adopted by carers and those with unstable care careers.[10]

Table 6.7
Mean age at survey by stability group per cent (standard deviation)

Carer adoption (n = 30)	Stranger adoption (n = 44)	Stable foster care (n = 63)	Unstable care (n = 37)	Total sample (n = 174)
12.3	10.3	13.4	14.4	12.6
(3.32)	(2.46)	(2.25)	(1.75)	(2.86)

The difference in average age between those in stable foster care and those with unstable care careers was not statistically significant for this sample, but this may be an anomaly as our analysis of the care careers of the much

---

[10]   One-way Anova significant at $p = <.001$ and Tukey test significant at $p = .05$.

larger census sample, presented in the previous chapter, found that the difference between these two groups was indeed significant.

Just over half (55%) of the children in our survey sample were male. There were no significant differences between the stability groups in terms of gender distribution.

Ethnic origin

The vast majority (82%) of the children in our survey sample were white. Half of the children from black or minority ethnic groups were of mixed ethnic origin. The next largest group were black, the majority of whom were of Caribbean origin, but few were of solely Asian origin, as shown in Table 6.8.

Table 6.8
Ethnic origin of survey sample (n = 196)

	%	(n)
White	82	(160)
Black	5	(10)
Asian (Indian sub-continent)	2	(3)
Mixed (black and white)	2	(4)
Mixed (Asian and white)	2	(4)
Mixed (other)	4	(8)
Other ethnic group	2	(4)
Missing data	2	(3)

Note: Percentages do not add up to 100 due to rounding.

The proportion of children from black or minority ethnic groups was lower in our survey sample than is the case for the population of children looked after in England as a whole, just 16 per cent compared to 22 per cent nationally during the year of our survey. The proportion of mixed ethnic origin was the same as the proportion nationally (8%), but the proportion of black children in our study (5%) was slightly lower than is the case for England as a whole (7%).

Around three-quarters of the children from black or minority ethnic groups in our survey sample came from our two London authorities. In the Outer London authority, 83 per cent of our sample was of black or other minority ethnic origin, and the black children in this authority accounted for half of all the black children in our sample. In our Inner London authority, 53 per cent of the children came from black or minority ethnic groups. Most of those were of mixed ethnic origin, followed by children who were black. Most of the remaining children of black or minority ethnic origin came from a single county. Children from these ethnic groups accounted for over a quarter of the sample in this county. In all of our other authorities, over 90 per cent of the survey sample were white. There were no significant differences in the age or gender profiles of children from different ethnic groups.

Children from black or minority ethnic groups were no more or less likely to have been adopted than white children. In total, 15 children from black or minority ethnic groups had been adopted. Around one-third of the children of mixed ethnic origin (five) had been adopted by strangers and half of the black children (five) had been adopted by their foster carers. Over half of the children of mixed ethnic origin (eight) were in stable foster care. However, numbers in these groups were too small for tests of significance.

Disability and health

We asked parents and workers whether young people had physical or sensory impairments, learning disabilities, mental health problems or emotional and behavioural difficulties. These matters can be difficult to define and people do not always agree on definitions. We accepted that young people experienced one of these difficulties if either a parent or a worker reported that they did. According to carers and/or social workers, one-quarter of the children had a disability.

The OPCS definition of disability includes children with emotional or behavioural difficulties (Bone and Meltzer, 1989). In our analyses, our categorisation of children as disabled/not disabled employed a narrower definition, encompassing only those with physical, learning or sensory impairments. Even on this relatively narrow definition of disability, one-quarter (50) of the children and young people in our survey sample were found to have a disability. In total, around one-third of the sample had a disability, chronic and serious health problems or both, as shown in Table 6.9.

Table 6.9
Children with a disability or serious health problems (n = 196)

	%	(n)
Disability only	11	(22)
Health problems only	7	(14)
Both disability and health problems	14	(28)
Total with a disability or health problems	**32**	**(64)**

The proportion of children reported to have a disability (25%) was the same as the estimate for the proportion of children with a disability among the national population of looked after children (Gordon *et al*, 2000). One-fifth of the sample was reported to have a statement of special educational needs. As data on this issue were missing for over half of the sample, this may be an underestimate of the true proportion with special educational needs.

Carers and social workers were asked to give details of any health problems or disabilities the children might have. In over half of these accounts, children were reported to have more than one difficulty, and it was clear that in many cases these difficulties were severe. It is therefore important to take account of these difficulties when we later consider questions of progress and outcomes in different areas of the children's lives.

Many children were reported to have developmental delay and/or emotional and behavioural problems. One in eight (25) were reported to have learning difficulties and for a substantial minority (10) these were severe. Nearly one in ten were reported to have emotional and/or behavioural difficulties and 12 of these children were reported to have Attention Deficit Hyperactivity Disorder (ADHD). These 12 children with ADHD represent six per cent of the sample, a proportion higher than that for the general population of 11–15-year-olds, for whom the prevalence of hyper-kinetic disorders is under two per cent (Meltzer *et al*, 2000). In a small proportion of cases (four per cent) the children were reported to have mental health problems. Nine children were reported to be on the autistic spectrum, two-thirds of them with a diagnosis of autism and one-third with Asperger's syndrome. Five of these children were said to have learning difficulties too.

Some children had chronic and serious health problems and/or a physical disability or sensory impairment. Five were known to be wheel-chair users, of whom all but one had cerebral palsy. Six children had other chronic health problems and two of these cases were reported to be the consequence of abuse. Details of the children's health and developmental difficulties are shown in Table 6.10.

Table 6.10
Health, developmental problems and disabilities (n = 196)

	Per cent of total sample	*Number*
Blind	2	4
Emotional and/or behavioural problems	9	18
Mental health problems	4	7
Mild/moderate learning difficulties	8	15
Severe learning difficulties	5	10
Autistic spectrum disorders	5	9
Cerebral palsy	3	6
Rare disease or syndrome	2	3
Epileptic	4	7
Other chronic/ongoing health problems	3	6

Most of the disabled children were in long-term foster care or had been adopted by their former foster carers, as shown in Table 6.11.

Table 6.11
Per cent of disabled children per group (n = 196)

	Carer adoption (n = 30)		Stranger adoption (n = 44)		Stable foster care (n = 63)		Unstable care (n = 37)		Other (n = 22)	
	%	n	%	n	%	n	%	n	%	n
Disabled	47	(14)	18	(8)	29	(18)	16	(6)	18	(4)

Nearly half of the children adopted by carers had a disability. Carer adoption clearly offers an important route to permanence for children with disabilities. One-quarter (four) of the children on residence or special guardianship orders were also disabled, two of whom were living with their former foster carers. Four of the disabled children in the unstable care group were living in residential placements.

Care history

Reason for last entry to care

We were able to gather information on the reason for the latest episode of care for just under three-quarters of the children. We asked social workers to distinguish between the main reason and a secondary reason for the child's last admission to care or accommodation. As we were concerned that we might receive fewer questionnaires from the social workers in relation to adopted children, we also asked adoptive parents to indicate the main reason why their child had entered care. Where no social worker questionnaire was returned, we have reported the reason given by the adoptive parent instead.

The reasons reported most often were parents' neglect and inability to care. Three-quarters of the children had last entered care for these reasons.

Table 6.12
Reasons for last entry to care

Reason	Main reason (n = 143)		Second reason (n = 50)	
	%	Number	%	Number
Parent unable to care	42	60	11	16
Neglect	34	48	9	13
Actual abuse	14	20	2	3
Potential abuse	6	9	9	13
Child's behaviour	2	3	1	2
Breakdown in parent–child relationship	<1	1	2	3
Adoption breakdown	1	2	–	–

There were no significant differences between our four stability groups in the likelihood of entering care for abuse, neglect or due to parents being unable to care. The rather patchy details given by social workers and carers suggested that an inability to care for their children was usually due to parents' mental health, drug or alcohol problems. In a few cases, parents had died. Abuse (actual rather than potential) or neglect was given as the main reason for entry for 48 per cent of the children. This is slightly lower than the national pattern since, nationally, 60 per cent of 10–15-year-olds in the care system (the largest age group in our study) are looked after for reasons of abuse or neglect (Department for Education and Skills, 2006).

Children in our sample were more likely to be looked after due to neglect rather than abuse. Numerous studies of reunification in the USA have found that children placed as a result of neglect are likely to remain in care longer than those placed for reasons of physical or sexual abuse. This may account for the smaller proportion placed due to abuse in this predominantly long-stay sample (Biehal, 2006). Another reason may be their age at entry, as Sinclair and colleagues' study of 596 children in foster care found that there was strong evidence of neglect for 56 per cent of those who entered care when under the age of five years (Sinclair *et al*, 2005b).

Age at entry to care

Nearly three-quarters (73%) of the children in our survey sample had first become looked after before they were five years old and, indeed, well over half (56%) had done so before the age of three. Placement outcomes varied considerably in relation to age at last entry to care. Adopted children had typically entered care at a very early age, with those adopted by strangers entering earliest of all. However, half of the children with unstable care careers had been five years old or over at their last entry to care.

Table 6.13
Age at last entry to care by group per cent (n = 168)

Age in years	Carer adoption	Stranger adoption	Stable care	Unstable care	% across groups
<1	40	59	15	3	28
1–<3	20	21	25	24	23
3–<5	10	9	27	22	18
5 and over	30	11	33	51	31
Total	**100**	**100**	**100**	**100**	**100**

Table 6.14 shows the mean ages at which the children in each group had entered the care system on both the first and last occasion.

Table 6.14
Mean age at first and last entry to care by group per cent (n = 168)

Age	Carer adoption	Stranger adoption	Stable foster care	Unstable care
	Mean (SD)	Mean (SD)	Mean (SD)	Mean (SD)
Mean age at first entry	2.5 (2.99)	1.4 (2.20)	3.7 (2.53)	4.9 (3.09)
Mean age at last entry	3.1 (3.50)	1.6 (2.30)	3.9 (2.49)	5.3 (2.91)

The difference in mean age at last entry to care between those adopted by strangers and those adopted by carers suggests that adoption by carers may offer a route to permanence for children entering care at an older age. Children adopted by their carers tend to remain longer in care prior to adoption than those adopted by strangers – an average of 4.27 years compared to 2.27 years for those adopted by strangers.[11]

Children in long-term foster placements typically entered care later than those who were adopted. The significant differences in the average age at which children entered care for the first and the last time (if they had more than one episode of care) lay between children who were adopted and those in both other groups. Although the mean age of children with histories of unstable care was higher than the mean age for those in stable foster care, this difference was not statistically significant.[12]

Age at last placement

Over half of the children had moved to their current placements before the age of five and the majority (80 per cent) of the sample had done so when under 10 years old. The children adopted by their carers had been, on average, over two years older when they were placed for adoption than those adopted by strangers and those on residence or special guardianship orders, as shown in Table 6.15.

Children in stable, long-term foster placements had typically entered their current placement at a similar age to those adopted by carers. Although the age at which these fostered children had moved to their current placement ranged from under one to 10 years old, three-quarters had been placed with their index carer by the time they were six years old.[13]

---

[11] Independent samples t-test significant at $p = <.001$ (n = 74).

[12] Chi-square tests, significant at $p = <.001$ for ages at both first and last entry to care. One-way Anova, significant at $p = <.001$ for both first and last entry to care. Post-hoc Tukey tests significant at $p = .05$.

[13] One-way Anova significant at $p = <.001$ for both age at last entry to care and age at last placement. Tukey-B test showed that there were significant differences in age at entry to care between those adopted by strangers and those in stable foster care ($p = <.001$) or unstable care ($p = <.001$); between those adopted by carers and those with unstable care careers ($p = .06$); and between those in stable foster care and those with unstable care careers ($p = <.001$). Tukey B test showed that the significant differences in age at last

Table 6.15
Mean age at entry to last placement by group (n = 174)

| | Mean age at entry to last placement | |
	Years	(SD)
Adopted (all)	2.92	(3.14)
Adopted by stranger	2.68	(2.71)
Adopted by carer	3.43	(3.73)
Residence/special guardianship order	2.3	(2.10)
Stable foster care	4.14	(2.58)
Unstable care	12.14	(2.61)

Duration of current placement

Most of the children had been settled in their current placements for a very long time – 77 per cent of them for five or more years.[14]

Over half of the children in the unstable care group had lived in their current placements for less than two years. However, 43 per cent (16) of them had been settled in their current placements for two to four years. For six of these children, these were their second long-term foster placements. Three others, two of whom had learning difficulties, had settled in residential care.

All of the children on residence/special guardianship orders had been in their current placements for five years or more, and 81 per cent had been living with the same carers for at least eight years. Children adopted by strangers had lived in their placements for a significantly longer time than children in all other groups, while those with a history of unstable care had naturally lived in their current placements for a shorter period of

---

placement lay between adopted by stranger and adopted by carer (p = .003), stable foster care (p = .002) and unstable care (p = <.001). Differences between the unstable care group and all other groups were significant at p = <.001.

[14] One-way Anova significant at p = <.001. Tukey-B test (significant at p = .05) showed that the significant differences lay between those in unstable care and all other groups and between those adopted by strangers and all other groups. There was no significant difference between carer adoption and stable foster care.

Table 6.16
Duration of current placement by group per cent (n = 174)

Duration (years)	Carer adoption (n = 30)	Stranger adoption (n = 44)	Stable foster care (n = 63)	Unstable care (n = 37)
	%	%	%	%
<2	–	–	–	57
2–4	7	2	–	43
5–7	23	55	29	–
8 or over	70	43	71	–
Total	**100**	**100**	**100**	**100**
Mean duration (SD)	8.74 (2.65)	7.26 (1.31)	8.84 (1.97)	1.46 (1.19)

time than all others. Among the children who had not left the care system, 61 per cent were in settled foster placements that had lasted for five years or more and nearly three-quarters of this group had been settled for a minimum of eight years.

Experience of loss

Many of the children and young people had experienced loss or disruption in their lives, either through bereavement or through the break-up of their adoptive or foster families. Data on these issues were incomplete, but it was reported that (at least) 28 per cent had experienced bereavement in their birth families. It was unclear whether a parent had died in all of these cases, or whether some replies referred to the death of other family members. Evidence from a study of a national cohort of over 35,000 Swedish young adults who had lived in care found that the likelihood of losing a parent before they reached the age of 18 was much higher for young people who had lived in long-term care than for those who had not been in care. Many had lost a parent due to substance misuse-related deaths, suicide or violence (Franzen and Vinnerlung, 2006).

Furthermore, nearly one-third of the children (32%) had experienced bereavement in their foster or adoptive families, although again it was unclear whether it was carers who had died or other family members. Indeed, seven children had experienced bereavement both in their birth families and in an adoptive family or foster placement. A small number had also experienced loss through the divorce or separation of their adoptive parents (eight per cent) or foster carers (eight per cent) at some stage in their lives.

Summary

- Placement patterns and stability for our survey sample (n = 196) were similar to those for our census sample. Thirty-nine per cent had been adopted (of whom 57% were adopted by strangers and 40% by their former foster carers), 32 per cent were in stable foster care and 19 per cent had experienced unstable care careers. Nearly three-quarters of those who had unstable care histories were in new foster placements, but just over a quarter of them were in residential care.
- One-fifth (22%) of the children were either fostered by relatives or looked after by them on residence/special guardianship orders. One-third of children in stable foster care and one-sixth of those with unstable care histories were in kinship foster placements.
- Children adopted by strangers were significantly younger and those with unstable care careers were significantly older, compared to other groups.
- One-quarter of the children had a disability or sensory impairment and one-fifth had a chronic health problem. Half of the children adopted by carers and 29 per cent of those in stable foster care were disabled.
- The most common reasons for the children's entry to care were their parents being unable to care for them (42%) and neglect (34%).
- Children adopted by strangers had begun their final care episode much earlier than others (mean age 1.5 years). Children adopted by carers had entered care for the last time later (mean age 3.1 years) and those in unstable care latest of all (mean age 5.3 years).
- The duration of current placements varied according to the children's stability groups. The mean duration was just under nine years for both carer adoption and stable foster care, just over seven years for adoption

by strangers but less than two years for those in the unstable care group. However, nearly half of those in the unstable care group had settled in a second long-term placement (in most cases foster care) for three to four years.

- Five per cent (ten) of the children had previously experienced the breakdown of an adoption or a placement for adoption. In most cases, this had occurred before they entered their index foster placements. All but two of the children had subsequently been successfully adopted by another family. Over one-quarter had experienced a bereavement in their birth families and one-third had experienced bereavement in their foster or adoptive families.

7 Planning for permanence

Chapters 5 and 6 described the different pathways taken by children in long-term foster placements or adopted from care. As we have seen, some were adopted while others remained in long-term foster care, became looked after on residence orders, experienced unstable care careers or returned home. In this chapter we explore permanency planning, which is one of a number of factors that may influence the pathways children take. We examine the ways in which plans for permanence were made and the rationale for them, drawing on both quantitative and qualitative data from our postal survey and on data from our focus groups.

The Children Act 1989 (S1 (2)) required the courts to be mindful that delay in decision making about children was likely to be prejudicial to their welfare. Despite this requirement, both research and findings from inspections have indicated that delay in decision making can reduce the likelihood that a child is adopted (Lowe *et al*, 1999, 2002; Social Services Inspectorate, 2000; Harwin *et al*, 2003). Selwyn and colleagues' study of adoption found considerable delay in permanency planning, with 41 per cent of children who entered care waiting a year or more before a plan was made. Although legal hold-ups, staff sickness and staff shortages accounted for some of the delay, much of it was due to poor assessment and a lack of active planning once the children became looked after (Selwyn *et al*, 2006). More recently, there has been renewed policy emphasis on active planning for permanence, for example, in the Adoption and Children Act 2002, the National Adoption Standards 2001 and the Public Law Outline 2008.

The original plan for the child

As might be expected, all of the stranger adopters in our study had considered themselves to be offering a family for life from the moment their children were first placed with them. However, initial plans had been quite different for most of the children who were in long-term foster placements or had been adopted by their former foster carers. Only half of the 60 long-term foster carers and carer adopters who answered this question considered that the original social work plan had been for them to offer the child a permanent home. For half of the children living in stable foster placements or with carer adopters at the time of our survey, therefore, plans had clearly changed over time. The children had originally been placed with these carers on a short- or medium-term basis, sometimes in preparation for another placement (13%), or with the intention that they would subsequently be reunited with their parents (7%). There were therefore two pathways to permanent foster care or carer adoption. Some long-term placements had been planned as permanent placements from the start. For others, plans for reunification or alternative placements had not come to fruition or had changed for other reasons, or relationships between carers and children had developed and the placement plan had changed from provision of short- or medium-term care to provision of a permanent home.

Where placements had not been intended to be permanent from the start, the time that had elapsed before plans changed was quite varied. In 40 per cent of cases the plan for the placement to become long term was made within one year of placement, while in 33 per cent of cases the plan had changed after the child had been placed for two years or more. In just over one in ten cases, the carers were unclear about when the plan for the child to remain with them long term had been made.

In many cases where plans for the placement had changed in this way, the foster carer had asked to keep the child long term, although in a small number of cases the request had come from the child as well as the carer. In some cases, too, the social worker had asked the carer to agree that the placement should become long term. Where carers had initiated the move to change the purpose of the placement to the provision of long-term care (either as a long-term foster placement or through adoption), in the majority of cases the response of social services had been positive. However, one-quarter (six) of the carer adopters who responded reported that social workers had initially been reluctant to agree to their proposed change of plan.

We also asked social workers about the original plan for the child's current placement. Excluding the responses of social workers reporting on children adopted by strangers, we had replies to these questions from 84 social workers. In over two-thirds (67%) of these cases, social workers told us that the child's current placement had been intended to be permanent right from the start, but in 31 per cent of cases they took the view that it had subsequently become permanent, although this had not been the original plan.

When we compared the responses in the 49 cases where both social workers and carers had answered these questions, we found some disparity in their views. In around one-third (17) of these cases, carers reported that they had always viewed the placement as permanent, whereas social workers reported that it had changed from being a short-term to a permanent placement as time progressed. It is possible, of course, that post-hoc rationalisation of events many years earlier might have coloured the views of some of these carers and that social workers' knowledge (or memory) of events several years earlier may have been faulty, but it remains a possibility that this was so in a proportion of these cases.

Reunification with birth families

The first permanency option normally considered is reunification of children with their birth families. As we have already seen, few children in our survey sample had been reunited with birth parents. This was due to the way our sample was drawn, as it was a sample of children in long-term care and the likelihood of reunification is known to decrease with time in care (Biehal, 2006). Social workers indicated that reunification had been attempted for nine children, but by the time of our survey just four of them remained with their birth parents. These four children had all entered care as a result of neglect or due to their parents' inability to care for them. Three had returned only once and had settled back at home, but the fourth was less settled, having experienced more than one return home. All four were teenagers (three of them aged 15–16 years at the time of our survey). For most of these children, return home was usually prompted by the breakdown of foster placements during adolescence, perhaps accompanied by the desire of children and parents to be reunited.

The failure of attempts at reunification may contribute to instability in children's placement careers. Return home has also been found to be one of the predictors of difficulties in social behaviour, along with poor school adjustment and attachment difficulties. For the five other children who returned home, all but one of whom had entered care due to concerns about potential abuse, placements with parents had proved unsuccessful. One had since been adopted, three were now in foster care and another was cared for on a residence order by his former foster carer. Social workers indicated that the "pull of the birth family" had contributed to the disruption of foster placements, but the attempted rehabilitation was sometimes unsuccessful:

> *Child's urge to return to mother triggered breakdown of first long-term foster placement. Lack of parenting skills contributed to breakdown of rehabilitation.* (Social worker)

Why were other children not reunited with their families?

We asked social workers why other children had not been reunited with their birth parents. Multiple reasons were often cited, the most common being that the home was too unsafe or damaging (40% in total) and that parents would be unable to cope (57%), as shown in Table 7.1.

In almost all cases where the home was viewed as unsafe, the children had last entered care as a result of neglect (39 children), and most of the remainder had entered following abuse (17). Neglect had also been the reason for entry to care where parents were viewed as unable to cope with their child. In most cases where parents were thought to be unable to cope, the home was also viewed as unsafe. In nearly one-quarter of cases, reunification had not been attempted partly because the courts would not have allowed it. Again, most of these children had been admitted due to neglect and the remainder due to abuse. In just over one in ten (16) cases, however, social workers reported that the child had no effective home to return to, because parents were either dead or out of contact.

The other reasons given concerned relationships. In nearly one in five cases children did not want to return to their birth parents, and in the majority of these cases social workers also indicated that the child's home

Table 7.1
Why child was not living with birth family per cent (n) (n = 146)

	Very much so		To some extent		Not at all true		Don't know/ not applicable	
	%	n	%	n	%	n	%	n
Child did not want to return (n = 59)	7	(10)	12	(17)	7	(10)	15	(22)
Birth parent opposed return (n = 60)	5	(7)	6	(9)	13	(19)		(25)
Home thought to be too unsafe/damaging (n = 67)	30	(44)	10	(15)	2	(3)	3	(5)
Parents would have been unable to cope (n = 68)	29	(42)	10	(15)	1	(2)	6	(9)
Child too bonded to foster carers (n = 40)	8	(12)	10	(14)	8	(11)	2	(3)
Courts would not allow it (n = 60)	19	(28)	5	(7)	3	(5)	14	(20)

was thought to be unsafe. These children had entered care due to neglect and/or abuse and most appeared to be settled with their current carers. Five of these children were adopted and in virtually all the other cases social workers indicated that these children were thought to be too closely bonded with their foster carers to return home. Indeed, in a total of 28 per cent of cases, the bond between child and carer was one of the factors that precluded the return of children to their parents.

Social workers considered that over one in ten parents (16) did not want their child to return and in ten of these cases it was thought that the child also did not wish for return. Most of these children had entered care due to neglect and in most cases social workers viewed the home as unsafe. Five of these children were disabled, and it is possible that their parents found it difficult to care for them for this reason.

If children cannot be reunited with their birth parents, social workers are usually expected to investigate whether they can be placed with other members of their families. As we saw in the previous chapter, one-third (21) of the children in stable foster care and one-sixth (6) of those with histories of unstable care were in kinship foster placements, half of them with grandparents. Another 11 children were cared for by relatives on residence orders. For nearly one-third (31) of the children who had not been adopted and who could not return home, however, social workers indicated that those children could not be placed with their extended families because no suitable relatives were available.

Decisions about adoption

Adoption by strangers

Our survey questionnaires asked carers why they had decided to offer a permanent home to the child. Some stranger adopters responded in quite general terms, replying that they had simply wanted to adopt a child. Other replies were more specific to the child in question, and generally indicated that they had felt the child belonged to their family right from the start. They spoke of the bond that had developed when the child had first been placed with them for adoption, or said that the child had seemed to fit in with their family very quickly:

We connected with her right from the start.

From the start, he bonded to me despite his interpersonal difficulties.

I'd been seeking to adopt a child her age and she settled into my family, who really accepted her.

Adoption by carers

Unlike stranger adopters, carer adopters already knew the children very well indeed before adopting them. Most told us they had adopted the child because a bond had developed between them, or said they had grown to love him or her, and several mentioned that the child had simply fitted in and felt like one of the family:

We all love her to bits and she loves us.

We had her for three years and we loved her dearly.

She'd lived with us since the age of six weeks and was part of our family. I wanted to give her stability and a normal life without lots of birth parent interference.

We love this child and they love us. They were part of our family. It was a natural progression. Let him know that people do care for him and love him.

It was my heart, you know, because, you know, we loved her, we'd grown to love her and care for her and she felt the same . . . She's, yeah, she's great, and even if she wasn't great, we'd still love her because she's part of our family, you know.

They often had additional reasons too. As they grew to love the children, they became concerned about their needs for a secure and stable future:

After having her for two years we loved her and wanted what was best for her, a permanent home.

Had grown to love the child. Thought of him as our own and wanted to protect him.

Sometimes, their anxiety about the child's long-term future was compounded by their concerns about what they viewed as unhelpful decision making by social workers. They wished for greater parental responsibility so that they could give the child greater security and also protect them better from the vagaries of the care system:

Part of our family. Fed up of social services' rules.

Social services were interfering too much, when we were the carers and we knew what was best. For example, making her see her sister even though it would disturb her.

I believe too much emphasis is placed on keeping siblings together. This delayed [child's] adoption until she was four-and-a-half years old . . . There was never a chance that she would return home or that all seven children could ever live together . . . Having seen her six siblings remain in foster care and be moved round and split up as placements broke down, I am happy that I gave her permanency and stability. She is my daughter and I love her unconditionally.

Several carer adopters mentioned that social workers had supported their decision to adopt, but two reported that they had encountered opposition from social services:

The first social worker wanted two parents [I'm one parent]. She left and the new social worker was all in favour.

She didn't want to leave and we had grown to love and care for her. If social services had had their way, we would not have adopted her. We had to take social services to the High Court where they overruled the decision against us.

There were also several cases where carers were prompted to consider adoption by social workers' decision to seek adoptive parents for the child and therefore remove the child from them. As several carers explained:

We did not want him to go to anyone else.

Some of these children had initially been placed with these carers at birth, or shortly afterwards. A few had not initially put themselves forward but, prompted by their love for the child, had decided to do so once it became clear that other adopters could not be found. It was apparent that in these cases, the child demonstrated an attachment to the carer and a mutually rewarding relationship had developed over time. An underlying desire to rescue a well-loved child from an uncertain future was also evident in some cases:

He was very attached and so was I. A couple had turned him down and I thought of this as a sign that we should be together. I'm so glad I did.

An adoptive family could not be found due to her health needs and past history . . . we grew to love her so much and had been through so much with her and her mum and she had got so attached to us.

Why were more children not adopted?

We also explored the reasons why adoption had not been pursued as a permanence option for the children in our sample who were not in adoptive homes at the time of our survey. As we saw earlier, the majority of these were in foster placements but a small number were on residence orders, in residential care or reunited with their parents. First we asked the social workers of non-adopted children why the child was not living with adoptive parents. The responses of 85 social workers are shown in Table 7.2.

Table 7.2
Why child had not been adopted % (n) (n = 85)

	% (n) of relevant children	
	%	n
Child did not want adoption (n = 23)	13	(11)
Birth family opposed adoption (n = 35)	34	(29)
Child thought too disabled (n = 24)	5	(4)
Too many behaviour problems (n = 32)	15	(13)
Child thought too old (n = 37)	25	(21)
Child too settled in foster care (n = 41)	40	(34)
Child bonded to birth family (n = 41)	32	(27)
Adopters sought but not found (n = 25)	6	(5)
Adoptive placement did not proceed to adoption (n = 20)	6	(5)

The reasons that adoption was not pursued fell broadly into four groups. First, the child or birth parent's opposition to adoption had discouraged social workers from pursuing this option. In over one-third of cases, parents were opposed to adoption and in eight of these cases, the children did not want adoption either. It is, of course, questionable whether parents' opposition to adoption is necessarily a legitimate reason for not pursuing this permanence option. A further three children were reported to be against the idea of adoption, even though there was no reported opposition from their birth parents. Some of the children were considered to be too bonded to their birth families to countenance adoption.

Second, the nature of the child's existing relationships had influenced decisions about adoption. Where children were placed with relative carers, some social workers indicated that either they or the foster carers felt adoption was inappropriate, although both adoption and residence orders had been discussed. Matters could be complicated precisely because these carers were related to the birth parents. For example, in one case, an aunt and uncle had decided not to apply for a residence order or adoption because of suspected opposition by the child's father. In some of these cases, carer adoption had not been pursued because the child was one of a group of siblings. Either carers did not want to adopt a whole sibling group placed with them, or adopt one but not others, or the children concerned did not wish to be adopted separately:

Siblings did not want a symbolic unravelling, with adoption by different family members. They wished to stay as a sibling group with the same status as each other.

Third, attributes of the child or the carer were given as the reason that the child was not in an adoptive home, most commonly because the child or carer was thought to be too old. The severity of the child's behaviour problems and, in a few cases, the severity of the child's disabilities, were also reported to have influenced decisions about adoption:

Discussions for foster carers to adopt children or look at residence order but worried about child's behaviour.

Child was placed with aunt for long-term fostering. He has requested adoption but his behaviour is causing indecision from his aunt and uncle.

Finally, the outcomes of permanency planning were also shaped by the availability of adopters for children. There were a few cases where adoption had indeed been planned but had not been achieved, either because no suitable adopter had been found or because an adoptive placement did not proceed to adoption. In two cases, a placement for adoption had broken down and in three other cases, a decision had been taken that the adoption should not proceed.

We asked social workers why these children had not been adopted by their current foster carers. All who replied reported that it was "not at all true" that their local authority was against adoption by carers and all also reported that it was "not at all true" that the foster carers' ethnic background made them unsuitable as adopters for the child in question (although evidence from our focus groups suggested that, in some authorities, concerns over ethnic matching could be a barrier to adoption, as we saw in Chapter 4). The most common reasons given were that the carers would not consider adoption (27%) and that the child's ongoing contact with their birth family made it unsuitable (34%). Nearly one-quarter of the carers (24%) were not considered to be suitable adopters for the child, and for half of these, the reason given was that the carers were too old to adopt this child. Some social workers also reported carers' concerns about a reduction in support if they adopted the child.

We also sought the foster carers' views on why they had decided not to adopt the children they were caring for. Fifty carers answered this question and two-thirds of them reported that they had not adopted the child because 'I see my role as a foster carer'. In five cases, they reported that they would have liked to adopt but had not been able to, and in another three cases, foster carers said they had considered adopting the child but decided against it. Three others reported that the child did not wish to be adopted.

As other studies have reported, concerns about the loss of financial and other support for themselves and for the children may make foster carers reluctant to consider adoption (Lowe *et al*, 2002). In our study, both foster carers and social workers described the carers' concerns about losing financial and other support:

This child is one of a group of three siblings. I know it would be difficult to put three children up for adopting together. I did not want them separated but could not afford to adopt myself. (Foster carer)

This placement has produced a high level of stability for the child. It is a shame, however, that the foster carers are not in a financial position to either adopt or take out a residence order. They do see the child as part of the natural family and treat him as such. (Social worker)

Financial factors would not allow the child and family the same standard of living if adopted. (Social worker)

The ideal outcome for [child] would have been either adoption or residence order with current foster family. However, the foster carers have been reluctant to take this step through a reasonable fear that fewer services would be available to the child and themselves as a family. (Social worker)

He has had a lot of problems with health and education. Social services have been very good. I feel at this time I need their support. (Foster carer)

His father was against it and because of his disabilities it was felt he would get more help if we carried on fostering him. (Foster carer)

The views of birth parents and children were also important to foster carers. Around half of these foster carers indicated that the agreement of both birth parents and social services would have had an impact on whether they proceeded with adoption. Foster carers of some children also commented that adoption was not an option due to the conflicting loyalties the children might experience, sometimes as a result of pressure from birth parents:

Child is still loyal to birth parents and thinks they may get upset if adopted.

Considerable [birth] family pressure to remain loyal and not to be adopted by us. We have offered adoption.

Child feels she has her own mum and dad and even though she can't live with either of them, they are still her mum and dad and very important to her, she does not want to replace them.

He has a good relationship with us and his parents. He knows he cannot return home so he feels and we feel also as if he has the best of both worlds. The plan and arrangements are working well.

Delay in permanency planning may be a further reason why children are not adopted, in circumstances where adoption might potentially be in their best interests. One study found that, for children permanently placed, the odds of not being adopted increased by 1.7 for every year of age at entry to care and by 1.6 for every extra year of delay in reaching a best interests decision (Frazer and Selwyn, 2005). Another study found that long-term plans had been formulated an average of one year sooner for children who were eventually adopted, compared to planning for children who remained in long-term foster care (Lowe *et al*, 2002).

Decisions about long-term foster care

When asked why they had decided to offer a long-term home to the child, the replies of the long-term foster carers who completed our question-naires were similar to those of the carer adopters. Most mentioned that they had formed a strong bond with the child, who had settled into the family and fitted in well:

Did short-term fostering for child and just fell in love with her.

Devoted to him, great affection for the boy.

Because we love him.

Because the child and her brother fitted in well with our family and seemed happy with us. We already had two adopted children . . . and they were all good company for each other.

He is part of the family.

Many of these foster carers felt they were acting in the children's best interests by offering to care for them long term. Like the carer adopters, some had decided to care for the child long term out of a desire to rescue him or her from an uncertain future, sometimes in situations where no suitable long-term foster carers or adoptive parents had been found. In the absence of alternative long-term carers, these foster carers were all too aware of the possibility that the children might move from placement to placement and wished to protect them from this. In a number of cases, these carers were also concerned to prevent the separation of siblings they were caring for:

> *Because the younger brother also wanted to stay with us – aged two, but we were told he could be adopted. We didn't want the brothers split up. They grew on us, became part of our family. The younger one called us mum and dad.*

Usually a mixture of circumstances led to both the decision that a permanent placement should be sought and the decision of the child's current foster carer to offer a long-term home, but always in the context of an established bond between carer and child:

> *Due to his mum's mental health problems and her continued stays in hospital, it was decided that a permanent placement was needed . . . They did try to place [child] with another carer, but he made it plain he didn't want to move . . . Because we have had [child] since he was 15 months old and have always been happy to have him back when the need arose. We were more than happy to keep him; he, in turn, had shown that he wanted to stay here.*

A few of the children in our "unstable" group, whose initial long-term placement had broken down, appeared to have settled in a second one. Again, this was largely due to the bond that had developed between foster carer and child, even if this had happened relatively recently. As well as genuine affection, some carers displayed remarkable altruism in difficult circumstances. For example, one foster carer, who had been looking after a 14-year-old girl for just one year, acknowledged the impact of placement breakdown on this child and said she intended to keep her long term despite her challenging behaviour:

> *Firstly, everyone wanted the placement to carry on. Secondly, because*

of Monica's behaviour and problems, finding another placement would have been hard . . . Apart from caring for Monica, we were very aware of how fragile she was as a result of her long-term placement breakdown. Monica is one of the most difficult placements we have had but to have her moved again would have made her feel rejection again.

The foster carers in our focus group expressed similar views to those who completed our questionnaires. They suggested that carers' decisions to offer a permanent foster home to a child initially placed short term were driven by a variety of factors. First, and crucially, carers and children had developed a strong relationship. Whether this happened was related to the child's capacity for forming positive relationships. Second, the "chemistry" between carers and children was important too, as sometimes the child just seemed to belong in their family: 'Sometimes you get a little soul that comes to you and they just fit.' Third, once carers had become attached to a child, they felt an altruistic desire to protect him or her from the potentially damaging effects of being in the care system, such as repeated moves. Their comments suggested that they often had multiple motivations to keep the child long term:

I couldn't bear for them to go back into the system. And part of that seems to be about the powerfulness of your relationship with those particular children. So, those children obviously got themselves to a sort of point where they could form a relationship with you

I think it's great if, if this child is going up for adoption and they've been with you for a period of time and they've settled in your household, why pick them up and move them to a set of strangers?

Social workers reported that in some circumstances, foster care was the preferred option for children with particular needs. For example, one child was placed with specialist foster carers due to his serious mental health problems and sexualised behaviour. Several social workers also indicated that they often saw long-term foster care as the preferred option for sibling groups, in order to keep siblings together and offer adequate support to carers. Carers, social workers and sometimes the children themselves also felt it was important not to treat siblings differently, through placing some for adoption but not others.

One-third of the children in long-term foster care were fostered by relatives, half of whom were grandparents. The relative carers in our survey sample were far more likely to remain as foster carers for the child or take out a residence order, than to adopt. Only one relative carer had adopted a child but one-quarter of them had taken out a residence order. Social workers often viewed residence orders as a more appropriate option than adoption for children fostered by relatives.

Kinship care often involved complex sets of relationships between siblings, carers and, sometimes, birth parents, in the context of which carers felt that adoption would be inappropriate, divisive or damaging, as well as being likely to deprive them of much-needed professional support. A social worker described the often complex situations faced by relative carers:

> The social work role has been to support grandparents since they undertook the care of three grandchildren they never knew existed when the crisis occurred in 1995. Because of their need for this, and because of the siblings' need not to be differentiated, they have feelings of solidarity from their experiences, and because of the uncertainties about Dad, who had a paranoid view of his own parents, we have never seriously entertained adoption ... It's a successful placement.

> The child hasn't gone on to adoption or residence order because the grandparents have felt the need for support over his health and education problems over the years and because there are no issues of stigma or conflict in their relationship with local authority.

Several managers in our focus groups and interviews emphasised that long-term foster care should be a positive choice for children who could not return home and who did not have a realistic chance of adoption. They acknowledged that short-term placements often became long term by default, but argued that sometimes the delay had occurred because unsuccessful attempts had been made to identify adoptive parents. Time passed as the search for adopters continued and during this period carers sometimes became strongly attached to a child and came forward to offer a permanent home. In these circumstances, converting the placement to a long-term one was a positive choice, they felt. Although sometimes social services were not convinced that these carers were the best possible match for a child, the development of a strong bond between carer and child, the lack of alternatives and a wish to offer stability, a decision would be made that, on balance, converting the placement to a long-term one was the best available option:

> *Because we haven't properly matched them at the start, we've placed them where there's a place. But sometimes it just gels and the child's had a lot of moves and you wouldn't want to move them for the sake of it.* (Manager)

> *Because it's a long-term placement and the young person's got some sort of attachment there, we're kind of constantly balancing whether it's be more destructive to move them to a better placement, which we probably haven't got anyway.* (Social worker)

However, several managers and fostering staff expressed concern that people approved as short- or medium-term foster carers might not necessarily have the skills needed to look after a child successfully in the long term, particularly once the child's behaviour became more challenging during adolescence. Foster carers with whom children were initially placed short term and who subsequently offered to care for them permanently were normally, therefore, assessed as long-term carers for these children. Such decisions were usually made at children's reviews and then, if assessment of the carers indicated that the plan was appropriate, approved at fostering panel. Occasionally, however, situations arose where authorities considered that a foster placement should become a permanent placement for a child but the foster carers were reluctant to make a long-term commitment. This posed dilemmas for social workers and managers:

I've got a couple of foster homes at the moment where we are trying to talk about long-term issues and the carers are frightened of committing themselves to permanence. In so many ways it's a perfect placement and there's a very strong bond . . . the child's attached and is doing really well and we probably won't be able to find better and that's, that's a real dilemma. (Fostering manager)

Managers and fostering workers were concerned about the impact that carers' refusal to keep children who had settled would have on the children, who might not understand the reasons for the bounded nature of short-term carers' commitment to them.

Conclusion

Plans for permanence may change over time and children for whom adoption was not the initial plan may eventually be adopted (Ward *et al*, 2006). Equally, adoption may not be achieved for all of those for whom it was originally planned. Delays may be occasioned by the failure of attempts at reunification, by an unsuccessful search for adopters, by the courts, by a change of plan or simply by a lack of timely planning. Long delays occasioned by a lack of timely planning, changing family circumstances or the search for optimal matches for children may, however, provide the time and opportunity for bonds to develop between children and their foster carers. Such relationships may depend on the "chemistry" between carer and child, which in itself may be influenced the carer's and child's capacities to develop mutually rewarding relationships and by the child's behaviour. In these circumstances, social services may set aside concerns that the match is not ideal and, given the strength of the bond, may make a decision that it is in the best interests of child to remain with these foster carers long term or be adopted by them.

The wishes and feelings of children and birth parents also play an important part in plans for permanence. Some children may wish to be adopted, while others are sure they do not wish this to happen, and some may state a strong preference for remaining with their foster carers until adulthood. The York studies of children in foster care found that some children strongly opposed the idea of adoption, but did not want to go home either. Many did not want to sever ties with their birth families and expressed a wish for what might seem a half-way house. These wishes were quite compatible with the desire of around four out of ten to continue living with their carers after the age of 18 (Sinclair *et al*, 2005b). If the children's views were to be followed, permanence for some might be sought through a positive choice of long-term foster care rather than through adoption or placement at home. The nature of relationships between children and their birth parents and the nature of any contact between them also has a significant influence on plans for permanence, as do carers' wishes to keep the children and their fears that they would lose support if they adopted children instead of fostering them.

However, all of these decisions occur at specific historical moments, in which there is a greater or lesser emphasis on permanency planning in general and on specific forms of permanence, such as adoption or reunification, in particular. They are shaped by the political, legal and social context, at both national and local level, in which decisions about policy and the use of resources are made. As we saw in Chapter 3, national adoption rates began to rise after the Government began its programme of adoption reform in 1998 and there is considerable local variation in rates of adoption and in the use of long-term foster care. Different authorities may be more, or less, likely to prioritise adoption as a form of perm-anence, due to local policy decisions, cultures and views about who is or is not suitable to adopt or be adopted. Local children's guardians and local courts also influence the nature and timing of decisions. National and local policy decisions about the provision of financial and other support to different types of carers may also influence carers' decisions about whether to adopt a child, apply for a residence order or continue to foster.

Decisions about permanent placement are therefore the product of complex processes whereby political, legal, institutional and individual decisions intersect to shape the pathways of children. Permanency plans are shaped by policies, organisational cultures, local decisions about resources and local courts, as well as by individual professionals and the wishes, feelings and behaviour of children, carers and birth parents. Some of these protagonists and institutions will have more power to shape decisions than others. Given these multiple influences on plans for permanence, it is perhaps not surprising that such decisions may sometimes be subject to change.

Summary

- Initial plans for short-term placement or for reunification often changed over time. Half of the long-term foster carers and carer adopters indicated that the original social work plan had been for them to offer the child a permanent placement, but for other children plans for the placement had changed with the passage of time and short-term placements became long term.
- Attempts had been made to reunite nine children with their parents, but in five cases the attempt at rehabilitation had failed. The most common reasons for not reuniting children with their families were that the home was thought to be too unsafe or damaging and that the parents would be unable to cope. In some cases, children or parents did not wish for reunification or the courts would not allow it.
- The main reason that carer adopters gave for adopting the children was that they had grown to love them. Children and carers had developed a strong bond and the children were felt to "fit in" and be part of the family. In these circumstances, some were prompted by social work decisions to look for an adoptive family, or by a failure to find stranger adopters, and some expressed a wish for greater parental responsibility.
- Social workers indicated that the main reasons children were not adopted were the child's or parent's opposition to adoption, the nature of the child's existing relationships with their birth parents, being fostered by kinship carers, the child's age or behavioural difficulties and a failure to find adoptive parents. Where foster carers had not adopted the children they cared for long term, this was most commonly due to the fact that they wished to remain as foster carers or were considered unsuitable as adopters by social services, or to the nature of the children's ongoing relationships with their birth parents. Several foster carers mentioned that they would not adopt because they feared a loss of practical and financial support.
- Long-term foster carers who had decided to offer the children a

permanent home were driven by the same motivations as carer adopters, principally the fact that they had grown to love the children and wished to protect them from the perceived vagaries of the care system. Relative carers were reluctant to adopt both because they feared they would lose financial and practical support and because of the complexity of family relationships. Some relatives had taken out residence orders.

- In situations where foster carers indicated that they wished to offer a permanent home to a child, managers and fostering staff were often concerned that children and carers had not been properly matched. However, given the development of a strong bond between carer and child, the lack of alternatives and a wish to offer stability, a decision would often be made that converting the placement to a long-term one was the best available option.

8 Predictors of adoption

The last chapter presented a descriptive analysis of the reasons for decisions about permanent placements, drawing on data from our survey, focus groups and interviews. In this chapter, we investigate the factors that made it more likely that some children in need of permanent placements would be adopted, while others would remain in care.

Multivariate analyses of the administrative data available on our census sample indicated that children were significantly more likely to be adopted if they had last entered care at a younger age, lived in particular local authorities and had never been placed with relatives.[15] We discuss each of these factors below.

Age at entry to care

Analyses of our administrative data showed that children who were adopted had entered care at a younger age, on average, than other children. The mean age at entry to care for children who were adopted either by carers or by strangers was 2.1 years, whereas the average age of those who were not adopted was 4.2 years.[16] Among the adopted children, 48 per cent had last entered care before they were six months old and 53 per cent had done so before the age of one year, compared to only 14 per cent of those not adopted.

However, there was considerable variation in age at entry to care between children adopted by carers and those adopted by strangers. As we saw in Chapter 6, children adopted by carers were, on average, nearly

---

[15] Logistic regression: the odds of being adopted decreased by .658 for each additional year of age (p<.001), and increased by 10.8 (p=<.001) for children living in County (North) and by 9.29 (p = <.001) for those living in Outer London Borough. The odds of being adopted decreased by .069 if children had had previous placements with relatives.

[16] Independent samples t-test, significant at p = .<.001.

twice as old when they last entered care (3.1 years) as those adopted by strangers (1.6 years).[17]

Compared to those who were in stable foster placements at follow-up, adopted children were more than three times more likely to have first entered care before they were one year old. They were also nine times more likely to have last entered care as infants under one year old, compared to those who experienced unstable care,[18] as shown in Table 8.1.

These findings reflect those from other research and national statistics. A study of over 7,000 children looked after in England similarly found that adoption was overwhelmingly restricted to younger children: the younger the age at admission, the greater the chance of adoption (Sinclair *et al*, 2007). Another study, of the pathways of 374 children in Northern Ireland, found that those who first entered care under one year

Table 8.1
Census sample: age at entry to care by group (n = 340)

Placement in 2006	*Age at first entry to care (age at last entry) %*				
	Under 1 year	*1–2 years*	*3–4 years*	*5 years and over*	*Mean age at last entry in years (SD)*
	%	%	%	%	%
Adopted (n = 136)	55	26	10	9	1.99 [2.52]
Stable foster care (n = 118)	15	28	28	29	3.81 [2.39]
Unstable care (n = 86)	6	29	27	38	4.87 [2.82]

[17] One-way Anova significant at p = <.001 for both first and last entry to care (n = 171). Tukey test for mean age at last entry, significant at p = .05, showed a significant difference between stranger and carer adoption, but not between carer adoption and stable foster care.

[18] One-way Anova significant at p = <.001 for mean age at both first and last entry to care. Tukey tests showed that there were significant differences between all three groups. Mean age at first entry to care was 2.55 years for those on residence orders, of whom 35 per cent had last entered care as infants and 64 per cent had entered before the age of three years. For children living with birth parents in 2006, mean age at first entry was 3.78 years, but 21 per cent had last entered care before they were one year old.

old were 2½ times more likely to be adopted than those who first entered care between the ages of one and two (McSherry *et al*, 2008). National statistics also indicate that children are far more likely to be adopted when under the age of five than over it. For those entering care at a younger age, there is clearly more time for decisions about permanence to be made and for adoptive placements to be found while the chance of adoption is still high.

Variation between local authorities

National statistics and research both indicate considerable local variation in the use of adoption (Sinclair *et al*, 2007). This was certainly true for the seven authorities in this study. Children in County (North) and in Outer London Borough were significantly more likely to have been adopted than those in other local authorities, while children in Inner London Borough were far less likely to be adopted than those living elsewhere.[19]

It was clear from our interviews and focus groups with local policy makers and practitioners that some authorities had more experience in, and were far more optimistic about, placing "hard-to-place" children for adoption than others. Equally, some may be more likely than others to encourage adoption by carers. Some local authorities may have had a stronger commitment than others to adoption and may have devoted more resources to recruiting and supporting adopters. Local policy and associated decisions about resources, together with local professional cultures and practice, are clearly highly influential. It is also the case that local courts have a key decision-making role in relation to the removal of children from their parents, whether contact with their parents should continue, and whether or not they should be adopted (Masson, 2008). These, too, may influence local adoption rates.

Placements with relatives

Children who were adopted were less likely to have been previously placed with relatives (10%) than those not adopted (40%). Decisions

---

[19]   Chi-square test significant at p = <.001.

about adoption are often influenced by whether or not a child has well-established relationships with members of their family. Local practice on placement with relatives may vary and some authorities may place greater emphasis than others on finding long-term relative placements for children as an alternative to adoption. Again, local courts may also influence these decisions.

As the range of variables in administrative datasets is limited, we also considered whether any additional data available to us from our survey might also predict adoption. The only additional factors which predicted that children would be adopted, as opposed to being placed in long-term foster care, were whether they had face-to-face contact with parents and whether face-to-face contact was forbidden. Age at entry to care appeared to be a somewhat weaker predictor of adoption once these two factors were taken into account, even when we considered stranger and carer adoptions separately.

Contact with parents

For our survey sample, the strongest predictor of adoption was having no face-to-face contact with either parent, and the second strongest predictor was face-to-face contact with parents being forbidden. Once these were taken into account, age at entry to care still had an impact on the likelihood of adoption. The odds that children would be adopted were three times higher if face-to-face contact with parents was forbidden, which was the case for 59 per cent of the adopted children compared to only nine per cent of those in stable foster placements. Adopted children were also far less likely to have any face-to-face contact with either parent than those in stable foster care (16% compared to 77% of those in stable foster care).[20]

Face-to-face contact may have been forbidden, or at least discouraged,

---

[20] Chi-square tests for adoption versus stable foster care by face-to-face contact with parents and by contact forbidden, both significant at p = <.001 (n = 119). Logistic regression significant at <.001 for face-to-face contact with parents (Exp.B = 9.349); significant at p = .03 for contact forbidden (Exp.B = 3.74), and significant at p = .003 for age at entry to care (Exp.B = 1.34).

due to concerns about the risk of re-abuse if parents were allowed access to the child. These issues were likely to have informed decisions about adoption taken earlier in the children's lives. However, where contact had not been expressly forbidden, it is difficult to know whether the adoption decision was informed by a perceived lack of appropriate contact by the parent, or whether contact was stopped as a consequence of the adoption decision, because a clean break was thought to be in the child's best interests.

Other studies have shown that an additional factor, not identified in this study, may also decrease the likelihood that children are adopted. They suggest that children are less likely to be adopted if they had been "tried at home", presumably because of the delay that this may occasion and the fact that such children are likely to have continuing relationships with their birth parents and therefore be less likely to have an adoption plan. Being part of a sibling group may also reduce the likelihood of adoption (Performance Innovation Unit, 2000; Sinclair *et al*, 2007).

For our sample, ethnic origin did not alter the likelihood that a child would be adopted, but this was possibly due to the particular characteristics of the two local authorities with the highest rates of adoption. In one of these authorities, all of the children were white, while in the other, the vast majority were from minority ethnic groups, so it was not possible to make within-authority comparisons.

Summary

- Multivariate analyses of administrative data on 374 children showed that children were more likely to have been adopted if they entered care at an early age, relative to those in long-term foster care. Children adopted by carers had entered at a later age than those adopted by strangers.
- Children were more likely to be adopted if they lived in certain local authorities, compared to those who lived in others. This is supported by our evidence from interviews and focus groups with professionals, which indicated that some local authorities more readily considered adoption than others.

- Children who had never been placed with relatives were also more likely to be adopted.
- Data from our survey indicated that, in addition to the above factors, children for whom face-to-face contact with birth parents was prohibited were more likely to be adopted.

9 Comparing emotional, behavioural and relationship difficulties

We asked the children's carers and social workers about their developmental progress and any emotional, behavioural and relationship difficulties they might have. Where both carer and social worker reports were available, we used the carer's rating but, if a carer questionnaire was not completed, for some of the measures we substituted the social worker's rating. Only social workers with recent contact with the children were asked to complete the measures discussed in this chapter.

Age at entry to placement

Previous research has shown that children's ability to recover from abuse and neglect is inversely related to the length of exposure to adversity (Rutter, 2000). Studies of adoption have found that children placed for adoption beyond infancy are at increased risk of poor psychosocial outcomes (Brodzinsky, 1993). Many studies have shown that children placed for adoption after the age of six months subsequently show higher levels of anxiety, insecurity and behaviour problems. Other adoption studies identify the cut-off point for late placement and increased difficulties in psychosocial adjustment at the age of 12 months (Howe, 1998). One study of attachment relationships in adopted children, for example, found that those adopted before the age of 12 months were as securely attached as their non-adopted peers, whereas those adopted after their first birthday showed less attachment security (van den Dries *et al*, 2009). In assessing the severity of the children's emotional and behavioural difficulties, we therefore took account of the age at which children entered their permanent placements.

As we saw in Chapter 6, the mean age at which children adopted by carers typically entered their permanent placements was greater (3.55 years) than that for children adopted by strangers (2.58 years). Nevertheless, over one-third of the children adopted by carers were placed with them (that is, initially fostered by them) before the age of one. This sub-group was larger than the proportion placed with stranger adopters and the proportion entering their permanent foster placements before they were one year old.[21]

Table 9.1
Age at entry to last placement by group per cent (n) (*n* = 174)

Age in years	Carer adoption (n = 31)		Stranger adoption (n = 43)		Stable foster care (n = 63)		Unstable care (n = 37)	
	%	n	%	n	%	n	%	n
<1	36	(11)	19	(8)	11	(7)		0
1 or over	64	(20)	81	(35)	89	(56)	100	(37)

Eight of the children who had entered their final placement before they were one year old were reported to be disabled (four in the stable foster care group and four in the carer adoption group).

Specific difficulties

First, we asked the children's carers and social workers to indicate whether a range of specific emotional and behavioural difficulties had been observed during the past year.[22] In relation to these difficulties, there were no significant differences between the two groups of adopted children, nor between the adopted children and those in stable foster care. The significant differences invariably lay between the unstable care group and the other groups.

---

[21] Chi-square test showed these differences were significant at p = <.001. Age one year was chosen as the cut-off point rather than six months, due to the small numbers involved.

[22] Where both social worker and carer questionnaires were returned, a behaviour or difficulty was taken as being present if either respondent indicated that it was.

Table 9.2
Specific emotional and behavioural difficulties per cent (n) (n = 164)

	Adopted by carers (n = 27)		Adopted by strangers (n = 37)		Stable foster care (n = 63)		Unstable foster care (n = 37)	
	%	n	%	n	%	n	%	n
Physically aggressive	26	(7)**	38	(14)	30	(19)**	57	(21)
Misuse of alcohol	4	(1)*		0**	10	(6)	22	(8)
Misuse of drugs		0*		0*	6	(4)	16	(6)
Running away		0*	11	(4)	3	(2)**	22	(8)
Depression	11	(3)*	8	(3)**	6	(4)***	35	(13)
Eating problems	7	(2)*	13	(5)	16	(10)	30	(11)
Sexualised behaviour	22	(6)	16	(6)***	14	(9)**	38	(14)
Sexual risk to self/others	7	(2)*		0***	10	(6)**	30	(11)
Stealing	7	(2)*	8	(3)*	22	(14)	32	(12)

* group comparison with unstable care group significant at p = .05 or less.
** group comparison with unstable care group significant at p = .01 or less.
*** group comparison with unstable care group significant at p = .001 or less.

Children in the unstable care group were reported to be more likely to experience depression and to engage in sexual behaviour that put themselves or others at risk than those in the other three groups. They were also more likely to be physically aggressive and to run away than children in stable foster care or adopted by carers, though not in comparison with those adopted by strangers. However, all other behaviours were significantly less likely to be reported in relation to the children adopted by strangers than for the unstable care group. Selwyn and colleagues' study of children for whom there had been a plan for adoption similarly found that the group who subsequently experienced unstable care had high levels of depression and were often violent (Selwyn *et al*, 2006).

Social performance

Carers and social workers were asked to rate the children's progress in nine developmental areas on a four-point scale covering the areas monitored by the Looking After Children programme, now incorporated into the Integrated Children's System (Ward, 1995). If no carer rating was available, we substituted the social worker's rating, if social workers had recent contact with the child.[23]

Other than health, which appeared to be good for the majority of children, the most positive ratings given for the sample as a whole were in relation to emotional ties. Nearly two-thirds of children were thought to be clearly attached to at least one adult. Many of the children had a range of other emotional and social difficulties too. Only one-third were considered to have no problems in their emotional and behavioural development and just over one-third were considered to display skilled/very acceptable behaviour in social situations. Less than half had several close friends. Progress in relation to "enjoying and achieving" was also limited. In total, just over half (52%) were making at least average educational progress (including 22% whose progress was rated as above average) and one-third were considered to have many special skills or interests. Table 9.3 shows the ratings by carers at the two extremes of this four-point scale.

There was no difference in mean scores between those adopted by carers, by strangers or in stable foster care, but scores for children with unstable care careers were significantly worse than for the three groups in permanent placements.[24] The main predictors of positive scores on this measure were being in a settled permanent placement (adopted or in stable foster care rather than unstable care) and not having a disability. Being under/over one year old at placement did not quite reach

---

[23] Where both carer and social worker ratings were available, correlations between the two ratings were moderate. Pearson correlations for the nine items were .3 (self-confidence and emotional ties), .33 special skills, .34 self-care, .35 health, .39 education, .43 close friends, .45 social behaviour, .53 emotional and behavioural development – all significant at either $p = .05$ or $p = .01$. Reliability was good for the combined version of the scale (Cronbach's alpha = .874). Mean scores ranged from 1.56–4. The mean for the total sample was 3.04 (SD = .640).

[24] Mean scores were 3.16 if adopted by carers, 3.24 if adopted by strangers, 3.1 if in stable foster care and 2.69 for the unstable care group. One-way Anova was significant at $p = .016$ for unstable by carer adoption, $p = .001$ for unstable by stranger adoption and $p = .008$ for unstable by stable foster care.

Table 9.3

Current status on developmental measures per cent

	Poor	*Good*
Health: frequently ill – normally well (n = 136)	2	87
Education: below average for ability – above average (n = 135)	23	22
Special skills and interests: none – many (n = 130)	7	32
Self-confidence: none – high (n = 133)	6	24
Emotional ties: not attached to anyone – clearly attached to at least one adult (n = 136)	2	63
Close friends: no friends – several close friends (n = 135)	5	43
Behaviour in social situations: unskilled – skilled (n = 134)	10	37
Emotional and behavioural development: serious problems – no problems (n = 134)	15	34
Self-care skills: not yet competent – competent (n = 136)	12	49

significance (p = .064). We then compared scores for children who were adopted with those for the stable foster care group (excluding those in unstable care from the analysis), and found that being adopted, rather than in stable foster care, was not a predictor of scores for developmental progress. Among children in permanent placements, the only significant predictor of poor scores on this measure was having a disability.[25]

Disturbance and strengths

We also asked the children's carers to complete a standardised measure of emotional and behavioural difficulties – the Strengths and Difficulties Questionnaire (SDQ) (Goodman, 1997). This measure comprises five

---

[25] Linear regression with LAC mean score as the dependent variable was significant at p = <.001 both for disability for under/over one at entry to current placement. Current age, sex and being in kinship care were not significant. The analysis was then repeated excluding the unstable group, since membership of this group was confounded with entering placement over the age of one year. Neither adopted/stable foster care (p = .427), age under/over one year at placement (p=.080), nor kinship care were significant. Disability was the only predictor of scores (p<.001).

sub-scales that give scores for emotional symptoms, conduct problems, peer problems, hyperactivity and pro-social behaviour. Scores on all sub-scales except the pro-social sub-scale are summed to generate a score for total difficulties.

Comparison with national samples

Cut-off points for SDQ scores have been calculated so that only 10 per cent of children in the general population would be expected to have scores over the clinical threshold for severe emotional and behavioural difficulties (Goodman, 1997). In our sample, scores for total difficulties and also for the individual sub-scales measuring conduct disorder, hyperactivity and peer problems were markedly higher than for the general population of children, as shown in Table 9.4.

Table 9.4
Per cent of total sample with clinically significant scores on SDQ (n = 136)

	Per cent of total sample
Total difficulties	38
Hyperactivity	33
Emotional symptoms	15
Conduct disorder	38
Peer problems	36
Pro-social behaviour	14

As Table 9.4 shows, the proportion of children in our survey who had scores above the clinical threshold for total difficulties and for conduct disorder was nearly four times higher than would be expected in the general population. In addition, more than three times as many children had high scores for hyperactivity (33%) and for peer problems (36%) than would be expected in the wider population.

We compared these findings to the results of the ONS survey of the mental health of 1,039 looked after children (Meltzer *et al*, 2003). Some caution is needed in making these comparisons, since the children in the national survey were all looked after. Although all of the children in our own survey had been looked after, many had been adopted by 2006. Also, the children in the national survey had been in care for a variety of durations, some of them only briefly, whereas all of the children in our survey had been cared for away from home for many years. We found that the proportion of children in our survey with a mental disorder was the same as the proportion for children in foster placements in the national survey (38% in both cases). However, the children in our survey were nearly five times more likely to have clinically significant scores for hyperactivity (33%) compared to those in the national sample of looked after children (7%).

Consistent with the ONS survey, we found that older children were more likely to have serious emotional and behavioural difficulties than younger children. In our sample, children aged 13 years or over had significantly higher scores than those who were under 10 years old, both for total difficulties (mean score 14.29 vs 10.21) and for conduct problems (3.61 vs 1.66). Those under 10 years old also had lower scores for peer problems than both 10–12-year-olds and those aged 13 years and over.[26] As in the national survey, the average score for total difficulties was significantly higher for boys in our sample, an average of 14.64 compared to 11.81 for girls, and boys were also more likely to have high scores for hyperactivity than girls (mean score 5.72 v 4.13).[27]

Children who were disabled had higher scores for total difficulties, with a mean score of 17.58 compared to 12.05 for those not reported to be disabled. They were also likely to have higher mean scores for hyperactivity than non-disabled children: 6.85 compared to 4.41 for children not reported to be disabled. As we saw in Chapter 6, the majority

---

[26] One-way Anova for age groups (7–9, 10–12 and 13–17 years) was significant at p = .041 for total difficulties, p = .01 for conduct problems and p.05 for peer problems (n = 137). Tukey test showed that both for total difficulties and conduct problems, differences lay between the 7–9-year-olds and those aged 13 and over. For peer problems, there were significant differences in mean scores between all three groups: 7–9-year-olds (1.86), 10–12-year-olds (3.23) and 13–17-year-olds (3.13).

[27] Independent samples t-test for gender was significant at p=.05 for total difficulties and p = .001 for hyperactivity (n = 137).

of the disabled children in the sample had learning difficulties or a diagnosis of autism.

Comparing groups

There was no significant difference in mean scores on the SDQ between children who were adopted and those in stable foster placements. Neither were there any significant differences between scores for children adopted by strangers and those adopted by carers or in stable foster care. However, scores for children in the unstable care group were significantly higher (i.e. worse) than those for children who were adopted by strangers (p = .023).[28]

Table 9.5
Mean SDQ scores by group (n = 123)

	Carer adoption (n = 22)	Stranger adoption (n = 34)	Stable foster care (n = 47)	Unstable care (n = 20)
Total difficulties mean score	12.68	11.68	13.43	17.65

Since disabled children tended to have higher scores on the SDQ, the high proportion of disabled children in the carer adoption group may help to explain why mean scores were higher than those for the stranger adoption and stable foster care groups. Table 9.6 shows the percentage of children in each group with SDQ scores above the clinical threshold.

There was no significant difference in the proportions of children adopted or in long-term foster care who had serious emotional and behavioural difficulties. Just over one-third of all adopted children and a similar proportion of those in stable foster care had clinically significant total scores for emotional and behavioural difficulties (35% of adopted

---

[28] Mann Whitney U test used to compare the groups in pairs. It is possible that the small numbers in each group for these comparisons may potentially have resulted in a failure to detect a significant difference between the other groups when in fact there was one.

Table 9.6

Per cent with clinically significant scores on the SDQ by group (n = 123)

	Carer adoption (n = 22)	Stranger adoption (n = 34)	Stable foster care (n = 47)	Unstable care (n = 20)
Total difficulties	41	32	36	50
Hyperactivity	36	29	29	45
Emotional symptoms	14	12	15	25
Conduct disorder	32	29	40	55
Peer problems	36	29	29	45
Pro-social behaviour	39	21	36	55

children compared to 36 per cent of those in stable foster care). A recent English study that also compared SDQ scores for adopted and fostered children came to similar conclusions, as it found no difference in levels of emotional and behavioural difficulty between a group of adopted children and others in long-term foster placements (Selwyn *et al*, 2006). Another study, in Northern Ireland, reported a higher proportion of emotional and behavioural difficulties among children in foster care (44%) compared to adopted children (33%, similar to this study), but this is likely to be because children in foster placements of any duration were included in this comparison, not just those in long-term placements, so that group might be the equivalent of a combination of the stable and unstable care groups in our study (McSherry *et al*, 2008).

We wanted to be sure that the similarity in levels of disturbance that we found between the adopted children and those in stable foster place-ments was not due to any bias in the selection of our sample of adopted children. First, we examined whether the group of adopted children might be overwhelmingly composed of children with especially severe difficul-ties. However, only one-third of the adoptive parents in our survey sample indicated that they had accessed adoption support from any source or had attended an adoption support group. Of course, receipt of support services is likely to be determined by the level of local provision as well as by need, but, nevertheless, this does suggest that our findings were not the result of inadvertent sampling bias due to the inclusion of a high number of adopted children with especially severe difficulties. We also investigated whether scores were significantly better for children in kinship foster placements, but this was not the case.

As nearly half of the children in the carer adoption group were reported to be disabled, we then considered whether this explained the lack of a significant difference between adopted and fostered children. However, among the sample of children for whom SDQ scores were available, the difference in the proportion of disabled children in the adopted group (29%) and the stable foster care group (24%) was not statistically significant.[29]

We then conducted multivariate analyses, which confirmed our findings: first, that the severity of emotional and behavioural difficulties was not associated with the type of permanent placement and, second, that children who were not in permanent placements (that is, our unstable group) were likely to have worse scores than those who were. We first examined whether adoption, as opposed to stable foster care, predicted SDQ scores once age at entry to the placement, age at the time of the survey, sex and disability were taken into account. In this analysis, the only significant predictors of higher SDQ scores were disability (p<.001) and entry to the placement after the age of four years (p = .003).

Next we compared scores for those in any type of permanent place-ment to those for children in the unstable care group. In this analysis, the three predictors of high scores for difficulty on the SDQ were being in the unstable care group (p = .001), being disabled (p<.001) and being male (p = .046). Current age and being in kinship care did not predict the level of emotional and behavioural difficulties. Our finding that experiencing unstable care was associated with higher scores on the SDQ is consistent with the findings of the ONS survey referred to above, which found that the prevalence of mental disorder decreases with the length of time in the current placement (Meltzer et al, 2003). It is also similar to the findings of an Australian study of the mental health of 347 children in care, which

---

[29] Chi-square test p = .654. Linear regression confirmed that, although disability predicted higher SDQ scores (p<.001), being fostered rather than adopted did not (p = .206).

reported that mental health difficulties were predicted by placement insecurity or lack of permanence, older age at entry to care (our unstable care group entered later than the other three groups) and intellectual disability (most of the disabled children in our sample had learning difficulties), as well as a history of physical, emotional or sexual abuse and recent adverse events (Tarren-Sweeney, 2007).

When all four placement groups were excluded from the model, we again found that the key predictors of high scores on the SDQ were entering the current placement at the age of four or over (p<.001) and having a disability (p<.001).[30] Entry to the placement at an early age and subsequent placement stability appeared to be crucial. We also found a correlation between a higher total number of placement moves and higher scores for conduct disorder, although this was only weak (.287, p = .001).[31] The direction of this association is not entirely clear, however. Children with more severe emotional and behavioural difficulties might be more vulnerable to placement disruption, but placement instability resulting from the actions of professionals or carers may also increase children's emotional and behavioural difficulties.

Relationship difficulties

We asked the children's carers to complete the Expression of Feelings in Relationships (EFR) measure, developed by David Quinton at the University of Bristol. This consists of 30 items and asks carers to rate, on a three-point scale, the manner in which the children display their feelings. Using the EFR, we were able to calculate a total score for attachment difficulties as well as scores for "inhibited", "disinhibited" and "disregulated" behaviour in relationships. High scorers on the inhibited sub-scale were said by their carers to bottle up emotions, show

---

[30] Linear regression analyses, with total scores on the SDQ as the dependent variable. When placement at under/over one year old was substituted for placement under/over four years old for the first analysis, this too was significant, p = 035. We could not include age at last placement in the second analysis as age at placement would be confounded with being in the stable/ unstable groups.

[31] Pearson correlation between placement moves and SDQ total difficulties score was .265, significant at p = .002.

little affection, hide fears and hide feelings of sadness. High scorers on the disinhibited sub-scale were said to seek attention by misbehaving, be more friendly with strangers than the carer would like, seek a lot of attention and show affection like a younger child. Children who are "inhibited" in their relationships tend to avoid investing in new relationships. They may display increasing emotional detachment as they grow older and become determinedly self-sufficient. In contrast, those who are "disinhibited" may be over-ready to elicit attachment behaviour, a trait often referred to as anxious attachment (Rushton *et al*, 1988).

We believe that the inhibited and disinhibited sub-scales on the EFR measure are conceptually related to the concepts of compulsive self-reliance and childlike attachment (Bowlby, 1979), but they have not been validated against other measures of these concepts. Sinclair and colleagues' earlier study of children in foster care drew on these two concepts to assess the attachment difficulties of children in foster care, including some of those in our own sample (Sinclair *et al*, 2005c). Other recent research on children in long-term foster care has also drawn on attachment theory, charting the progress of those referred to as "open book", "closed book" and "on the edge" children. These, too, are categories based on attachment theory, which are therefore conceptually similar to the three EFR groups described above (Beek and Schofield, 2004).

There was a significant difference in total scores on the EFR between children with unstable care careers and those who were adopted or settled in stable foster placements. Children in our unstable care group had higher scores for inhibited behaviour in relationships and also higher total scores for relationship difficulties than those who were adopted or in stable foster care.[32] This suggests that children who display greater inhibition in their relationships may be more likely to experience unstable care

---

[32] Independent sample t-test comparing unstable groups with adopted children and children in stable foster care (grouped together) were significant at p = .005 for EFR total score and p = .022 for inhibited score (n = 124). Mean scores for "inhibited" were 2.77 (SD 2.43) for the stable group compared to 4.14 (SD 2.88) for the unstable group. Mean total scores on the EFR were 18.45 (SD 10.94) for the stable group compared to 26.4 (SD 12.95) for the unstable group.

careers. However, these findings should be taken as merely indicative. Caution is needed in generalising from these results, as the EFR measure was completed in relation to only 22 children in the unstable care group.

There was also a correlation between children's scores on the EFR and their scores for emotional and behavioural difficulties on the SDQ. The correlations with the SDQ score for total difficulties were particularly strong for the EFR total difficulties score (r = .842), the disinhibited score (r = .729) and the disregulated score, and was moderate for the inhibited score (r = .320).[33] Higher scores on the "inhibited" sub-scale were moderately correlated with SDQ scores for conduct problems (r = .386, p = <.001). In particular, it seems likely that disinhibition is in some way related to behavioural disturbance. Scores for disinhibition were strongly correlated with SDQ scores for hyperactivity (.701, p = <.001) and quite strongly correlated with SDQ scores for conduct problems (.669, p = <.001). There was also a moderate correlation between disinhibition and peer problems (.506, p = <.001), so the children's disinhibited approach to social relationships was clearly affecting their peer relationships as well as their relationships with adoptive parents or carers.

Relationships with carers: parenting, family integration and rejection

We used a number of measures of parenting and carer–child relationships that had been previously used in the foster care studies of Sinclair and colleagues. Details of these measures were given in our chapter on research methods. The Child Orientation Measure, developed by Marjorie Smith at the Thomas Coram Research Unit, contains ten items that refer to activities which the parent might undertake with the child and which the child might be expected to like. Each item is measured on a three-point scale. Scores for the items were added together and a mean score was calculated. We also asked social workers to rate carers on six four-point scales, which explored how caring, accepting and consistent they were in their approach to the child, and used these scores to create a parenting score.

---

[33] Pearson correlations significant at p = .01.

A family integration score was calculated from the carers' answers to six questions, which explored how far the child was perceived to be fully part of the family. An exclusion score was similarly based on answers to questions about whether the child felt the odd one out, wanted to leave or felt picked on. The rejection score was calculated on the basis of five items that aimed to measure how carers felt about looking after the child and how children and carers were getting on.

Scores for child orientation were significantly worse for the carers of children in the unstable care group, compared to all other groups. When we compared child orientation scores for adoptive parents and the foster carers of children in long-term foster care, we also found that scores were slightly more positive for adoptive parents compared to the foster carers. However, there were no significant differences in scores for the carers of children in our four stability groups on any of the other parenting measures.[34]

Children's total scores for emotional and behavioural difficulties on the SDQ were correlated with carers' scores for family integration and rejection, and with social worker ratings of parenting. Carers of children with severe emotional and behavioural difficulties were likely to have lower scores on our family integration measure and higher scores on our rejection measure. Their parenting of the child was also viewed less positively by social workers.[35] More specifically, there were moderate correlations with SDQ scores, indicating that children with more severe conduct problems appeared to be experiencing poorer family integration, greater rejection and poorer parenting by their carers. Higher scores for rejection by carers were also correlated with higher scores for hyperactivity and for peer problems on the SDQ. Carers whose scores indicated a greater degree of family integration were more likely to rate children's

---

[34] One-way Anova significant at p = .008 for child orientation score. Tukey test indicated that the only significant difference was between unstable care and all other groups, significant at p = .05. Independent samples t-test comparing child orientation scores for adoptive parents and long-term foster carers significant at p = .004 (n = 102). Mean score was 2.624 for adopters and 2.454 for foster carers.

[35] Pearson correlations (n = 136) for total difficulties by family integration r = −.345, significant at p = <.001; total difficulties by rejection r = .528 p = <.001; total difficulties by parenting score r = −.421, p = .001.

capacity for pro-social behaviour positively on the SDQ, while carers with higher scores for rejection tended to give children lower scores for pro-social behaviour.[36]

Scores for family integration and rejection, and social worker ratings of parenting, were also correlated with children's scores on the Expression of Feelings in Relationships (EFR) measure. The carers of children with higher scores on the "disinhibited" sub-scale of the EFR were likely to have higher scores for rejection, and these carers were rated less positively by social workers. Carers of children with higher scores on the "inhibited" sub-scale also had higher scores for rejection by carers and were viewed by them as less fully integrated into the family. Children with high scores for "disregulation" were also more likely to experience rejection. Where scores for disinhibition or deregulation were higher, carers received less positive ratings from social workers on our parenting measure.[37]

Conclusion

To sum up, children with greater emotional, behavioural or relationship difficulties were less likely to be accepted and perceived as integrated into their substitute families, and more likely to have experienced unstable care careers. How far the children were integrated into their adoptive or substitute families, and the likelihood that they would be rejected by their carers, were closely correlated with the severity of their emotional and behavioural difficulties and attachment difficulties. Children with greater emotional and behavioural difficulties and/or greater attachment difficulties were likely to be less integrated into their substitute/adoptive families and were more likely to experience rejection.

---

[36] Pearson correlations for conduct problems (n = 136) by family integration r = −.383, p = <.00; conduct problems by rejection r = .556, p = <.001; conduct problems by parenting score r = −.392, p = .002.

[37] Pearson correlation for disinhibited by rejection (n = 134), r = .434 significant at p = <.001. Pearson correlation for inhibited by rejection r = .469 (n = 125) and by family integration (n = 109) r = −.575, both significant at p = <.001. Pearson correlation for disregulated by rejection (n = 125) r = .511, significant at p = <.001. Pearson correlation for social workers' parenting score (n = 57) by disinhibited r = −.328, significant at p = .013; by disregulated r = −.414, significant at <.001.

As we saw earlier, children who had experienced unstable care had significantly higher (worse) total scores on the EFR than those adopted by carers and their scores for emotional and behavioural difficulties on the SDQ were also higher than those of the children in stable foster care. Children with greater emotional, behavioural and attachment difficulties were more likely to have experienced disruption, but it is equally possible that disruptions to their care may, in turn, have reinforced these difficulties. Causation may be complex, as children with attachment or behavioural difficulties may unwittingly elicit rejection from carers and, similarly, carers who are less accepting of a particular child may reinforce that child's emotional and behavioural difficulties. In these circumstances, the carer may succeed with a different child and the child may settle more successfully with a different carer.

Summary

- Many children displayed serious emotional and behavioural difficulties.
- Children in long-term foster care were more likely to have positive scores for developmental progress and less likely to have clinically significant emotional and behavioural difficulties, as measured on the SDQ, than those with unstable care careers.
- There were no significant differences in scores for developmental progress or for emotional and behavioural difficulties (on the SDQ) between children who were adopted and those in stable foster care. It was entering the current placement at the age of three or under that made the difference to SDQ scores.
- Boys were likely to show less developmental progress and more severe emotional and behavioural difficulties than girls, and children with disabilities similarly showed less developmental progress and more severe difficulties compared to those who were not disabled.
- Carers' scores for child orientation were significantly worse for the carers of children in the unstable care group, compared to all other groups. Adoptive parents had slightly higher scores for child orientation than long-term foster carers.
- Children with more severe emotional and behavioural difficulties

were likely to experience less family integration and greater rejection by carers, and their carers' parenting was rated less positively by social workers.

- Children with higher scores for inhibition, disinhibition and dis-regulation in relationships were likely to have worse scores on carers' ratings of family integration and rejection as well as on social workers' ratings of the carers' parenting. Causation may be complex, as children with attachment or behavioural difficulties may elicit rejection from carers and carers who are less accepting of a particular child may reinforce that child's emotional and behavioural difficulties.

10 Exploring change in emotional, behavioural and relationship difficulties

In this chapter we examine outcomes for the 90 children in the York sample who were previously surveyed by Sinclair and colleagues in 1998 and 2001 (Sinclair *et al*, 2005b, 2005c). Within this group we explore changes that took place between 2001 and 2006 and ask three questions:

- What happened to the children over this time?
- How far and in what way did they change?
- What explains any changes?

In asking these questions we focus particularly on whether adopted children do "better", "worse" or "much the same" as those not adopted. As described in more detail below, our judgements of what is doing "better" or "worse" depend on changes on four measures: one of these deals with a wide range of emotional and behavioural difficulty, two with attachment, and one with general social performance. In this way, we are asking whether the children become better adjusted, better able to make relationships and more socially competent.

What happened to the children?

In 2001, over half (57%) of the children originally surveyed in 1998 were still living with the same carers, either adopted by them or continuously fostered by them. All of the others had been adopted by strangers. By 2006, just under three-quarters (67) of the children in this sample had left the care system, either through adoption (62%), residence orders (10%) or discharge home (2%). Just 17 per cent remained with their index foster carers. Nine per cent (8) had had less settled care careers since 2001. Five had moved to new foster placements, one was at home but unsettled and two were in residential placements. Given the small size of the original York sub-sample, for the purpose of analysis we have also included in the unstable care group two children who had recently returned to parents, both of whom had experienced multiple placement moves prior to this return. The stability groups for the York sample are shown in Figure 10.1.

The proportions of children in the York sample in the different placement groups should not be viewed as representative of those likely to be found among the wider population of children placed long term. This sample comprised children whose carers or social workers had participated in our earlier follow-up survey in 2001, and at that point the response rate from adoptive parents was particularly good. However, the availability of data on these 90 children at three points in their lives means there is much we can learn about patterns of change for children with different pathways through, and out of, the care system.

Our measures

So far we have been looking at changes of placement. These are important. However, we also want to know how, if at all, the children changed psychologically and in their social performance. To do this we need a measure of behaviour and psychological state. We are fortunate in having data on the York sample from 1998, 1999 and 2001, which we are able to

Figure 10.1
The York sample: number at follow-up by group (n = 90)

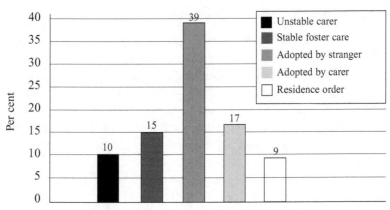

draw on in our analyses of outcomes for the children in 2006. However, caution is needed in generalising from these results, as numbers are often small.

In the previous chapter, we presented our analysis of the children's emotional and behavioural difficulties in 2006, as measured by the Strengths and Difficulties Questionnaire (SDQ). The SDQ was also completed by the carers of children in the York sample in 1998, 1999 and 2001. However, it is only designed for children age three years or over, so since many of the children were very young in 1998, fewer SDQ scores are available for that year. This limitation also applies to 1999, along with the additional constraint that these and other measures were only available for children who remained with the same foster carer.

In the previous chapter we also described the EFR (Expression of Feelings in Relationships) measure, which we used to assess the children's relationship difficulties. Eight items from an earlier version of the EFR (the Expression of Feelings Questionnaire, or EFQ, also developed by David Quinton) were included in questionnaires to carers in our 1998 and 2001 surveys. These same items were used in both studies to calculate scores for inhibition in relationships (referred to as the "stoicism" score in the earlier surveys) and for disinhibition (referred to as the "childlike attachment" score in the earlier surveys). We were therefore able to compare scores for children whose carers had completed the EFQ in 1998 and 2001 with scores for the same eight items on the EFR in 2006. In relation to the children's carers, we have the rejection scores and the child orientation scores of their carers in 1998 and 2001.

Changes on the SDQ

Although the SDQ was designed as a screening measure rather than a change measure, the opportunity provided by the fact that we had earlier scores on the SDQ for many of the York sample led us to investigate whether any changes in scores could be discerned. Table 10.1 shows the average scores on the SDQ for the total York sample at four points in time.

This table has many "missing children". In 1998 and 1999 these were mainly children under the age of three, for whom the SDQ was not

Table 10.1
Scores on SDQ 1998–2006: sample sizes and means (n = 90)

	SDQ total 1999	*SDQ score 2001*	*SDQ score 2006*	*SDQ score*
score 98				
Valid	39	40	82	65
Missing	51	50	8	25
Mean	**14.5897**	**12.8500**	**12.4576**	**11.9231**

appropriate. By contrast, the children who did not have SDQs in 2001 are significantly older than the others, as are the children without an SDQ in 2006. So we need to be careful that the apparent steady decline in average scores between 1998 and 2006 does not simply reflect a tendency for children with "high scores" to appear in one set of measures but not in the next. To do this we need to look at changes in individuals.

We therefore compared the children's SDQ total scores for emotional and behavioural difficulties for 1998, 1999, 2001 and 2006. Overall, there was no significant change in mean SDQ scores for total difficulties between any of these points in time.[38] However, these figures are averages. They do not, of course, mean that individual children did not change. Between 2001 and 2006, there was a marked improvement in SDQ scores for one-fifth of the children (a fall of 5–13 points), while for 15 per cent there was a marked deterioration (a rise of 5–13 points), but for the majority (65%) there was little or no change in scores during this period.[39] The pattern was similar for change in the scores of individual children between 1998 and 2001. All of this suggests that the severity of emotional and behavioural difficulties may change little over time for most children (although it is also possible that the SDQ was insufficiently sensitive to detect changes that did indeed occur for some children).

---

[38] Paired samples t-tests showed no significant change in mean SDQ scores 1997–1998 (p = .59, n = 29), 1998–2001 (p = .980 n = 33) or 2001–2006 (p = .767, n = 58).

[39] Range for SDQ Total Difficulties is 0–40. Minimum change for 2001–2006 was –13 and maximum change was 11 points. Mean difference was –.148 with a standard deviation of 5.2.

Comparing groups

We saw in Chapter 9 that there were no significant differences in the SDQ scores of children who were in stable foster care or adopted, but scores were significantly worse for children in our unstable care group. When we compared scores from 1998, 2001 and 2006 for each of our groups, we found that mean scores for each group did not change significantly across any of the three time periods (although for some children *within* each group scores improved or worsened).[40] On average, children who experienced unstable care after 2001 had significantly higher SDQ scores in both 1998 and 2001 compared to the children in all other groups, as shown in Table 10.2.[41]

Consistent with the earlier York studies (Sinclair *et al*, 2005b, 2005c) these analyses suggest that children who experience unstable care careers may already have significantly greater emotional and behavioural

Table 10.2
Current stability group by mean SDQ scores in 1998 and 2001

Current group (2006)	SDQ score 1998 (SD) (n = 39)	Current group (2006)	SDQ score 2001 (SD) (n = 82)
Carer adoption (n = 5)	7.8 (3.19)	Carer adoption (n = 17)	10.94 (5.23)
Stranger adoption (n = 9)	14 (8.49)	Stranger adoption (n = 39)	10.67 (4.96)
Residence order (n = 5)	14.4 (4.39)	Residence order (n = 5)	16.6 (7.20)
Stable foster care (n = 11)	14 (5)	Stable foster care (n = 13)	12.72 (4.90)
Unstable care (n = 9)	19.78 (4.89)	Unstable care (n = 8)	21.38 (8.07)

---

[40] Paired samples t-tests were used to compare mean SDQ scores from 1998–2001 (n = 34) p = .980; 2001–2006 (n = 59) p = .844; 1998–2006 (n = 23) p = .646.

[41] One-way Anova and post-hoc Tukey tests were used to compare the 1998 and 2001 SDQ scores for our stability groups. Group differences in mean SDQ scores in 1998 are significant at p = .015. Group differences in mean SDQ scores in 2001 are significant at p<.001. In 2001, the key difference in SDQ scores lay between those for children in the unstable care group and those who were in stable foster care or adopted. As explained above, the two children discharged home to parents were included in our unstable care group for these analyses.

difficulties at an early stage in their care careers, compared to other children who go on to experience greater stability. The high scores in 1998 for the small unstable care group were recorded three or more years before they moved on from their long-term foster placement. The perhaps surprisingly high mean score in 1998 for children adopted by strangers is possibly due to the fact that the three children in this small group who had particularly high scores were disabled and, as we saw in the last chapter, disabled children tended to have greater emotional and behavioural difficulties.

Table 10.2 shows the current placement groups for the 39 children for whom we had SDQ scores in 1998 and also for the 82 children for whom scores were available in 2001. We then compared SDQ scores for the sub-sample of children for whom we had SDQ data from both 2001 and 2006.[42] The unstable care group are excluded from this analysis as scores were available at both points in time for only two of the children in this group.

As Table 10.3 shows, there was no significant change over time for any of the groups. Neither did the extent of the, albeit limited, change in scores vary significantly between the groups.[43] These findings are consistent with our conclusion that, for most children, the severity of their emotional and behavioural difficulties changes little over time. The

Table 10.3
Change on SDQ 2001–2006 (n = 54)

	Carer adoption (n = 14)	Stranger adoption (n = 30)	Stable foster care (n = 10)
2001 score	11.57	10.25	13.94
2006 score	12.07	10.97	10.8
Significance p	.776	.317	.074

---

[42] Wilcoxan Signed Ranks Test for paired samples. We did not repeat this analysis for children for whom the SDQ scores were available in both 1998 and 2006, as scores at both these points were available for only 20 children.

[43] Wilcoxan Signed Rank test used compare scores from 2001–2006 within each group. Kruskal Wallis test comparing the extent of change across groups was not significant p = .081.

Table 10.4
Correlations between SDQ scores 1998–2006

		SDQ total score	SDQ score 1999	SDQ score 2001	Av. SDQ 98 to 01	SDQ score 2006
SDQ total score 1998	Pearson Correlation	1	.809**	.602**	.889**	.481*
	Sig. (2-tailed)		.000	.000	.000	.020
	N	39	29	34	39	23
SDQ score 1999	Pearson Correlation	.809**	1	.857**	.966**	.591**
	Sig. (2-tailed)	.000		.000	.000	.001
	N	29	40	35	40	26
SDQ score 2001	Pearson Correlation	.602**	.857**	1	.942**	.730**
	Sig. (2-tailed)	.000	.000		.000	.000
	N	34	35	82	82	59
Av. SDQ 1998 to 2001	Pearson Correlation	.889**	.966**	.942**	1	.702**
	Sig. (2-tailed)	.000	.000	.000		.000
	N	39	40	82	88	63
SDQ score 2006	Pearson Correlation	.481**	.591**	.730**	.702**	1
	Sig. (2-tailed)	.020	.001	.000	.000	
	N	23	26	59	63	65

** Correlation is significant at the 0.01 level (2-tailed).
* Correlation is significant at the 0.05 level (2-tailed).

relative stability of these different groups suggests that individual children who score high or low relative to others at a particular point in time will be likely to hold this position at a later point. This does, indeed, seem to be the case. Table 10.4 gives the correlations between the scores of children at different points in time.

Table 10.4 shows a relatively high degree of correlation. For example, children who had high scores in 1998 tended to have high scores in 1999, 2001 and 2006. Two factors influence the extent of this correlation: the length of time between the two measures and whether or not the child was still in the same family and rated by the same carers. In 1999, children only had an SDQ score if they remained with the carer who had filled in the original questionnaire: given this, and the short follow-up period, it is unsurprising that the correlation was high ($r = .81$). By 2006, the correlation had dropped quite substantially ($r = .48$).[44]

A second feature of these changes is that large drops in score are more likely among those with high scores. There were no very large drops (big improvements) among those with SDQ scores of five or less. This is not surprising. The "best possible" score on the SDQ is "0". So these children could not have change scores greater than this. Rather similar conclusions apply to those who score between five and 10. They cannot make an improvement of more than 10 points as this would mean they improved on every "symptom" they are supposed to have.

An additional explanation may be that this trend represents "regression to the mean". On this analysis, unusually high (or low) scores are more likely to be found among those who, for reasons of chance, happen to be measured during an unusually good or bad time for them. Later measurements are likely to be made at a more usual time and thus show a rise or drop in score. Hence, there is likely to be a positive

---

[44] We were able to test this explanation on the original data. Among the 111 children who remained with the same carer from 1998 to 2001, the correlations were .79 (98-99), .66 (98-01) and .83 (99-01). Among the 253 who had moved from their original foster placement to a new placement, or who had been adopted, the correlations were .73 (98–99), .48 (98–2001) and .51 (99–2001). As might be expected, the correlations are consistently lower for those who move placement.

correlation between a measure of improvement and an initial score that measures the severity of the problem. As we will see, this consideration is important when we come to do some more elaborate analysis.

We investigated whether our findings on change over time might be biased by the loss of some children from the York sample by 2006, as no questionnaires were returned on 26 children at follow-up. When we compared the SDQ scores in 2001 for children included in our change analysis to those for children lost to follow-up, we found that those included in the change analysis had had more severe difficulties in 2001 than those lost to follow-up. However, this was true for similar proportions of the adopted and fostered children, so our findings on change over time for the adopted and fostered groups did not appear to be biased as a result of sample attrition.

The fostered children included in our analysis of change on the SDQ had somewhat lower SDQ scores in 2006 than the total group of long-term fostered children in our survey sample. On average, they appeared to have less severe difficulties and may not, therefore, have been representative of all children in the sample who experienced stable foster care. We also considered whether there was a higher proportion of disabled children in the adopted group, which may have raised the mean SDQ score for this group, but we found a similar proportion of disabled children in the fostered group. A fuller discussion of the possible effects of sample attrition on this analysis is presented in Appendix 2.

Expression of feelings in relationships

We similarly considered whether scores for the children's expression of feelings in relationships had changed over time. As already explained, in 2006 we collected a more developed measure of these by using the Expression of Feelings Questionnaire (EFQ). As this measure was only available for 2006, we could not use it as a measure of change. However, our four measures of disinhibited attachment correlate highly with the relevant full EFQ measure.[45] The correlations for the inhibited

---

[45] The correlations are .56 (1998), .43 (1997), .6 (2001) and .83 (2006). The correlation for the average of the 1998, 1999 and 2001 scores with the 2006 score is .65.

measure are rather less good but still highly significant.[46]

Comparing scores for disinhibition (or childlike attachment) between 2001 and 2006, we found that by 2006 nearly half of the children were perceived as *less* disinhibited and a smaller number were perceived as *more* disinhibited, while for a small group scores remained the same.[47] Correlations between age and the children's disinhibited attachment scores tended to be negative (i.e. the older they were the less disinhibited they seemed to be). So it is possible that, in part, scores improved simply because the children were growing older.[48]

In relation to inhibition (or stoicism), scores changed significantly from both 1998–2001 and 2001–06. Across both periods of time, around one-fifth of the children were perceived to have become *less* inhibited (or stoical), but nearly three times as many children were perceived as *more* inhibited. It appears from this that, for many of the children considered inhibited in their relationships, stoicism was likely to intensify rather than reduce.[49] In this case, there were positive correlations between this score and age at all the points at which we measured it.[50] So it is likely that much of the "deterioration" in the scores may simply reflect the children's older age.

In the last chapter, we saw that the children in our unstable care group had significantly higher scores for inhibition than those in stable foster

---

[46] The correlations are .56 (1998), .58 (1999), .3 (2001) and .55 (2006).

[47] Wilcoxan Signed Ranks test for changes in disinhibition over time. For 2001–06, exact significance was p = .05 (n = 59): 25 scores reduced, 15 scores increased. Kendall's tau-b test found no significant correlation between age and the change in scores for disinhibited attachment: −.160, p = .106. Between 1998 and 2001, there was no significant change in scores for disinhibition p = .424 (n = 34).

[48] The significant non-parametric correlations were Rho =.25 (p<.05) for 2001, Rho = .33 (p<.05) for average score for 1998, 1999, 2001.

[49] Wilcoxan Signed Ranks test for changes in inhibition over time. For 2001–06, exact significance was p = .001 (n = 61): 12 scores reduced, 31 scores increased. For 1998–2001, exact significance was p = .013 (n = 52): 11 scores reduced, 32 scores increased. Kendall's tau-b test found no significant correlation between age and change scores for inhibited attachment: −.176, p = .182.

[50] The significant non-parametric correlations were Rho = .78 (p<.001) for 1998, Rho = .59 (p<.001) for 2001, Rho=.65 (average for 1998, 1999, 2001) and Rho = .24 (p = .056) for 2006.

care or adopted (although there was no relationship between stability group and scores for disinhibition). However, it was not possible for us to test whether unstable care was predicted by children's earlier attachment scores, due to the small number of children in the unstable care group for whom earlier scores were available.

As in the case of the SDQ, there was evidence that high scores on either inhibited or disinhibited attachment predicted a change for the better. This was true for those who improved on either score between 2001 and 2006.[51] Once again, this was something that we needed to take into account in further analysis.

Changes in social performance

The earlier studies used a measure of social performance that indicated the children's developmental progress. We asked social workers, foster carers and adoptive parents to rate the children on their health, education/work, skills, close ties, friendships, social behaviour, social and emotional difficulties, and ability to look after themselves. The ratings were separately defined for each variable but basically involved a four-point scale ranging from one (well below average) to four (well above average), as described in the previous chapter. When both social workers' and carers' ratings were available, we took the average rating and otherwise, the social work or carer rating, depending on which we had. The ratings were not suitable for young children who, for example, might not be at school. So in this study we have looked only at the overall scores (the sum of the ratings) for 2001 and 2006 and at the way they changed.

On average, there was no difference between these scores in 2001 and 2006. As in the case of the attachment variables, there was quite a strong correlation between the scores ($r = .57$, $p<.001$), so children who scored high or low at one point in time also tended to do so at the other. There was also a significant negative correlation between the score at one point

---

[51] The relevant non-parametric correlations were Rho = .51 ($p<.001$) for the correlation between the 2001 disinhibited attachment score and "improvement" on the score between 2001 and 2006, and .51 for the corresponding improvement for the inhibited score.

in time and positive change ($r = -.37$). In other words, children who scored well in 2001 tended to do worse, while those who scored "badly" tended to do better.

What predicts change?

We wanted to know what might explain change for the better. Our first question was whether, as in our original studies of foster care, children who were adopted tended to have improved outcomes. The answer to this question was: "no". Between 2001 and 2006, adopted children either improved less or deteriorated more on their SDQ scores and their disinhibited and inhibited attachment scores (all at $p<.05$). There was no difference on the social performance score.

These associations do not necessarily mean that adopted children were really doing "worse". As pointed out earlier, children with high scores were generally more likely to change for the better. So adoption may have been a victim of its early success. For this reason, we needed to take account of the children's scores in 2001, a point at which adopted children were doing significantly better than others. Once we had done this, the differences were no longer significant. Only in the case of the SDQ score did adopted children even appear to be doing "worse", but this result was not significant ($p = .071$).

Obviously, adopted children differed from others and not only in their scores. So we needed to take account of other variables that might affect improvement or deterioration. In selecting these variables, we took account of our previous research and also of what we expected. We looked first at four "personal" characteristics:

- age, which had been associated with less improvement in some of the analyses in the earlier studies;
- age at entry, on the assumption that those entering at a later date would be less responsive;
- age at joining the current family, for similar reasons;
- disability, on the grounds that some disabled children would have genetic disadvantages that could make change difficult.

We tested these hypotheses using regression analyses that still took account of the scores in 2001. In none of these analyses did age appear to have a significant negative effect on change. It did, however, verge on a significant negative effect in the case of the inhibited attachment score (p = .069) and the social performance score (p = .094).

With one exception, age at entry to care was similarly unrelated to change. The exception was inhibited attachment. It is possible that children who first enter care when relatively old have had time to grow a "shell", behind which to guard their emotions, and that this shell is hard to change. Table 10.5 gives the relevant regression equation. The table shows that a high score in 2001 predicted a drop. After taking this into account, children who first enter the care system later tended either to change less for the better on this variable or to change more for the worse.

Table 10.5
Regression equation predicting change in inhibited attachment 2001–2006

Model	Unstandardised coefficients		Standardised coefficients		
	B	Std. error	Beta	t	Sig.
1 (Constant)	5.536	.745			
inhibited attachment 2001	−1.036	.149	−.767	7.426	.000
age at first entry to care			−		
(903 data)	.315	.105	.331	6.951	.000
				3.000	.004

Age at placement with their current parent or carer proved a more general predictor. Children who were placed at an older age did significantly worse on their social performance (p = .019) and inhibited attachment (p = .016) scores. They also scored worse on their SDQ change scores, but this difference was not quite significant (p = .067). Taking account of these associations did not change our conclusion that adopted children were not doing better or worse on these changes.

We looked at the association between disability (as defined in Chapter 7) and change while taking into account both age at placement and the relevant score in 2001. In this context, disability proved to have strong significant associations with worse changes in both the social performance score (p = . 001) and the SDQ (p = .006). Table 10.6 gives the regression equation for the SDQ. As can be seen, in this equation age at placement also becomes significantly associated with worse change scores.

Table 10.6
Regression equation predicting change on SDQ score 2001 to 2006 (1)

Model	Unstandardised coefficients		Standardised coefficients		
	B	Std. error	Beta	t	Sig.
1 (Constant)	.801	1.583		.506	.615
Inhibited attachment 2001	−.337	.122	−.374	−2.753	.008
Disability	4.535	1.571	.387	2.886	.006
Age placed here	1.131	.528	.272	2.141	.037

Once again, we checked that these findings did not shake our conclusion that adopted children were not doing better or worse on these change measures. We found that they did not.

We next asked whether the kind of parenting provided by the parents or foster carers influenced change for better or worse. Our previous work had suggested that the most important predictor would be acceptance as against rejection. Table 10.7 gives the results of adding in a measure of "rejection" in 2001.

At first sight, our rejection score was not significantly associated with change in SDQ. It does, however, significantly increase the ability of the regression to predict these changes. If age at placement is removed, rejection is significant (p = .041). Age at placement, disability and rejection also combine to predict worse change on the social performance score, as shown in Table 10.8.

Table 10.7
Regression equation predicting change on SDQ score 2001 to 2006 (2)

Model	Unstandardised coefficients		Standardised coefficients		
	B	Std. error	Beta	t	Sig.
1 (Constant)	−.653	1.736		−.376	.708
SDQ score 2001	−.535	.161	−.595	−3.331	.002
Disability	4.781	1.542	.399	3.100	.003
Aged placed here	.948	.526	.228	1.801	.078
Rejection in 2001	.990	.535	.319	1.850	.070

Table 10.8
Predicting change on the social performance score 2001–2006 (a)

Model	Unstandardised coefficients		Standardised coefficients		
	B	Std. error	Beta	t	Sig.
1 (Constant)	3.106	.485		6.408	.000
Social performance 2001	−.745	.116	−.757	−6.449	.000
Age placed here	−.086	.042	−.208	−2.062	0.43
Disability	−.443	.122	−.362	−3.625	.001
Rejection in 2001	−.113	.039	−.333	−2.906	.005

(a) Dependent variable: difference in LAC score 2006–2001.

As seen earlier, age at placement was associated with worse change on the inhibited attachment score. However, the other variables in this set were not. The findings on disinhibited attachment were more complicated. Rejection in 2001 went with worse change scores on disinhibited attachment over the period. This, however, was only true if we took account of the degree of disinhibited attachment in 2001 and even then was not significant (p = .12). If we took account of both inhibited and disinhibited attachment, the association between rejection in 2001 and

Table 10.9

Predicting change on the disinhibited attachment score 2001–2006 (a)

Model	Unstandardised coefficients		Standardised coefficients		
	B	Std. error	Beta	t	Sig.
1 (Constant)	4.412	.837		5.272	.000
Disinhibited attachment 2001	−.453	.107	−.517	−4.226	.000
Inhibited attachment 2001	−.614	.144	−.453	−4.253	.000
Rejection in 2001	.372	.154	.289	2.412	.019

(a) Dependent variable: 2006–2001 scores for disinherited attachment.

Table 10.10

Predicting change on the SDQ score 2001–2006 (a)

Model	Unstandardised coefficients		Standardised coefficients		
	B	Std. error	Beta	t	Sig.
1 (Constant)	−7.162	3.167		−2.262	.028
SDQ score 2001	−.497	.129	−.548	−3.845	.000
Disability	3.937	1.502	.327	2.621	.012
Age placed here	.785	.515	.189	1.523	.134
Mean rejection score 2006	8.879	3.098	.406	2.866	.006

(a) Dependent variable: SDQ 2006–2010.

change for the worse on disinhibited attachment does become significant, as shown in Table 10.9.

The associations between rejection and worse change scores remains or becomes significant if we substitute a measure of rejection in 2006 for the one we have for 2001. This is true for all our change variables including inhibited attachment. Table 10.10 gives the change for the SDQ as an example.

Carers were more likely to have high rejection scores in 2006 if they also had them in 2001. However, the main predictor of rejection in 2006 was a high SDQ score in 2001 and, if we took this into account, the association between the two rejection scores was no longer significant.

These findings are rather complicated and confusing. A possible explanation is that high scores for disinhibited and inhibited attachment work in two ways. They allow or lead to better change scores for disinhibited attachment. They also reflect or lead to rejection, which in turn leads to worse change scores. So it is only if we take account of their direct association with change that the baneful effect of rejection comes to light. At the same time, carers are also more likely to find it difficult to manage children who have the kind of behaviour problems identified by the SDQ. So rejection is itself made greater by the behaviour it may help to bring about.

Our case studies and other analyses not reported above support the explanation we have given. We should, however, make it clear that this is not the only story the statistics could support. As we have seen, rejection reflects difficult behaviour, which most probably also brings it about.[52] So it could be that our measure of rejection predicts negative change not because it causes it but because it reflects difficult behaviour that is not directly measured by the other variables we have put in our equations. It may be these unmeasured difficulties rather than rejection itself that brings about changes for the worse. So our judgements on how this process works can only be partly based on our statistics. They also have to reflect our thoughts about what is plausible as well as other evidence (our own case studies, other research, and experience in the field).

Conclusion

Some of the findings in this chapter seem clear, others less so. One clear conclusion is that the changes for which we have been looking are not easy to bring about. Although change was observed in relation to some individual children, on average the children did not change at all on the SDQ or on our social performance score. On average again, their scores on disinhibited attachment improved while on the inhibited attachment

---

[52] The correlations between rejection in 2001 and our various 2001 measures are very high ranging, from .72 (with the SDQ) to -.56 (with good social performance).

score they got worse. Both of these changes, however, came about at least in part because the children grew older.

A second clear conclusion is that the adopted children did not do better on our scores than those with whom we were comparing them (predominantly slightly older children in stable foster care or on residence orders). At first sight they did worse. This, however, seemed to reflect their better starting position. Our earlier research on children in foster care suggested that there were initial advantages to adoption (Sinclair, 2005c). If so, they may mainly be reflected in comparison with a wider sample of foster children and/or in the early years. At least three years into the adoption, they did not improve more quickly on our measures than the other children.

A third probable conclusion is that most children may find it easier to improve on some scores if they are placed quickly and at a young age in their final placement. Late placement seemed to reduce the chance of improvement on the inhibited attachment, SDQ and social performance scores. So carers and adoptive parents may find their task easier if their children have come into care early and have quickly found the place where they expect to grow up.

A final – and less certain – conclusion is that even high-class parenting may find it difficult to produce change. The variables that predicted good outcomes in the earlier studies of foster care – particularly a measure of authoritative parenting and child orientation – did not predict positive change between 2001 and 2006.[53] Similarly, children with unstable care careers were already disturbed before these careers began. There is no reason to think that the great majority of the parents and carers were not excellent. Our measure of rejection (perhaps better phrased as lack of full acceptance) did indeed seem to identify those

---

[53] Our measure of child orientation tended to predict "good outcomes" in our earlier studies but did not predict positive change between 2001 and 2006. In this case, it is possible that the good effects had, as it were, been already discounted. For example, there is a significant, if low, positive correlation between the 2006 social performance score and the 2001 measure of child orientation. This effectively disappears when we take account of the 2001 measure of social performance. It remains possible that this is "unfair", since the 2001 measure of social performance could itself be influenced by the 2001 measure of child orientation.

children who were going to improve on certain variables. As we have pointed out, however, the apparent effect was quite weak and could have other causes.

If children's mental health is influenced by the degree to which carers are rejecting (or accepting) towards them, this is certainly not surprising. Child and carer relationship styles and behaviours can create a downward spiral. Children exhibiting more disturbed behaviour, particularly those with demanding, childlike attachment styles, may elicit more rejecting responses from carers. Equally, perceived rejection by carers may elicit more demanding, clingy and difficult behaviour. In these very difficult circumstances, foster carers may need additional support in coping with children whose serious emotional, behavioural and attachment difficulties make them hard to love.

Practically, then, the first lesson may be that change on the variables we have been considering is possible and should continue to be an objective. Second, such change is, however, hard won and may not occur even with excellent parenting. Parents should not be blamed or blame themselves for lack of progress. Third, children should, insofar as this is possible, achieve their "final placement" as early as possible. Finally, every effort should be made to interrupt the negative spirals that can occur when difficult behaviour leads to lack of acceptance, which in turn leads to more difficult behaviour.

Summary

- This chapter examined change in scores for emotional and behavioural difficulties (SDQ), attachment difficulties (EFQ/EFR) and social performance at four points in time between 1998 and 2006.
- On average, there was little change on the SDQ and on the social performance score. On average, scores for disinhibited attachment improved and those for inhibited attachment got worse, in part because the children grew older.
- Change on these measures of emotional and behavioural difficulties, attachment difficulties and social performance is nevertheless possible and should continue to be an objective.
- The adopted children did not show greater improvement on these

scores (from 2001 to 2006) than those in stable foster care or on residence orders, but this may be because they had often made substantial improvement prior to 2001.

- Late placement seemed to reduce the chance of improvement on the inhibited attachment, SDQ and social performance scores. Every effort should be made to ensure that, as far as possible, children are placed in their final, long-term placement as early as possible.
- Even with high-quality substitute parenting, it may be difficult to produce substantial change. Children in our unstable care careers group in 2006 already had significantly worse scores in 1998, compared to children who were subsequently adopted or who settled in long-term foster placements.
- Effort should be made to interrupt the negative spirals that can occur when difficult behaviour leads to lack of acceptance by carers, which in turn may lead to more difficult behaviour.

11 Education: comparing progress and outcomes

There has been much concern about the poor educational achievement of many children who are looked after (Biehal *et al*, 1995; Jackson and Martin, 1998; Wade, 2006). Failures in corporate parenting, involving low expectations, a failure to prioritise education and the disrupted schooling that may result from placement instability, may contribute to this picture of low attainment (Berridge and Saunders, 2009). However, discussions of the low educational achievement of looked after children have relied heavily on official statistics, which provide a cross-sectional picture of achievement by those looked after on an annual census date but cannot take account of individual progress. Explanations of underachievement have sometimes failed to acknowledge the complexity of this issue and have not always taken account of children's disadvantaged backgrounds (see Berridge, 2007 for a fuller discussion). Studies that have taken account of the age at which children entered care have provided a more nuanced picture of progress (Dixon *et al*, 2006).

Adopted children have also been found to experience problems with school life. One study, which compared children adopted at a mean age of 3.2 months to a matched sample of non-adopted children, found that the adopted children did worse on teacher ratings of school behaviour and achievement. Among the adopted children, girls did worse than boys at the age of six to seven years, but this pattern was reversed by the age of 10 to 11 years. The authors concluded that even these children who, in most cases, were adopted as infants, were vulnerable to educational problems (Brodzinsky *et al*, 1984a). Another major follow-up study, which compared children adopted as babies to fostered/late-adopted and non-adopted children, found poorer school adjustment for adopted boys, though not girls, at the age of 10–11 years, but differences between the adopted and non-adopted groups had diminished by the time the boys reached 15 years of age (Bohman and Sigvardsson, 1980). School problems may be worse for children placed for adoption at a later age, as another study found that levels of maladjustment at school when children were seven years old rose sharply for those placed for adoption after the age of six months and even higher for those placed after 12 months (Seglow *et al*, 1972).

We asked carers and social workers about the children's participation, attainment and general progress in education. In our analyses we used carers' replies to these questions wherever possible, as they were more likely to know the details of the child's schooling. However, if no carer reply was available, we substituted the social worker's reply if there was one.

Educational provision

Three-quarters of the children were reported to be attending a mainstream school.

Table 11.1
Educational provision (n = 184) per cent (n)

Type of provision	%	*n*
Mainstream school	75	(137)
Special school (day)	12	(21)
Residential school	2	(4)
Pupil referral unit	3	(5)

Children with unstable care careers were significantly less likely to be attending mainstream school and two of them were refusing all educational provision at the time of our survey.[54] The proportion of those with unstable careers attending mainstream school was only 54 per cent, much lower than for those in stable foster care (76%), adopted (82%) or on residence orders (86%). Nearly one-quarter of all children in the sample were receiving additional educational support at a learning support unit within school.

---

[54] Chi-square test significant at p = .007.

One-third of those who were not in mainstream education had a learning disability or were autistic. A further eight per cent of those who were not in mainstream school had serious health problems. Nevertheless, 57 per cent of those with a disability and/or a serious health problem did attend ordinary local schools. Among the children with a disability and/or chronic health problem, a substantial minority (32%) attended a special day school and one child attended a residential school. However, no educational provision was available for two of the disabled children, both of whom were adopted.

Participation in education

One-fifth of the children had truanted in the past six months. Those with unstable care careers were significantly more likely to have truanted at least once and also more likely to have truanted frequently during this period.[55]

Table 11.2
School attendance in past six months by group per cent

	All *(n = 180)*	*Adopted* *(n = 65)*	*Stable foster care* *(n = 59)*	*Unstable care* *(n = 40)*
Always attends	80	89	81	65
Occasional truancy	13	11	14	10
Frequent truancy	7	0	5	25

There was no significant difference in relation to truancy between children in stable foster care and those who were adopted. Fifteen per cent of the children who were of school age at the time of our survey had been temporarily excluded from school during the previous six months and five children had been excluded permanently during this period. Children who had been adopted and those in stable foster care were far less likely to have experienced exclusion from school than those with a history of unstable care. However, the children in stable foster care were more likely

---

[55] Chi-square test significant at p<.001.

to have been excluded than those who were adopted. Nearly half of the children in the unstable care group had been excluded from school in the past six months and for three of these children the exclusion was permanent.[56]

Table 11.3
School exclusion by group per cent (n) (n = 159)

	Adopted (n = 64)	*Stable foster care (n = 61)*	*Unstable care (n = 38)*
Exclusion (temporary or permanent)	3 (2)	15 (9)	47 (18)

Attainment

We asked about exams taken or planned, but the numbers reported were small as respondents could only answer questions appropriate to the age of the child concerned and there was also a great deal of missing data on this topic. Just over one-quarter of the children were aged 14 or over and only just over half of this group (55%) were reported to be planning, or to have taken, GCSEs. This figure may be low partly due to the substantial minority of disabled children in the sample, the majority of whom had learning difficulties, but it might also be an underestimate. National figures for looked after children indicate that 68 per cent of eligible children sit at least one GCSE, but only 15 per cent achieve five or more GCSEs at grades A*–C (Department for Children, Schools and Families, 2009b). The national figure is indicative but not strictly comparable as our sample included children who had been adopted. Also, we had no data on this issue in relation to over one-third of the eligible children in our sample. Table 11.4 shows the number of GCSEs taken or planned.

---

[56] Chi-square tests significant at p = .016 for adopted vs fostered and at p = <.001 for unstable care versus adoption and stable foster care.

Table 11.4
GCSEs planned or taken (n = 56)

Number planned or taken	Per cent of children age 14+
None	5
1–2	4
3–4	5
5 or more	46
Not applicable	4
Don't know/missing	36

Although one or more GCSEs had been planned or taken by a higher proportion of the adopted children than those in other groups, the differences were not statistically significant (possibly due to the small numbers involved).

Overall progress at school

We also asked carers and social workers to rate children's overall functioning at school on a scale taken from the Assessment and Action Records of the Integrated Children's System, which ranges from 1 (all well below average for ability) to 4 (all well above average for ability). Nearly half (45%) of the children were reported to be "below" or "well below" average for their ability, but nearly one-third (31%) were reported to be functioning at a level that was "above average" for their ability and 24 per cent were rated as "well above average". Children who had experienced unstable care had significantly lower mean scores on this measure than those adopted or in stable foster care.[57] Three-quarters of the children in the unstable care group were reported to display behaviour problems at school, and they were significantly more likely to do so than children in permanent placements. However, reports of behaviour problems at school were reported far more frequently in

---

[57] One-way Anova significant at p = .001. Tukey test significant at p = .05 showed that the significant difference was between unstable care (mean score 3.31) and those adopted, in stable foster care or on residence orders, whose mean scores ranged from 4.53–4.8.

relation to children in stable foster care (60%) than for adopted children (35%).[58]

Using these two measures – together with data on whether or not children truanted, had recently been excluded from school or were enjoying school – we created a composite measure of doing well at school, which we called "schoolwell". This took the form of a scale ranging from 0–7. We found that children with more severe emotional and behavioural difficulties, as measured on the SDQ, were generally doing worse at school. This correlation was strongest for those with high scores for hyperactivity on the SDQ. Children who were disabled also had significantly worse scores on our schoolwell measure than those who were not disabled.[59] Children with unstable care careers also did worse on our schoolwell measure than those in stable foster care. Our finding that children in our unstable care group were doing worse on measures of participation and progress at school is consistent with the findings from another recent study, which found that children with unstable care careers were more likely to be excluded from school or to truant than children who were adopted, and they had therefore received little education (Selwyn et al, 2006). Among children who were looked after, those in kinship care placements had slightly better scores on this measure, but this difference did not quite reach significance (p = .058).

There is some evidence that children with attachment difficulties may encounter greater difficulties at school (Phillips, 2007). We therefore considered whether there was any relationship between scores on the Expression of Feelings in Relationships questionnaire (EFR) and how

---

[58] Chi-square tests significant at p = <.001 for unstable care vs adopted and stable foster care, and at p = .004 for adopted vs stable foster care.

[59] The Pearson correlation between "schoolwell" and the total difficulties score on the SDQ was −.607, significant at p = <.01 and the correlation with the SDQ hyperactivity score was −.483, significant at p+<.001. One-way Anova significant at p = .001 showed that children in the unstable group had a mean score of 3.14, compared to between 4.49 and 4.8 for those in the other three groups. Tukey test (significant at p = .05) showed that the difference lay between the unstable group and the other three groups. Children who were disabled had a mean score of 3.5 compared to 4.73 for those who were not disabled: one-way Anova significant at p<.001.

children were getting on at school. We found that children displaying disinhibited or disregulated behaviour in relationships were likely to be doing significantly worse at school. There were moderate negative correlations between those with higher scores for disinhibited (r = −.448) and for disregulated (r = −.452) behaviour in relationships, and a weaker negative correlation with scores for inhibited behaviour (r = −.301) in relation to scores on our schoolwell measure.[60]

We then used multivariate analyses to further examine the factors associated with doing well at school. We considered the child's age at entry to care, age at entry to their current placement, their current age, total number of placement moves, total scores and sub-scale scores on the SDQ and on the EFR, whether they were disabled, whether they had had stable or unstable care careers, whether they were adopted or in stable foster care, and whether they were in kinship care placements. We did not include scores for SATs or GCSEs as there were so many missing data in relation to these measures.

By far the strongest predictor of doing well at school was having low scores for emotional and behavioural difficulties on the SDQ. Scores on the SDQ predicted 36 per cent of the variance on our schoolwell measure. On this composite measure of participation and progress, adopted children and those in stable, long-term foster placements were equally likely to be doing well at school.[61] However, children who were adopted or in long-term foster placements were more likely to have high scores for doing well at school than those with unstable care careers. As we have already seen, the latter were less likely to be in mainstream schools and were more likely to truant and to be excluded from school. Not having a disability also predicted doing well at school, but to a lesser degree. Together, these three variables accounted for 43 per cent of the variation

---

[60] Pearson correlations between schoolwell and the EFR (n = 125), significant at p = <.001 for disinhibited and disregulated and at p = .001 for inhibited.

[61] Mann-Whitney U test was not significant p = .277. A comparison of scores for stranger adoption and stable foster care also proved to be non-significant (p = .185). In this multivariate analysis, being in kinship care was not a predictor of performance on the schoolwell measure.

in scores for doing well at school.[62] However, scores on the EFR did not predict doing well at school, once SDQ scores, placement stability and disability were taken into account. This suggests that disturbance, and the placement instability with which it is associated, may be stronger predictors of doing badly at school than attachment difficulties.

Conclusion

The children in stable foster care were more likely to display behaviour problems at school than adopted children and were also more likely to truant (although the proportion doing so was very small). Overall, however, on our composite measure of participation and progress at school, they were doing as well as those who had been adopted. However, our unstable care group was doing worse on all measures of participation and progress in education. Compared to the children who were adopted or in stable foster placements, they were more likely to have truanted and also more likely to have been excluded from school in the previous six months, to display behaviour problems at school and to do worse on our measures of educational progress.

For children whose foster placements endure over time, therefore, educational outcomes may be no worse, on average, than those for children who are adopted, although both may do worse in comparison with the general population of children. Our evidence suggests that poor participation and progress in education for looked after children may be less of a problem for those who experience placement stability and significantly more of a problem for those with unstable care careers. A study of young people leaving care, which similarly found that those who experienced unstable care had worse educational outcomes (Dixon *et al*, 2006). Assessments of educational outcomes should differentiate between outcomes for children who enter care at an early age and settle in long-term, stable placements and those for children who enter care at a later

---

[62] Linear regression. SDQ total difficulties score Beta −.484 significant at p = <.001; stable care *vs* unstable care Beta .258, p = <.001; whether disabled Beta −.178, p = .016. The same three variables were also found to predict scores on the Looked After Children Education scale, but for this scale having a disability was a stronger predictor than the severity of emotional and behavioural difficulties.

age, who may be at risk of greater placement instability.

The strongest predictor of doing badly at school, however, on a composite measure of participation and progress, was having high scores for emotional and behavioural difficulties on the SDQ, which predicted 36 per cent of the variance in doing well at school. Being in unstable care and having a disability were also predictive, but together accounted for only seven per cent of the variance in school progress and participation. The main reason for the unstable care group's poor integration and progress at school was, therefore, the fact that they were likely to have more serious emotional and behavioural difficulties. We know from our analysis of the SDQ scores of the York sample over time, presented in Chapter 9, that the unstable care group had these difficulties from an early age, so it is likely that their school problems were also long standing. The Government's new policy of using the SDQ to screen children looked after for one year or more for emotional and behavioural difficulties may therefore help to identify those in particular need of support to ensure their integration and progress at school.

Summary

- Three-quarters of the children attended mainstream school and 17 per cent attended special schools or pupil referral units. One-third of those not in mainstream education had a learning disability or were autistic.
- Children who were adopted or living in stable foster placements were more likely to be attending mainstream school than those in the unstable group. They were also far less likely to have truanted or to have been excluded from school in the previous six months.
- Over half (55%) of children aged 14 or over were planning to take, or had taken, at least one GCSE.
- On a composite measure of participation and progress in school, children with high scores for emotional and behavioural difficulties, and particularly those with high scores for over-activity, were doing worse. Children with high scores for disinhibited or disregulated behaviour in relationships were also doing significantly worse at school.
- Adopted children and those in stable foster care had similar scores on

our composite measure of educational progress and participation in school, but children in our unstable care group were doing significantly worse than these two groups. The unstable group was significantly more likely to display behaviour problems in school than the stable foster care group, while adopted children were least likely to do so.

- The strongest predictor of doing well at school was having low scores on the SDQ, our measure of emotional and behavioural difficulties. Having a stable (foster or adoptive) placement and not having a disability were also predictive, but to a lesser degree. The main reason for the unstable care group's poor integration and progress at school was, therefore, the fact that they were likely to have more serious emotional and behavioural difficulties. The Government's policy of using the SDQ to screen children looked after for one year or more for emotional and behavioural difficulties may therefore help to identify those in particular need of support to ensure their integration and progress at school.

12 Contact with birth families

Prior to the mid-1980s, it was almost unheard of for adopted children to have continuing contact with their birth families, but in the last 20 years there has been a substantial shift in policy and practice, partly as a result of the increasing numbers of older children adopted, some of whom may have significant relationships with members of their birth families. However, there is only limited evidence on the extent and nature of both face-to-face contact and indirect contact between adopted children and their birth families. There has also been very little research on how adopted children view the issue of contact (Thomas *et al*, 1999). Continuing contact with birth parents is believed to be so important for looked after children that the Children Act 1989 imposed a new duty on local authorities to promote contact between children who are looked after and those who are connected with them. Local authorities are required to allow reasonable contact with the child's parents or any other guardian the child was living with before entering care. While the proportion of children in long-term foster care who have face-to-face contact with birth parents has remained at around 60 per cent, since the Children Act 1989 the frequency of such contact has increased (Cleaver, 2000; Neil and Howe, 2004).

Enthusiasm for promoting contact with birth families has been based largely on arguments regarding the rights of children and families and on research claiming that it has positive effects (Family Rights Group, 1986). Claims have been made, for example, that contact may have positive effects on children's emotional and behavioural development, reduce the risk of placement disruption, and promote reunification of children with their birth families (see Biehal, 2007 for a summary). However, Quinton and colleagues' critical review of the research revealed that the evidence on the effects of contact is weak and inconclusive. There is no strong evidence that contact with parents either is, or is not, beneficial to children (Quinton *et al*, 1997). They concluded that the evidence suggests that contact can work amicably and that, as one study found, contact may be associated with greater placement stability (Fratter *et al*, 1991).

However, little is known about how and why any such association between contact and placement stability may operate.

Brodzinsky has distinguished between "structural openness" and "communicative openness" in adoption (Brodzinsky, 2006). This chapter focuses principally on structural openness, that is, on the nature and frequency of contact with birth families. We asked the foster carers, adoptive parents and social workers who took part in our survey about the extent and nature of the children's contact with their birth families and how they felt about this contact, or lack of it. We felt that carers would be more likely to have detailed knowledge of these issues, so where both carer and social worker responses were available to us, we took the carer's response. However, if no carer data were available, we used the information provided by social workers.

We also asked the 37 children and carers whom we interviewed about any contact that existed between children and birth relatives and sought the children's views on the contact they had.

Face-to-face contact with birth families

Seven or more years after they had entered care, only half of the children still had face-to-face contact with their mothers and less than 30 per cent saw their fathers at all. Nearly 70 per cent of those who had siblings sometimes saw one or more of them and over half saw other relatives (in most cases grandparents). Some children had had no contact with relatives for many years.[63]

As might be expected, the proportion of children who had face-to-face contact with birth parents varied considerably between those who were adopted and those who were looked after. Forty-six per cent of the sample had no face-to-face contact with either parent and, unsurprisingly, children who were adopted were far more likely to fall into this group.[64] The

---

[63] In this chapter we have compared results for children adopted by strangers or by carers with those in stable foster placements and those with unstable care careers. However, children in other types of placement are included in any totals given for all placements.

[64] Chi-square tests significant at $p = <.001$ for both contact with parents and contact with other relatives.

children in the unstable care group had the most contact of all, as shown in Table 12.1.

Table 12.1
Per cent with face-to-face contact with parents (n = 157)

Contact with:	Adopted (all) (n = 62)	Adopted by stranger (n = 34)	Adopted by carer (n = 28)	Stable foster care (n = 57)	Unstable care (n = 38)
Mother	11 (7)	3 (1)	21(6)	74 (42)	75 (29)
Father	6 (4)	0	14 (4)	37 (21)	44 (16)
One/both parents	15 (9)	3 (1)	29 (8)	77 (44)	86 (31)

Among the adopted children who were in direct contact with birth parents, all but one had been adopted by carers. In total, only 15 per cent (nine) of the adopted children saw either one or both parents, a figure remarkably close to the figure of 17 per cent among a group of 64 children adopted from care, who were followed up by Selwyn and colleagues seven years after the decision that adoption was in their best interests (Selwyn *et al*, 2006).

Patterns of contact for children on residence or special guardianship orders were similar to those for children in foster care. In total, 81 per cent of this group were known to have face-to-face contact with one or both parents. Half of them had face-to-face contact with their birth mothers and just under half had contact with birth fathers.

The adoptive parents interviewed generally showed the kind of "communicative openness" in relation to the fact that the child was adopted that has been thought likely to promote the healthy psychological adjustment of adopted children (Brodzinsky, 2006). Furthermore, some adoptive parents of children who did not see their birth parents nevertheless indicated a willingness for them to do so. Two carer-adopters described how birth parents had broken off contact. Alastair's adoptive mother reported that his birth father had 'disappeared' once Alastair was placed for adoption and Tania's adoptive mother considered that her birth mother and grandmother had 'never shown any interest . . . she didn't want to know'. Caitlin's adoptive mother, who was a stranger adopter, explained that she had agreed to yearly contact with her child's birth mother because she thought it would benefit the child, but due to her own difficulties Caitlin's birth mother had been unable to keep to this arrangement. This had been hard for the child to understand.

One child adopted by strangers did see his birth mother occasionally, but no other relatives. There was some confusion as to who his father was and he was distressed by the fact that he could not see his birth father. This child had disabilities resulting from foetal alcohol syndrome. He had been adopted at the age of six by people who, although they had never previously looked after him, already knew him slightly in a professional capacity. His adoptive parents viewed the contact as beneficial for him: 'He has questions we cannot answer. It is an honesty issue. He will always know who his birth mum is and why he is like he is.'

All of the other adopted children in our study who had face-to-face contact with a parent had been adopted by their foster carers. Contact established prior to the adoption had simply continued in these cases, although not always with the same frequency. Some adopters mentioned having grown to know and like a child's birth parent while the child was fostered by them. Adoptive parents who are willing to allow contact between the children and their birth families often do so because they feel it is in the best interests of the child (Berry *et al*, 1998). This was certainly the case for some of the adopters in our study, who were motivated to continue contact because they felt it might be beneficial for the child to keep in touch with relatives:

> *One of the reasons that we adopted her was that I didn't want her to lose contact with her sister, I didn't want her to lose contact with her mum, because I quite liked her mum, even though she was an addict, and she had begged me to adopt Philippa and I wanted to keep that contact going. But then eventually anyway her mum died.* (Adoptive mother of Philippa, carer adoption)

I mean we're happy for the contact to go ahead and I, I think it's good for them . . . for them to be . . . to keep in touch and we would encourage it. (Adoptive mother of Alastair, stranger adoption)

Foster carers generally also had a positive attitude to contact with birth parents and in a number of cases felt it did benefit the child. The carers of some children who had experienced unstable care careers appeared to feel particularly strongly that the children should have contact with their birth parents:

Because I think he needs, he needs to know that they're still there and he really does love his mum and dad. (Carer of Daniel, unstable care)

She needs an identity, she can't identify with us, she's our foster daughter. Yeah, she can care about us but, you know, deep down she needs a sense of who she is. And that, I feel, needs to go back to the birth family and she needs those questions answered, from them, not by a social worker, not by a foster mum but by her parents. (Carer of Monica, unstable care)

I like his mum and dad so I don't mind, you know, the contact, and sometimes I do wish it was more, that he had more contact. But because he is one of six and the fact that the birth parents work, you know, I understand that it's difficult so I don't want to encourage something that's not going to happen. (Carer of Johnny, unstable care)

However, some foster carers and carer adopters were concerned about the impact of face-face contact with parents on the child:

It just screws him up, just screws his head up all the time. (Carer of Maurice, stable foster care)

It used to be awful. He used to be very anxious before a contact so that he would misbehave and be really naughty at school, because all he could think about was this contact that he was gonna have. And then when he went back to school the next day after contact, again we'd have some upset because of what had gone off during the contact. (Carer of Brian, stable foster care)

Several of the children interviewed indicated that they were happy with the contact they had with one or both parents and thought the frequency was about right. Often, these were children who had had unstable care careers:

I like to see my mum and dad. Once a month, but when that can't happen I don't really mind as long as I can see them. (Daniel, unstable care)

I do quite enjoy it but when I come back here I feel real guilty because I can't like say what we've done and everything, can I? And I think other children in here they don't see their mum as often as I do, so I don't really tell them. (Laura, unstable care)

While some did not indicate that they felt upset during or after these encounters, others clearly did find these occasions troubling:

Yeah, it's like, it's like you get picked up during the day and then the night you just suddenly drop, it's like this really thin like rope and then like when they leave it's like it's cut and it all has to start all over again, you have to build yourself back up to see them again and then it all goes again when you've done it . . . it's hard. (Monica, unstable care)

A few children in long-term foster care had managed to reconcile the fact that, while they identified principally with their foster carers, who they called mum and dad, they also belonged to their birth families. Sarah, for example, often spent weekends with her birth mother and sometimes took friends along with her on these visits. She felt the contact was sufficiently frequent and enjoyed her visits but had no desire to live with her mother. She and her mother appeared to have established a comfortable modus vivendi:

Well it is about right, 'cos . . . I like going and see her, so . . . she's

*really nice, just like, she's quite small [laughs] like me. She has a
laugh as well. She likes to take us out but sometimes she can't. Like,
she likes to do more with us, like more contact, so she's already got
like more contact and everything now, so we see her every other
weekend and stuff. She buys us sweets. Then she buys us presents and
everything, so, basically things like a normal parent as well.* (Sarah,
stable foster care)

Other children in long-term foster placements who saw birth parents from
time to time were more ambivalent, as they wished to remain in contact
with their parents but felt ashamed of them. Nathan visited his maternal
grandmother regularly and sometimes saw his mother while he was there,
but according to his carer, never wanted to be seen in public with her.
Aidan saw his mother three times a year and also telephoned her roughly
every three weeks. When asked how these visits went, his reply indicated
his ambivalence:

*Absolutely embarrassing. 'Cos she doesn't look . . . 'cos she wears
second-hand clothes, she stinks of smoke, she, I don't know, does she
buy second-hand toilet roll? [laughing] . . . It goes quickly 'cos I
enjoy it but it's more slow 'cos I'm so embarrassed. So I just stay that
one yard away from my mum [laughing] behind her pretending I'm
not part of her. 'Cos [his brother] just walks ahead of us, I walk behind
him and mum walks in the middle and wonders what's going on.*
(Aidan, stable foster care)

Some children expressed no desire to see their birth parents at all. For
example, Niamh said she did not wish for any contact with her birth
mother, whom she referred to as 'a witch', and was clear that she did not
wish to see her birth father either:

*Don't know my birth dad whatsoever. I have one picture and I know
his name, which I've got in my life story book . . . I don't know him.
I just don't know him and I don't think I'll ever want to really get into
contact with him, to be honest, not like I do with [her brother] type
thing.* (Niamh, carer adoption)

Others, like Reece, who were placed at an early age with adoptive families or in foster placements that were quasi-adoptive in nature, said they were content to wait until they were older before making contact with birth parents:

> *I don't mind actually if I can't see my real parents because I need to get . . . when I'm old enough I'm allowed to see them, but I've just got to go and see my brother first and then after that go and see my mum and dad.* (Reece, stable foster care)

Several children, though, found contact unpredictable and difficult. Nine-year-old Terry, who had been adopted by his carer and was happily settled, said he felt 'a bit stressed' whenever he visited his birth mother. He had not lived with her since he was a baby, felt uneasy when he was with her and was reluctant to be embraced by her. Maurice's visits to his mother could be stressful in other ways:

> *It's all right some, some of the time, but we argue a lot [pause] just about random things, I don't know why, I think she likes the argument or the attention or something because most of the time I'd go and she'd say something and then it'll just lead to a big argument, she just deliberately tries causing an argument. Sometimes she like goes into one of these moods.* (Maurice, stable foster care)

Lexi felt let down by her mother, who visited only twice a year. She clearly felt ambivalent about her and often angry, and said was relieved when these visits were over:

> *Sometimes I say I miss her and sometimes I don't . . . Another reason I don't really like her is because she used to come round every Saturday, but then she didn't and we'd not seen her for three years and . . . and then she just comes up out of the blue, calls my dad saying that she wants to see us. So we've all agreed to see her and she came and saw, seen us for Christmas, and bought us a selection box and a little bit of metal, that kind of does break off a necklace, and that's another reason why I don't like her.* (Lexi, residence order)

Face-to-face contact with siblings and other relatives

Nearly one-third of the children saw at least one of their siblings daily because they lived in the same adoptive home or foster placement. Some lived with one or more siblings but not with others, who were in different placements.

Table 12.2
Placement with siblings by group per cent

Contact with:	Adopted (all) (n = 66)	Adopted by stranger (n = 39)	Adopted by carer (n = 25)	Stable foster care (n = 60)	Unstable care (n = 34)
All in same placement	6	8	4	25	3
Same placement and elsewhere	23	31	12	17	12
All elsewhere	59	51	68	55	79
No siblings	12	10	16	3	6

Table 12.3
Face-to-face contact with siblings by group

Contact with:	Adopted (all) (n = 49)		Adopted by stranger (n = 29)		Adopted by carer (n = 20)		Stable foster care (n = 49)		Unstable care (n = 39)	
	%	n	%	n	%	n	%	n	%	n
Some contact	29	(14)	24	(7)	35	(7)	86	(42)	97	(37)
No contact	71	(35)	76	(22)	65	(13)	14	(7)	3	(1)

Among those children who had siblings, far fewer adopted children saw their siblings at all compared to children who were looked after, as shown in Table 12.3.[65]

---

[65] Chi-square test significant at p = .001 for contact with parents and p = .008 for face-to-face contact with siblings.

Most of those who had some face-to-face contact with a parent also saw siblings. However, only a very small proportion of the adopted children (5%) saw their siblings but not their parents, as did a similar proportion of the fostered children (6%).

Most of the children interviewed who saw siblings appeared to be happy with the nature and frequency of contact:

> *[I'm] happy that I can see them . . . Like most of the time we just go out and enjoy ourselves, go to town, then get something to eat and talk, go to the Pound Shop, spend money.* (Daniel, unstable care)

> *It was just exactly the same as when I go to a friend's house who's got children, she quite happily joins in with them. I'm not quite sure that she sees them any differently, just going to somebody else's house, but she knows he's her brother and she just got on and, they all played, they all played together.* (Adoptive mother of Olivia, stranger adoption)

Sometimes, however, there was conflict between siblings. For example, Laura met her sisters regularly but often fell out with them. Gray and his adoptive mother both reported that Gray's older brother often used to beat him up when he saw him, possibly, according to Gray's mother, because Gray had been adopted and he had not. Now aged 18, the brother had not been in contact for a while. Gray very much wanted to be in contact with his brother, but had found the contact they had quite difficult:

> *I asked if me and Carl could stay together 'cos I was the youngest one in the family, and I felt fairly close to Carl at the time, and it seemed to me that Carl, me and Carl would stick together, like always stay together and never be split apart . . . I, I feel a bit of security with him . . . (but now) well I don't really know because every now and again we phoned him, and I never could think of anything to say, but as soon as, I suppose if I had more time with him, more like days and days, I suppose I could like just bond with him even more.* (Gray, stranger adoption)

Two other children longed to renew contact with younger siblings or half-siblings whom they had not seen since shortly after they were born:

> Yeah, 'cos I still adore him [laughs] but I haven't seen him in 11 years. I've always asked questions whether who's seen him and who hasn't, how is he, all that thing but he doesn't actually know I exist ... I know he exists because I left when he was a baby, I ... I was moved to here when he was a baby, so he doesn't know me. (Naimh, carer adoption)

Jacob was one of ten children in a variety of foster and adoptive homes. Social services arranged meetings that brought most of these children and their carers together for days out. These encounters were supervised because some of the children posed a risk to their siblings. Jacob very much wished to see his youngest brother, now seven, whom he had last seen when he was one day old:

> There should be a law saying that you can see your brother until a certain age, because like what's he going to do when he finds out when he's 18 that he's got brothers and sisters out there? What's he going to do? He's going to be heartbroken. (Jacob, unstable care)

Some of the children had some form of contact with other relatives, in most cases grandparents. It was not uncommon for the children we interviewed to see their grandparents as well as, or sometimes instead of, their birth parents. This contact was often, though not always, viewed as less problematic than contact with parents and children often enjoyed it:

> I think it was very good, yeah. She showed her lots of old pictures of Philippa's mum when she was little and yeah, she looks like her great nan as well. (Adoptive mother of Philippa, carer adoption)

> I quite enjoy staying with my grandma to be honest. Yeah, we have a good laugh but she's, I mean she wouldn't be able to cope with me living there, to be honest, I don't think 'cos she's 87 now, so. (Nathan, stable foster care)

A few children, including those in long-term foster care, were also reported to maintain contact with former foster carers.

Frequency of contact

As expected, frequency of face-to-face contact was very different for adopted children compared to those who were fostered.

Table 12.4
Frequency of face-to-face contact with parents per cent (n)

	Birth mother			Birth father		
	Adopted (n = 63)	*Stable foster care (n = 55)*	*Unstable care (n = 38)*	*Adopted (n = 62)*	*Stable foster care (n = 55)*	*Unstable care (n = 36)*
Weekly	0	18 (10)	8 (3)	0	3 (2)	6 (2)
Monthly	2 (1)	13 (7)	29 (11)	2 (1)	9 (5)	14 (5)
Less often	10 (6)	42 (23)	40 (15)	5 (3)	24 (13)	28 (10)
Never	87 (56)	27 (15)	23 (9)	93 (58)	64 (35)	53 (19)

For the adopted children, the frequency of face-to-face contact with birth parents was similar to that in a recent study of contact after adoption (Neil *et al*, 2003). However, the percentage of fostered children with weekly or monthly contact with parents was substantially lower than the figure of 70 per cent found in a recent study of long-term foster care. The majority of the children in that study had entered their foster placements in the previous two years, whereas all the children in our study had been with their carers for six or more years (Schofield *et al*, 2000; Neil *et al*, 2003).

For some children in long-term foster care, contact with birth parents may decrease with the passage of time. For just over half of the children, nothing had changed in the previous three years. Either the frequency of contact had remained the same or they continued to have no contact at all with their birth families. However, the remaining children experienced either an increase or a decrease in face-to-face contact with their birth families. For some, the picture was complicated, as contact with some family members had increased but contact with others had decreased, as shown in Table 12.5.

Table 12.5
Changes in frequency of contact by group (n = 169)

	All placements per cent (n)		Adopted per cent (n)		Fostered per cent (n)	
	%	n	%	n	%	n
No contact	29	(49)	57	(41)	10	(7)
No change	26	(44)	22	(16)	32	(23)
Increase in contact	18	(30)	6	(4)	22	(16)
Increase some, decrease others	14	(23)	4	(3)	22	(16)
Decrease in contact	14	(23)	11	(8)	15	(11)
Total	**101**	**(169)**	**100**	**(72)**	**101**	**(73)**

NB: Figures do not total 100% due to rounding.

In the previous three years there had been a slight decrease in the frequency of contact for adoptive children. Selwyn and colleagues also found a reduction in face-to-face contact as time passed for a sample of adopted and fostered children (Selwyn *et al*, 2006). Another study found that a reduction in contact between birth and adoptive parents (that is, in indirect contact), was more likely to be initiated by the birth parents than by adoptive parents. However, some adoptive parents in that study had initially agreed to contact because they feared they would not be allowed to adopt if they did not, and then subsequently reduced or stopped that contact (Berry *et al*, 1998).

Children in all three unstable groups were likely to see siblings more frequently than birth parents, and, as before, those in stable or unstable care were more likely to have frequent contact than those adopted, as shown in Table 12.6.

Although the children who were adopted were far less likely than others to see any members of their birth families, contact arrangements appeared somewhat more settled for them compared to children in foster care. The latter were more likely to have experienced a change in the

Table 12.6
Frequency of face-to-face contact with siblings by group per cent

	Adopted (n = 62)		Stable foster care (n = 61)		Unstable Care (n = 38)	
	%	n	%	n	%	n
Weekly		0	23	(14)	29	(11)
Monthly	8	(5)	23	(14)	21	(8)
Less often	15	(9)	25	(15)	45	(17)
Never	56	(35)	13	(8)		0
Not applicable (no siblings)	21	(13)	16	(10)	5	(2)

frequency of contact in the previous three years.[66] In a few cases, contact had increased as children in foster care grew older and they and/or their parents had chosen to see each other more regularly. Sometimes carers felt less concern about contact as children grew older because they were more confident that the children could now take care of themselves on these visits:

> *It was supervised up until her being 16 with mum, but now she's 16, we talked about it and just said that she's sensible enough to, if anything, know if anything's not right when she's on contact. She will walk away, she is quite a sensible girl.* (Carer of Laura, unstable care)

In 15-year-old Monica's case, contact had increased substantially due to a change of placement. She had been placed with long-term foster carers at the age of two and had remained with them for 11 years until the placement disrupted, partly due to the carers' divorce and partly due to Monica's difficult behaviour. Those foster carers had fiercely resisted her birth families' attempts to maintain contact but the new carers she had moved to following the placement disruption took a different view:

> *Because what I want, what I'm doing now with Monica is re-introducing her to her birth family slowly and building up relationships that*

---

[66] Chi-square test significant at p = <.001.

*have been damaged by this other foster carer with the birth family and
it's coming on, it's really coming on well, because . . . Monica was
very anti-family, couldn't stand them when she came here. But it
wasn't her, when we actually explored more about where Monica was
coming from with regards to her feelings towards the birth family. It
wasn't about her choices, it was the foster carer's choices that she'd
taken on board because she was identifying with them, you know. She
wanted to be one of them, to be one of them she had to join forces and
side, she hadn't got the other side of the argument.* (Carer of Monica,
unstable care)

In most cases, though, our interviews suggested that change in the
frequency of contact was in most cases the result of a change in the birth
parents' capacity to maintain contact, for example, due to a deterioration
in their mental health, or problems with their behaviour, or an apparent
decline in their commitment to seeing their children:

*But their dad has always been in and out of their lives. He can, he
would go for a couple of months and he would phone, he'd phone
them every week or even more than once a week and then they
wouldn't hear from him for, for months. He occasionally comes over.*
(Carer of Aidan, stable foster care)

*I seen that bond slipping, mainly because of what she was doing when
they went to visit her, you know, and the boys used to turn up she'd
never be up for them, she'd never have food in for them for the day,
there'd be strange people there that frightened the boys. And, you
know, I think in the end they'd have been quite happy if somebody had
made that decision for them not to go there again, and in the end they
did because she was taking illegal substances as well. So they, they
stopped it on the drug thing.* (Carer of Nathan, stable foster care)

*[Birth mother] kept contact up with Alex until he was about five. She
used to come down to our house and was, she would come down to
our house if social services would lay a taxi on for her, she would
come down to see Alex but there was no real, her heart was never in*

it, you know, it was just like a duty she used to come down and see him and go again . . . And eventually she said she didn't even want to do that, she never even sent him a birthday card a Christmas card or anything ever. (Carer of Alex, stable foster care)

Telephone and letterbox contact

Some children had telephone contact with family members and, again, this contact was most likely to be with siblings. Telephone contact was rarely an alternative to face-to-face contact between children and birth parents, as 95 per cent of those with telephone contact with parents also had some face-to-face contact. Children, parents and siblings who had face-to-face contact often mentioned texting each other too. However, for most of the children who had telephone contact with birth families, this was infrequent, as shown in Table 12.7.

Table 12.7
Telephone contact with birth family per cent

Contact with	Weekly	Monthly	Less often	Never	Total with this contact
A parent (n = 169)	14	10	15	60	39
Siblings (n = 143)*	20	7	19	39	46
Other relatives (n = 172)	13	9	15	63	37

* Children without siblings excluded from this count.

As we might expect, children who were adopted were far less likely to either see or be in telephone contact with their parents, as 84 per cent of the adopted children had neither form of contact compared to 20 per cent of the fostered children.[67] For nearly half of the children who were adopted there was letterbox contact, in most cases between adoptive parents and

---

[67]   Chi-square test significant at p = <.001.

birth parents. This was infrequent, occurring less than once a month for almost all of the children.

Contact prohibited

For 35 per cent (68) of the children, face-to-face contact was not the plan and for 24 per cent, no contact of any kind was allowed. In most cases, contact was forbidden with the child's father or mother, or both, but in a few cases, contact was forbidden with all members of the birth family. Face-to-face contact was forbidden for 59 per cent of the adopted children but only one-quarter of the fostered children, although there was no significant difference between fostered and adopted children in the likelihood that any form of contact would be forbidden.[68] The use of online social networking sites such as Facebook is likely to make it increasingly difficult to prevent children and parents establishing contact with one another in circumstances where professionals consider that contact is likely to be harmful to the child.

Quality of contact

Nearly two-thirds of the children (103) had face-to-face contact with one or more of their birth relatives and, as we have seen, very few of this group were living with adoptive parents. We asked the carers and social workers of these children for their views on the nature of this contact and its impact on the children concerned. Carers' views are shown in Table 12.8.

Contact was viewed as positive for over half of those who had contact and it was rated as a positive experience at least "to some extent" for over 80 per cent. However, around one-third of the children were reported to be upset by the irregularity of contact, a problem also identified by Sinclair and colleagues (Sinclair et al, 2005c). There were also concerns that just under one-third were exposed to serious risk during contact.

Carers and social workers often had very different views about the impact of contact on children. Where the views of both were available to us, we compared their responses and found that on the whole, social

---

[68]   Chi-square significant at p = <.001 for face-to-face contact.

Table 12.8
Carers' views of quality of contact with birth relatives per cent

	Not at all	To some extent	To a large extent	Don't know
Good contact with at least one relative (n = 76)	9	34	54	2
Child has as much contact as s/he wants (n = 72)	25	25	44	6
Particular relatives undermine placement (n = 70)	69	13	8	10
Problems over regularity of contact (n = 71)	59	27	11	3
Child upset by irregular contact (n = 71)	65	22	13	0
Exposed to serious risk during contact (n = 71)	66	20	10	4
Mixes with undesirable people during contact (n = 71)	76	10	3	11
Upset by way treated during contact (n = 71)	69	15	3	13
Overall contact is a positive experience (n = 71)	11	32	51	6

workers were generally more likely to rate the quality of contact as positive. For questions that asked about the positive impact of contact, there was agreement in only 38–56 per cent of the cases compared. However, there was much closer agreement (in 78–86% of cases compared) in relation to questions about specific, negative effects of contact on the child. Selwyn and colleagues' study of a similar sample found that social workers generally assumed that contact would be good for the child, but that contact plans were not always well thought out (Selwyn *et al*, 2006).

Contact with particular family members may be detrimental as well as beneficial to children. Four children were reported to have experienced abuse during the course of contact with a relative during the previous year. Sinclair and colleagues' earlier study of children in foster care found that the only variable that predicted re-abuse was weekly contact with a relative. In that study, for children who had previously been abused, re-abuse was significantly more likely if no one was forbidden contact (Sinclair *et al*, 2005c).

Carers often thought that contact was a positive experience for the children, as mentioned above, but several mentioned their concern at the impact on children when parents failed to turn up for visits. In a few cases, carers expressed concern about the care children received while visiting their birth parents:

> *He's been a bit naughty, he's had them down sometimes and he's not fed them properly, he's given them sweets if they've said they're hungry, he's not given them a meal. He's let them stop up all night watching television till they come back, so they're not, they're no good for school, big bags under their eyes, whacked out, you know, and he knows he shouldn't do it.* (Carer of Josie, stable foster care)

> *I'm very dubious about that because, I've said to their social worker, if it starts affecting their behaviour, I'm gonna stop this because I'm not having it. 'Cos we've had days with their mum when they've come back and just turned into little monsters because they've been allowed to do what they please.* (Carer of Sarah, stable foster care)

> *The birth mother, she'd be saying 'They're coming to take you away' and they're going here, there, and course being their mum they believed her, and then we decided to move.* (Carer of Nathan, stable foster care)

Some carer adopters or foster carers of children in long-term foster placements spoke of their relief that contact had ceased:

> *I think once the contact with mum stopped, it was better for me because when it was contact with mum, you were sort of over the top worrying all the time, what's it going to be today, is she going to turn up, is Sheila going to be upset 'cos she's got to have to come home early 'cos mum's not going to be there, is mum going to get upset and start crying and, which she did sometimes, you know, and she'd, some*

days she'd be really good with her and other days she didn't want to know. (Parent of Sheila, carer adoption)

In my experience, I think that it's been better for 'em to have limited or no contact with their own mum and dad, because there's been no influence, no, it's just been easier. I've been able to get on with looking after 'em without having to think, I feel really terrible because that's, they're her children and she can't, do you know what I'm saying? I've been able to make decisions without, without upsetting anybody else. (Carer of Reece, stable foster care)

Children's feelings about contact

We asked carers about the children's feelings about their contact, or lack of it, with birth relatives. If no questionnaire was received from carers of children who had not been adopted, we substituted the social worker's response to the same question. Clearly, these responses can only tell us the adults' perceptions of the children's feelings in this respect, but they nevertheless give us some indication of the children's feelings about contact. First, we asked whether the children (in all types of placement, including residential placements) felt that they had sufficient contact their birth relatives. Most respondents thought the children were happy with the degree of contact they had, that is, happy with whether they had any contact at all and if so, the extent of this contact. However, a substantial minority of children were reported to feel they had too little contact, ranging from 29 per cent for contact with mothers and siblings to 34 per cent for contact with fathers, as shown in Table 12.9.

Just one child was reported to think that the amount of contact was 'too much', and this was indicated solely in relation to his sibling. However, some of the children we interviewed did wish for more frequent contact with birth parents in particular, while others wished for less, as other research has found (Thomas *et al*, 1999). For example, while Johnny (in unstable care) wished for weekly rather than monthly contact, Nathan (in stable foster care) found contact with his mother 'a bit depressing' and thought that monthly contact was enough.

Table 12.9
Children's views of extent of contact with birth relatives per cent

Contact	About right	Too little
With birth mother (n = 91)	71	29
With birth father (n = 64)	66	34
With siblings (n = 100)	70	29
With other relatives (n = 83)	86	14

Table 12.10
Children distressed by lack of contact with birth mother per cent

	Adopted per cent (n = 40)	Fostered per cent (n = 24)
Distressed	5	29
Ambivalent	23	25
Content	72	46
Total per cent	**100**	**100**

Table 12.11
Children distressed by lack of contact with birth father per cent

	Adopted per cent (n = 34)	Fostered per cent (n = 21)
Distressed	9	24
Ambivalent	6	33
Content	85	43
Total per cent	**100**	**100**

We also asked carers and social workers about the feelings of children who had either very little or no contact with their birth relatives. Again, it is important to bear in mind these data are based on adults' perceptions of the children's feelings. Adopted children were reported to be far more accepting of a lack of contact with birth parents than children in foster care, as shown in Tables 12.10 and 12.11.

It is possible that adopted children felt a stronger identification and sense of belonging to their adoptive families and so expressed less need for contact with their birth families. Alternatively, if they did yearn for this contact, they may have been reluctant to express this to their adoptive parents. Children in foster care appeared more likely than those adopted to be distressed by a lack of contact with either parent, and also more likely to feel some ambivalence in relation to this lack of contact with fathers. However, children in both types of placement were regarded as more or less equally likely to feel some ambivalence about a lack of contact with their mothers.

Although a few of the older children interviewed appeared to have reached some resolution of their feelings about their birth families, most showed a degree of ambivalence and some were clearly distressed by birth parents' failure to keep in touch with them. Lexi, who had been placed with her current carers when only a few days old, spoke at some length of her parents' erratic contact with her and her ambivalent and often angry feelings towards them, saying that she was 'really unhappy' with her mother in particular:

> *My real dad, well, I wouldn't, I love him but not really love him because he hardly comes and visits, he hasn't visited . . . the last time he visited me was on the 21st of December 2006. My real mum . . . never comes and visits, especially when she's got a man in her life. She, when she's not got a man in her life, she's, like, my darling little children, which is really annoying me. So she comes and visits, visits now and then, but not often.*

Speaking of a particular visit, she added:

> *It was me and my brother, no, just me actually, I pretended to actually, like, love her and like her and that, but it weren't, I didn't really because she left me alone, she didn't try to stop them from taking her away, being took away, but I'm glad about that . . . If she knew I didn't really like her then she would probably never come round.* (Lexi, residence order)

Maurice, too, was upset by the fact that, although his mother occasionally texted him, she did not visit and his father did not keep in contact. When asked if his father ever telephoned, he answered:

> *I've got his number, he's got my number but he's never tried calling me ... And so if he's not going to bother trying to call me I'm not going to bother trying to call him.* (Maurice, stable foster care)

Fostered children were also reported to be more likely than adopted children to be either distressed (30% versus 6%) or ambivalent (30% versus 17%) about a lack of contact with their siblings. Nearly four-fifths (78%) of the adopted children were thought to be untroubled by a lack of contact with brothers and sisters, compared to only 41 per cent of children in foster care.[69]

Conclusion

Our interviews with children and their carers suggest that whether or not contact was a positive experience for children was related to some extent to parents' past and recent behaviour towards them and the meaning that children ascribed to both this behaviour and separation. The attitudes of foster carers and adoptive parents were important too, as their willingness to support contact, despite any reservations they might have about it, could encourage children to stay in touch with their birth families. The age at which children had entered care and the attitudes of their carers to contact also played a part. It should be noted, however, that our conclusions are based on interviews with children who had been separated from parents for many years and some of the children had no memory of living with their parents. It is possible that children more recently separated from birth parents may have a somewhat different view of contact.

The reasons for children's long-term separation from birth parents were important. It was easier for children to make sense of the fact that

---

[69] Chi-square tests significant at p = .019 for no contact with mother, p = .049 for no contact with father and p = .006 for no contact with siblings.

they were no longer with their birth parents if they understood this as being due to parents' inability to care for them, due to their learning disabilities or mental health or substance abuse problems. Although, as in the case of Nathan and Aidan, children might feel embarrassed by such parents or, in Terry's case, feel no real sense of belonging to them, they did not always experience separation as a personal rejection. Such children were ambivalent about, or even uninterested in, seeing birth parents and had no desire to see them more often, particularly if they were happily settled in long-term foster placements or adoptive homes. Nevertheless, as this contact did not appear to trouble them too much, it allowed them to maintain a sense of connection with birth families that might become more important to them as they grew older. For other children, knowledge or unhappy memories of abuse, neglect or rejection could make them feel angry or ambivalent towards birth families. The narratives they developed to make sense of their histories could make them yearn for more contact or wish for none at all. These representations of past experiences were often affected by children's interpretations of parents' commitment to staying in touch with them and the quality of contact when they saw them.

Age at separation from parents also played a part, though in a variety of ways. Some children who entered care at a very early age and had no memory of any abuse or neglect, or those at high risk of maltreatment who had been removed before these could occur, had never known their birth parents and did not have face-to-face contact with them. Some of this group showed no longing for contact, although a few thought they might like to meet birth relatives when they were older. A few of these early-separated children did have some contact with birth parents, however, and their feelings about it were closely linked to their feelings about their parents' past and recent actions. For example, children like Lexi, who felt that parents had abandoned them long ago, interpreted their subsequent erratic contact as continuing evidence of rejection.

For children who had entered care at a later age, memories of early experiences of abuse or neglect could leave them angry with birth parents and keen to distance themselves from them, like Jacob and Niamh. Others, despite unhappy memories, might nevertheless yearn to see parents and have a closer relationship with them. Sometimes, with the passage of time, children reached some resolution of their feelings about birth families and, like Sarah, had developed a better relationship with birth parents and began to see them more frequently. These issues concerning contact are also related to the broader question of the interaction between children's feelings about their birth families and their relationships with their carers or adoptive parents, which are discussed in the next chapter.

Summary

- Three-quarters (74%) of children in stable foster care and 86 per cent of those with unstable care histories had some face-to-face contact with one or both birth parents. In contrast, only one child adopted by strangers had any face-to-face contact with a birth parent, although 29 per cent of those adopted by carers did so.
- Children were often keen to retain contact with siblings, although sibling relationships could be difficult for some. Nearly all (97%) of those with unstable care careers and 86 per cent of those in stable foster placements had some face-to-face contact with siblings, compared to only 35 per cent of those adopted by carers and 24 per cent adopted by strangers.
- For those who did have face-to-face contact, contact with both birth parents and siblings was more frequent for those who were fostered compared to those adopted. The frequency of contact had changed over time for around one-fifth of those fostered.
- Face-to-face contact was prohibited for 59 per cent of the adopted children and one-quarter of the fostered children.
- Telephone contact was only rarely an alternative to face-to-face contact. For around half of the adopted children there was letterbox contact between birth parents and adoptive parents. Face-to-face contact was prohibited for 59 per cent of the adopted children and one-quarter of the fostered children.
- Quality of contact was an important issue. Nearly three-quarters of the children were thought, by social workers, to have good contact with at least one relative. However, for around one-third of the children there

were problems over the regularity of contact and nearly one-quarter were thought to have been exposed to serious risk during contact.

- Children in foster care were thought more likely to be distressed by a lack of contact with birth parents and to be preoccupied with their birth parents than those who were adopted. This may be related to the fact that those who were adopted were more likely to have been separated from their parents as infants.
- Children's feelings about contact were related in complex ways to how they made sense of their parents' past and recent actions, their age at entry to care and, to some extent, their carers' attitudes to contact.

13 **A sense of belonging**

This chapter draws on interviews with 29 children in long-term, stable foster placements or adopted, and their carers, to explore the children's perceptions of emotional and legal security. After six or more years settled in permanent placements, where and with whom did these children feel they belonged? How far were children with different characteristics, histories and circumstances able to reconcile the fact of having two families? These perceptions may be complex and may shift over time. We examine the children's and carers' perceptions of belonging – looking in turn at children in stable foster placements, those adopted by foster carers and those adopted by strangers. In this chapter we use an older terminology and refer to the children's foster carers as their foster families, because for these children in stable, long-term foster homes, carers were perceived as another family.

Some caution is needed in interpreting our findings, because the carers and children who agreed to be interviewed were a self-selected group. Our typology of perceptions and experiences should therefore be viewed as illustrative of the patterns we might expect to find in the wider population of children in permanent placements, but not necessarily a reflection of the proportions we would expect to find in each group.

Stable foster care

There was immense variety in the degree to which children in stable foster care felt they belonged to their foster families. In situations where there had been no face-to-face contact with birth families for many years, some children and foster carers perceived their relationship as a quasi-adoptive one. In other foster families, both children and carers appeared comfortable with the fact that the child belonged to two families. However, for some children and carers, the situation was more fraught. Some foster carers felt that the child "belonged" to them emotionally, but the children's preoccupation with their birth parents (often a hurt, angry or conflicted preoccupation) could undermine the stability of relationships within the foster home.

Primary identification with foster family: quasi-adoptive placements ("as if")

Three boys were living in foster families that appeared to be perceived as quasi-adoptive by carers and children, in that carers perceived themselves as "parents" to the children, replacing absent birth parents. Reece and Alex had been placed in infancy and had lived with their foster carers for nine and 12 years respectively, while Noah had lived continuously with his carer for ten years, since he was four years old. All three foster carers spoke of how much they loved the children and the children's accounts revealed that they clearly felt unequivocally loved.

A key factor which made these quasi-adoptive situations possible was the fact that none of these children was in contact with their birth parents, although two had had some contact many years earlier. The exclusive nature of these foster placements created the conditions in which it was possible for both child and carer to view them as quasi-adoptive. In Noah's case, face-to-face contact with parents had been prohibited, although he occasionally received letters from them.

There were some similarities between the other two children. Both had chronic and serious health problems and both had been rejected by their drug-dependent mothers, neither of whom had been in contact for many years. Reece had never had direct contact with his birth mother, who had problems of both drug and alcohol dependency. Until a few years earlier, she had occasionally telephoned his brother, who lived in the same placement, but according to his carer, she had never shown any interest in Reece:

> *She never actually asked to speak to Reece, it was always [his brother], it's really just like Reece didn't even exist. I mean she knew that he'd been really poorly and not once did she ring up and say 'How's Reece?' – never even asked, you know, so.*

Alex's foster carer said she had encouraged visits by his mother, but the mother's intermittent visits had ended seven years earlier due to her apparent lack of interest in continuing them. His carer mentioned that the last time Alex ever saw his birth mother, she had asked him his name. This lack of contact with birth parents gave foster carers a greater sense of entitlement to act as if they were indeed parents, partly because they no longer felt obliged to take birth parents' wishes into account. As Reece's foster carer explained:

In my experience, I think that it's been better for them to have limited, or no contact with their own mum and dad, because there's been no influence, no, it's just been easier. I've been able to get on with looking after 'em without having to think, I feel really terrible because that's, they're her children and she can't . . . do you know what I'm saying? I've been able to make decisions without, without upsetting anybody else.

In these very settled situations, where children had been placed at an early age and there was no contact with birth parents, the children's perception of family belonging appeared to mirror the carers' perceptions. The children's primary identification was with their foster families. They appeared able to hold in mind their "real mum and dad" (Noah), but nevertheless live *as if* their carers were "Mum" and "Dad", as they called them.

For both Reece and Alex, their sense of belonging to their foster home was reinforced by the fact that they remembered no other home, as both had lived continuously with their foster carers since infancy. These children were all very settled and appeared to have no anxiety that these foster families were anything other than a family for life. However, although he was settled and felt that he "belonged" to his foster family, Alex was troubled by the past and by his feelings about his birth family. His carer felt that the past 'eats into him' but that he had nevertheless 'learned to deal with it'. When asked about his birth mother, Alex distanced himself from her, perhaps because he was reluctant to talk about her or possibly because he did not remember much about the occasional contact he had had with her when younger, explaining, 'I met her once, it was quite a few years ago'.

In contrast, Noah, who had joined his foster family at the age of four, idealised the birth parents who had abused him, and this led to some emotional conflict and occasional ambivalence towards his foster carers. He received occasional letters from his birth parents and sometimes saw his brother, who still lived with them. He looked forward to the time when he would be old enough to see them again, but appeared to have accepted that this could not happen until he was an adult:

> *I don't mind, actually, if I can't see my real parents because I need to get, when I'm old enough I'm allowed to see them but I've just got to go and see my brother first and then after that go and see my mum and dad.*

Noah's behaviour was often very difficult, but his carers viewed it as a manifestation of his underlying anxiety and need for reassurance and said they accepted and coped with it saying, 'It's been difficult, but we love him'. Despite his occasional ambivalence towards them, Noah nevertheless felt unreservedly loved by his foster carers, who, he said, 'chose me' and who, in day-to-day life, he referred to and treated *as if* they were his parents, while perhaps feeling a stronger connection to his birth family than the other two children. His carers' understanding of the roots of his behavioural problems, their willingness and ability to cope with his difficult behaviour and their expressed love for him meant that, despite his anger and ambivalence, Noah felt secure in his sense of belonging to this family and his primary identification was with them.

Although absent parents were psychologically present for these children, they were not physically present and this made it easier for foster carers and children to live their everyday lives *as if* these foster families were indeed the families that the children belonged to. This shared perception that 'I belong to you and you belong to me' appeared to be implicit in the day-to-day practices of family life and contributed to the children's sense of emotional security. While holding in mind their birth families, these children nevertheless identified principally with their foster families. Calling their foster carers "Mum" and "Dad" was of considerable symbolic significance, a marker that the children wished to live as if their carers were indeed their parents.

Belonging to two families reconciled ("just like")

Another three children expressed the view that they belonged both to their birth families and to their foster families. All three had entered these placements between the ages of five and nine years, later than those whose primary identification was with their foster carers, and they were now between 14 and 17 years old. They had been settled in these place-ments for between seven and ten years. Two of them had previously experienced unstable care careers before settling in their current long-term foster placements.

These children were in direct contact with their birth mothers, although in one case this contact was only occasional, so birth parents were physically as well as psychologically present for the children. Neither they nor their carers felt that birth parents had in any sense been replaced. Instead, the young people had managed to reconcile their feelings of belonging to two families. Instead of viewing their foster carers *as if* they were indeed their parents, they viewed them *just like* another set of parents. These children felt that they loved, and were connected to, two kinds of parents. For example, Sarah's carer reported that she had told her, ' "I love being here and I love you but I want to be with my mum. Does that make sense?" I say "Of course it does".'

However, although these children saw birth parents reasonably regularly and were happy with that contact, they expressed no desire to live with them either in the near future or when they were older. As Kate explained:

> *I think my mum expects me, when I come out of foster care, to go to [home town] and live there, but 'cos I've grown up round here and I feel that if I go back there, it sounds bad, but I don't want to end up like my sister . . . I'd rather stay round here . . . 'cos I've sort of got my own life here.*

Two of the children called both their birth mothers and their foster carers "Mum", while the third addressed her carer by her name but always referred to her as "Mum" when speaking to others. Sarah had chosen to call her carer "Mum" when very young, wishing to emphasise the normality of her circumstances in response to questions from other children. As a teenager, however, she often took her friends along with her on regular visits to her birth mother and was open about the fact that she had two different "mothers" in her life. Her foster carer was more troubled than Sarah was by the question of how she should be addressed:

I think because when I started fostering I was always told they must never call you mum . . . you must keep remembering they have their own parents . . . I keep thinking well I'm not their mum and I try to keep just one step back, which is probably not a good thing but it's just the way I've grown over the years with all the kids I've had, I've just kept them that little bit further away.

Although this carer felt she had maintained a degree of emotional distance, Sarah was either unaware of this or reluctant to acknowledge it. She described how her "belonging" to her foster family was enacted in its day-to day practices, which positioned her as a "normal" member of a "normal" family, enabling her to feel fully part of it:

Just like any normal family, really. It's just like they act, they act the same as they would with their children . . . They're just basically my parents, to be honest. I probably do really love them, 'cos they're just like my parents . . . I feel really safe here.

Although she visited her birth mother regularly and often stayed for weekends, she had no desire to live with her and was sure that she would stay with her foster carers until she felt ready to live independently.

The carers of the other two children unequivocally expressed their love for them, felt that they "fitted in" naturally to the family and said they would always "be there" for them. Both were positive and supportive about the children's contact with their birth mothers, and able to accept that although they might 'feel like a mother to her', as one of them put it, the children had other mothers too.

However, 17-year-old Nathan's carer explained that, although she and her husband loved him and knew that he loved them, his preoccupation with his birth relatives meant that his identification with his foster family was somewhat ambivalent. He saw his mother, and a brother in foster care, only occasionally and was somewhat preoccupied with his connection to blood relatives, particularly with a younger brother he had never met. He also mentioned that he 'didn't like' his birth father, but wondered if he might like him if he ever saw him again. Nevertheless, Nathan also felt he was very much part of his foster family and felt settled and secure there, viewing them as a family who would be there for life. He felt grateful to them for 'how it's turned out' and was working hard at school in order to get to university. However, he also felt that a foster home 'can't be the same as your real home'. Aware of his ambivalence, his carers were anxious that he might one day leave them 'if something better came along'.

In two cases, carers attributed the success of the long-term placements to the child's temperament, their willingness to "fit in". As Sarah's carer commented, 'she accepts everything . . . she's just gone with the flow'. However, in Kate's case there was some indication that, when she had first arrived, at the age of nine, her compliance, emotional control ('she doesn't cry') and efforts to be accepted may have been influenced by her early experience of neglect and her two previous placement disruptions (in one case the result of emotional abuse by her carer). Her carer described her as being 'desperate to please' and 'accepting everything' when she first arrived, at the age of nine years, which no doubt made it easier for relationships to develop. Despite her earlier difficult experiences in her family and in care, she appeared happy, settled and emotionally secure in her long-term foster placement.

In these circumstances, where children and young people had been able to reconcile the fact that they had two families, albeit to varying extents, children felt able to love both their carers and their parents, apparently without significant emotional conflict. Despite some evidence of ambivalence and anxiety on the part of both children and carers, these children were doing well in stable, loving foster homes and felt secure in the knowledge that their substitute family would be a family for life. All were in contact with their mothers but none of them appeared to idealise their parents, although one was somewhat preoccupied with them. The carers' openness and inclusiveness facilitated this contact and none of the children indicated that they were troubled by conflicts of loyalty.

Qualified belonging: ambivalence and perceptions of permanence

Five other children in long-term foster placements were more obviously troubled by feelings of ambivalence, hurt and anger towards their birth parents. Although settled in their foster placements, their feelings about their birth parents led to divided loyalties and a qualified sense of belonging. These children had entered their current placements when they were between two and seven years old and had been settled there for between seven and 11 years. They were all teenagers at the time of interview, their ages ranging from 13 to 16 years. All had experienced some rejection by parents and all but one had also experienced neglect or abuse.

Most had some contact with parents, although for four of them this was intermittent due to parents' failure to keep to contact arrangements. For example, Gordon and Rachel had been placed with their maternal grandparents at the age of six and seven years respectively, following the discovery of persistent and serious physical abuse by their mother's partner. Their mother had elected to remain with her partner and had maintained only intermittent contact with the children over the following seven years. The plan was that contact should be monthly but she had made no effort to see them for over a year. Both children remembered the exact date of her last visit. Both felt hurt and angry about their mother, the boy externalising his distress through difficult behaviour at home and at school and the girl manifesting hers through anxiety and clingy, demanding behaviour towards both carers and friends.

For Gordon and Rachel, their sense of family belonging was clear, as they were cared for by their grandparents. Being with relatives helped them feel secure, as one of them explained: 'I know they are related to me and that I can trust them.' They believed that their grandparents would be their family for life, yet they also understood that these grandparents expected them to leave as soon as they were 18 years old. Motivated partly by a sense that they had an obligation to care for the children, these grandparents were offering only qualified permanence as they felt they would have done all that could be expected of them if they looked after the children until the age of 18. In stark contrast, the grandparents' own younger daughter, who was in her early 20s, was still living with them.

In the other three cases, both relative and non-relative carers had an unequivocal commitment to the children and viewed themselves as parents to them, but the children themselves were ambivalent about their sense of belonging. Maurice's and Aidan's carers thought the children had completely come to terms with the separation from their parents and fully accepted that they belonged emotionally to their substitute families, but Josie's carer was saddened by the fact that the child did not 'want us too close', which she felt was due to Josie's strong allegiance to her mother. All three carers expressed their love for the children and claimed them as their own. For example, Maurice's carer, his aunt, fully understood that he 'loves his mum to bits' but nevertheless felt that, 'He sees himself more as our son now . . . He's like our own son . . . He's mine.'

Both she and Aidan's carer believed that the child's sense of belonging mirrored their own perceptions that 'I belong to you and you belong to me', but the accounts of the children themselves indicated a degree of ambivalence about this. These children's complex feelings of hurt, anger and allegiance towards parents who had been rejecting and unreliable gave them a sense of ambivalent, qualified belonging to their carers. When asked if they felt they belonged in their foster families, the young people answered:

> *Not all the time, but some of the time . . . It's like when, when we have stuff like family get-togethers and things and you just think, hang on, I'm not really part of this.* (Maurice, 15 years old)

> *I don't feel this is my family . . . I feel I'm in the middle and most people just fall away from me. I feel so, being so spaced out, I don't feel loved.* (Aidan, 16 years old, autistic spectrum disorder)

Despite their qualified sense of belonging, all five considered that these placements were permanent and would last until they were at least 18 years old, if not longer. Maurice had even told his foster carer that he 'would stay until he was 50'. Thirteen-year-old Josie, who felt a strong allegiance to her birth mother, worried about where she would live when she grew up. Wishing to remain in touch with both her birth mother and her foster family, she imagined that she would settle in a town half way between the two. Furthermore, all of them also considered that even once they had moved on, their substitute families would be families for life, who they would see regularly and who, according to some, would act as grandparents to their children.

Provisional belonging

Finally, for Brian, a 12-year-old boy who had been settled in his foster placement for seven years, the placement appeared close to breakdown. This child displayed serious behaviour problems and had been diagnosed with an attachment disorder. His mother had serious mental health problems and was said to have displayed similar behaviour to his as a child. His foster carer's husband had died a year earlier. Her grief about her husband's death and her distress at Brian's extremely difficult behaviour and angry rejecting words had led to her growing ambivalence regarding whether she could continue to care for him. She now doubted the wisdom of having fought to keep him with her when he was younger and mourned the loss of the 'loving little boy he used to be' as well as the loss of her husband.

The relatively recent stress occasioned by the loss of a husband/foster father and the child's mental health problems and deteriorating behaviour were compounded by the actions of social workers, the birth mother and the foster family. Brian very much wanted to remain with his foster family and had wanted to be adopted by them in the past, but social workers had not proceeded with this because his birth mother had objected. Although he called his foster carers "Mum" and "Dad" and they had told him that they loved him and saw him as a son, he had clearly received mixed messages about how permanent this home might actually prove to be.

He had initially been placed with this family at the age of one, but unsuccessful attempts at reunification meant he did not finally settle there until the age of five. After that, his mother had phoned to tell him he would eventually return to live with her. His carer recounted:

It was, he was about six or so. And he was sad and I said, 'What's the matter?' He said, 'I don't have to go home to my mam, do I?' I said, 'Well, it would be a situation where if mummy was thought to be well enough to look after you and this was going to go on for, you know,

the rest of your life until you were old enough to look after yourself,
then yes maybe they would place you back home with mummy then.'
And he said, 'I'd feel sad if I left here'.

More recently, his carer and her adult children had made it clear to him
that unless his behaviour improved he might have to leave. This child had
only occasional contact with his mother and did not wish to return to her:
'I don't really want to live with my mum any more ... because I don't
really know her much now. She's a person what I see, so.'

Despite the love that carer and child clearly had for one another, the
lack of legal security for this child meant not only that any sense of
belonging was only provisional but also that his carer, at a time of grief,
loss and immense stress, felt able to consider giving him up when his
social worker suggested this as an option. Clearly aware of the uncertainty
of his situation, when asked if he felt loved, Brian replied 'sometimes'.
When asked if he felt fully part of his foster family, his reply indicated his
anxiety about how far he really belonged: 'No, not really, 'cos my foster
mum's daughters don't really like me ... I feel a bit sad. I like it here,
sometimes.'

Adoption

Nine children who had been adopted by their former foster carers and
eight adopted by strangers were interviewed, along with their adoptive
parents. Of these 17 children, 14 felt a reasonably straightforward sense
of belonging to their adoptive families, but three were troubled by a more
qualified sense of belonging and their adoptive placements were under
strain.

Adoption by carers: primary identification with the adoptive family

Six of the children adopted by carers had been fostered by these families
as infants, some shortly after birth, and so remembered no other home.
These were the only families they had ever known. Although a few
showed some curiosity and concern for parents, these children identified
principally, or solely, with their adoptive families. These adoptive parents

felt that these children saw themselves as fully part of the family and viewed them as if they were their own:

I think she just accepts, you know, she's grown up with that, she accepts that, she's known no, no other thing, no other way of living really, so to her that is the norm. (Adoptive mother of Tania)

But from having him from birth it's just been like an ongoing process, just like having your own child really, isn't it? I think with us having him since he was born he's just like he's been sort of part of the family anyway. (Adoptive mother of Jordan)

Two children had moved to their adoptive homes at the age of five. Niamh, now 16 years old, had experienced abuse, neglect and also a great deal of instability, as she had been in and out of care until this point. The situation was somewhat different for Terry, a nine-year-old with learning difficulties. His adoptive mother had previously cared for Terry's teenage mother, who had also had learning difficulties. She had been present at his birth and kept in touch with him throughout his early years, as a "grandmother" figure. She remained in contact during his time in care and his placement with a previous carer adopter, who had been abusive and neglectful, and from whom she eventually rescued him.

Both children now felt very secure and happy in their adoptive homes. Given the unhappiness and instability of their early lives, these two children were happy to feel loved and safe at last, and immensely relieved to have the legal security of adoption. With this legal security came a greater sense of emotional security. When asked what she thought about being adopted, Niamh replied:

Oh my God, you feel like a weight's been taken off your foot. It's, I don't know, you feel absolutely brilliant in a way, you feel like you've got a family that actually likes you for who you are. Like they love you for who you are, not because of what you are, it feels brilliant.

Her carer, who also fostered other children, explained the difference that adoption made:

Niamh's very much, you know, 'This is my home, this is my mum and dad. I'm here until I decide otherwise and that's the way it is and that's the way it's staying.' Whereas with foster children there always seems to be a little question mark always hanging around.

Terry, too, expressed his relief at being adopted after such troubled early years:

My mum and dad say they're going to keep me forever ... I like everyone, everyone's being nice to me ... I think they should have started here and ended here, that's what I would like to think of.

His carer also explained how important the adoption had been to him:

I took a lot of advice and I said, I need to make him safe, I need to make him secure, he needs to know that nobody can take him away or fight to take him away ... 'Cos he used to write at school, all I want is to be called Terry [adopters' surname] and I want to stay with this mummy and daddy ... He felt loved and wanted and a part of somebody's life really, you know.

For three children, fostered as infants with their current adopters, earlier attempts had been made to have them adopted by strangers. For Morgan and David, initial placements for adoption by strangers were made, but rapidly disrupted. After these disruptions, they returned to their foster carers who then applied to adopt them themselves. Another child, Tania, had been threatened with being moved from her carer (formerly her foster carer) to an adoptive family. Her carer recounted that she had said at the time, 'I don't want a new mummy and daddy, I want to stay here'.

All of these children had wished to remain with their carers. Terry and Niamh had been old enough to understand and wish for the legal security of adoption. Both spoke of their joy when the adoption order was finally granted and described the family celebrations that had ensued. For these two children, their sense of being actively chosen by carers who made it clear that they loved them was of great symbolic significance, enhancing their sense of truly belonging to these families.

A key ingredient in the success of all these carer adoptions was that the children were not preoccupied with seeing or returning to their birth parents. Although it might be easier for children placed as infants, who remembered no other home, to avoid a troubling sense of divided loyalty, two of the successful carer adoptions involved children who were late-placed. These two children expressed no desire to see their birth mothers and there was nothing to suggest that they felt any emotional pull towards them. Niamh was old enough, at 16, to make it clear she had no desire to see her birth mother, whom she referred to as 'a witch'. Terry saw his birth mother monthly but, according to his adoptive mother, he found these meetings stressful.

As well as Terry, another child had face-to-face contact with his birth mother, who visited him twice a year. The circumstances of carer adoption appeared to lend themselves more readily to open adoption of this kind, as adoptive parents continued the contact arrangements that had been in place while the children were fostered by them. A third child had occasional letterbox contact with his mother and for a fourth there was letterbox contact between the adoptive and birth mothers, of which the child was unaware. For half of these children, however, there was no contact of any kind.

Although one or two of those not in contact were curious about birth parents or siblings, none of them gave any indication that, at this stage in their lives at least, they felt they belonged to their birth families in any real sense. They could not imagine living, or wanting to live, anywhere but in their adoptive homes. As far as the adoptive parents of two children (both placed with them in infancy) were aware, the children did not appear to have a strong sense of belonging to any other family but theirs:

I don't think she can visualise herself anywhere else but here. (Adoptive parent of Tania, 10 years old)

She feels we're mum and dad, this is her home and she's safe, yeah, this is where she belongs. (Adoptive parent of Sheila, 11 years old)

A few of these children wondered about their birth parents. However, the absence of a strong preoccupation with birth parents or divided loyalties, in the context of loving adoptive families who claimed these children as their own, gave these children a strong sense of belonging to their adoptive families.

Another important reason for the success of these carer adoptions was the fact that the carers already knew and loved the children before making the decision to adopt them. Children and carers had bonded long ago and shared a sense that the children were already part of the family. In all cases, relationships were already strong before the application was made, so adoption was not a leap in the dark for either carer or child.

Children adopted by carers indicated that they felt a strong sense of belonging to their adoptive families. Although a few wondered about their birth parents, there was no apparent sense of divided loyalties at this stage in their lives, despite the fact that two were late-placed with these carers. The late-placed children expressed their relief at having achieved the legal security of adoption. The fact that carer–child relationships were already strong before the adoption application was made contributed to the success of these carer adoptions.

Adoption by strangers: primary identification with adoptive family

As with carer adoptions, for six of the eight children adopted by strangers, their primary identification at this stage in their lives was also with their adoptive families. Again, most of the children who had a relatively straightforward sense of belonging to their adoptive families had been placed with them in infancy, but two had been placed in these families at the ages of four and six years.

The two children who had been late-placed appeared to be as settled and happy in their adoptive families as those who had been placed as infants. Gray, age 14, had joined this family at the age of six and had not seen his mother since he was 18 months old. Until the age of six he had experienced repeated attempts at reunification and several placements, including an earlier adoption that had disrupted, before being placed in his current adoptive family. During his first few years in this family his behaviour had been very difficult, but he had eventually settled down. When asked if he thought about his birth parents at all, he vehemently expressed his identification with his adoptive family:

No, definitely not. Yeah, I suppose if I had the chance to be born into this family, like mum was my real mum, I suppose it'd be even better really, because I haven't, yeah, so. I don't, just think these were my real parents really 'cos, like I've got best friends, I've got a niece, I've got a sister, I've got three brothers, four brothers sort of, sort of a sister-in-law, brother-in-law, auntie, uncle, things like that, so I've a really good family and relationship with everyone.

Twelve-year-old Caitlin, who had joined her adoptive family at the age of four, had initially had face-to-face contact with her birth mother and two sisters, but this had drifted and eventually stopped. She now had letterbox contact with them. She appeared happy and settled, able to talk openly about both her families but her account indicated that her primary identification was with her adoptive family:

We're all together, I just like spending time with my family basically and I just like being here 'cos I've been here for a long time so I'm used to here ... Yeah, I do belong here, yeah ... I just like being altogether in sort of like, as a big family.

Unlike some of those adopted by their former foster carers, none of these children had face-to-face contact with birth parents. Just two of them had letterbox contact with birth relatives. As well as Caitlin, Jenny had continued letterbox contact with her grandmother after her birth mother had died a few years earlier. None of these children gave any indication of a yearning for or idealisation of their birth parents. However, those placed in infancy, who had no memory of birth relatives, were inquisitive about them. Some cherished hopes of meeting parents and birth siblings once they were adult, but did not appear to be preoccupied with thoughts of meeting them any sooner than that. Jenny, who had been placed as an infant and was clearly settled and happy did, however, suggest that the existence of birth relatives (and her letterbox contact with her grandmother) had some bearing on her perception of belonging to her adoptive family. When asked if she felt she belonged in this family, she answered:

Well a bit, kind of, and, like, when I'm 18 I'd like to go looking for my nana and my dad, which I'd, well my birth dad, who I haven't quite found out where he is, or whether he's still alive, but that's what I'd like to find out. (Jenny, nine years old)

Another, when asked what she would wish for if she had three wishes, said she would like to see her birth mother one day. Although these children had a sense of genealogical connectedness to birth relatives, they appeared to be able to hold in mind their two families without major emotional conflict, at least at this stage in their lives. While aware that they also belonged, in a genealogical sense, to birth relatives whom they had no memory of, their primary identification appeared to be with their adoptive families.

Adoption under strain

For three children, one adopted by carers and two by strangers, the adoption was under strain although none of these situations showed signs of imminent disruption. All three children had been placed relatively late. Niall, whose father was schizophrenic, was an extremely disturbed child who had had nine placements before joining his adoptive family at the age of three. He had been diagnosed with an attachment disorder and, at the age of eight, was displaying severe behavioural problems at home and at school. Despite the difficulty of caring for him, his adoptive family were fighting to support him and to obtain the mental health and educational help he needed. According to his adoptive mother, he was unwilling to talk about being adopted. When asked if he remembered anything about coming to live in this family when he was three years old, his reply indicated how troubled he was by his past experiences, 'Don't talk about my baby, because I get upset'.

Elspeth (age 15 years) and Alastair (age 16 years) had both joined their adoptive families at the age of seven and both had learning difficulties. Elspeth was also thought to have Asperger's syndrome, and this may have contributed to the difficulties that she and her adoptive mother had had in bonding with one another. Both she and her adoptive mother expressed ambivalence about their relationship and after a difficult period the family had asked social services for respite care, to no avail. Neither she nor Niall had any contact with their birth families, but Elspeth had some memories of this family and hoped to see her older sister again one day. However, although her adoptive placement appeared more troubled in comparison to the other adopted children, she did not appear to be overly preoccupied with her birth family.

Alastair was the only adopted child interviewed who expressed a desire to be with his birth parents instead of his adoptive family. He had letterbox contact with his birth mother and saw his siblings two or three times a year. During adolescence, he had become angry and challenging to care for and had become preoccupied with issues of where he belonged. This was deeply hurtful to his adoptive father, who nevertheless tried to support Alastair through this emotional turmoil. The adoptive father ascribed this turmoil to insecurity resulting from the severe neglect Alastair experienced during his first four years of life and also to his developmental problems, which made it hard for him to make sense of his situation.

Alastair appeared very confused. On the one hand, he spoke of his attachment and closeness to his adoptive family and said he felt loved by them:

I can't really tell how much they love me. They probably love me more than any other family would, they love me the same as every other family loves their child. So really they're just the same as any other family.

At the same time, he harboured a wish to rejoin his birth family. His account of this desire for reunification suggests that, perhaps due to his cognitive difficulties, he did not appear to truly understand the meaning of adoption: 'So hopefully, probably in about few years, my mum will probably adopt me and I'll spend my next years with mum and play tennis.' Unable to reconcile belonging to two families, he felt angry and frustrated and blamed the adoption for preventing him seeing his birth family:

Since this adoption thing, since I've been adopted, I just keep on getting angry and frustrated 'cos I want to be with my other family . . .

*I'm missing them a long time and it just makes me angry that I can't
go and see them and I just can't, you know, break, like, in other words,
it's like a prison cell and the key's just chucked in the river.*

Alastair appeared unable to reconcile belonging to two families and his
account indicated some confusion as to whether the boundaries between
the two family systems were rigid or more permeable:

*I belong in both families really . . . I more belong in the other family
than I do in this one, cos they're really both the same.*

A common feature of all three cases where adoption was under strain,
along with the case of the fostered child whose sense of belonging was
only provisional and whose placement appeared close to breakdown, was
that the children were late-placed and also had special needs. Two
appeared to have incipient mental health problems and two had moderate
learning disabilities. In addition, three of them had difficulties that were
likely to make the formation of close parent–child relationships particularly difficult, as two had attachment disorders and one had Asperger's
syndrome. All four also had severe externalising behaviour problems.
Although, as we have seen, late placement or having special needs did not
in themselves appear to be a barrier to the development of children's sense
of belonging and emotional security, the cumulative effect of these
circumstances and difficulties was that these children were more confused
and less secure in their sense of belonging to their adoptive or substitute
families. These children and families were clearly in need of support.

Discussion

For children who are looked after long term and for those who are
adopted, their sense of belonging to foster or adoptive families is often
intertwined with perceptions of their birth families. A key factor in
whether a child feels a sense of belonging is the way they locate their
foster family in relation to their birth family (Sinclair *et al*, 2005c).

Some of the children in our study clearly found the boundary between
their two families difficult to come to terms with. Although their birth
parents were physically absent, they were nevertheless psychologically

present. This group included children who had only intermittent contact with birth parents or none at all. They were preoccupied with their birth parents and troubled about where they belonged. Ambivalence towards, or yearning for, their birth parents could make it more difficult for them to identify with, and feel emotionally secure in, their permanent substitute families.

Children who are adopted or looked after long term may experience the ambiguous loss of their birth families. Although birth families may be physically absent from their day-to-day lives some, or all, of the time, they remain psychologically present (Wright *et al*, 2007). Family systems theorists have conceptualised such situations as family boundary ambiguity. They argue that where an individual's physical and psychological presence in a family is incongruent, family members may find it more difficult to determine whether they are inside or outside that family. In their view, it is an individual's perception of a situation and the meaning they ascribe to it that determines the existence and nature of boundary ambiguity (Fravel *et al*, 2000; Carroll *et al*, 2007). For example, some birth mothers of children placed for adoption have been found to experience boundary ambiguity, as these children often remain psychologically present in their birth mother's everyday life (Fravel *et al*, 2000).

Children in apparently similar situations may or may not experience family boundary ambiguity depending on their perceptions of their birth parents and the meaning they ascribe to their experiences. How children process their knowledge of why they were separated from their parents is crucial. Children who have been abused, rejected or severely neglected may, like Alastair, yearn to be accepted by their birth families and feel they truly belong with them. They may develop strategies to manage the ambiguous loss of the birth family by creating their own definitions of family permanence, affirming their membership of the "real family" that has been lost (Samuels, 2009). Where adopted adolescents have high levels of preoccupation with adoption, they may develop a sense of alienation from their adoptive parents (Kohler *et al*, 2002). Alternatively they may, like Niamh, respond to early negative experiences by emotionally distancing themselves from abusive birth parents and seeking to identify wholly with their substitute families.

Other children may find it easier to make sense of their situation in ways that do not reflect badly on either themselves or their parents. For example, Terry understood that his mother had been unable to care for him due to her learning difficulties (which he had inherited). His adoptive mother ran a hostel for adults with learning difficulties and he knew that his birth mother's own difficulties were similar to those of the residents. According to his adoptive mother, he understood that, 'she couldn't really care for him, you know, it wasn't her fault. It's not that she doesn't love him, sort of thing.'

In some cases, where birth parents were physically absent, either completely or intermittently, children could be preoccupied by feelings of hurt, anger or ambivalence towards them and this could make them feel confused or ambivalent about where they wanted to be. For these children, the symbolic presence of birth parents influenced their thoughts and feelings about their foster or adoptive families. Where birth parents remained a strong and troubling psychological presence in their everyday lives, children appeared less likely to feel a secure sense of belonging to their substitute families.

For other children, the psychological presence of birth parents was less strong and the children appeared to be inquisitive about them rather than troubled by them at this stage in their lives, making it easier for them to view themselves as belonging principally to their substitute families. The accounts of several children indicated that they wished to represent their current family life as "normal" and some emphasised that they were treated no differently to other children in the family. At this stage in their lives they appeared able to reconcile, both cognitively and emotionally, the two family systems that they belonged to. They did not appear to idealise their birth parents or wish to return to them and were not overly preoccupied with them. Some of them had reasonably regular, although not necessarily frequent, direct contact with their birth parents and the quality of this contact was relatively unproblematic, but others had not seen their birth families for many years and several, separated in infancy, did not remember them.

In a sense, this group of children had bracketed their birth parents out of their everyday lives and so were able to view themselves as members of their foster or adoptive families in a relatively unproblematic way. This was likely to be easier for those who had joined these families in infancy, remembered no other home and had no contact with birth parents, but was also possible for some children who had been separated from their birth parents later in their lives but had no desire to be with them. Some late-placed children, such as Gray and Niamh, who had responded to their earlier experiences by emotionally distancing themselves from birth parents, did not idealise and yearn for absent parents and so did not appear to experience any conflict of loyalties. Their emotional investment was in their adoptive families and this was reciprocated by these families.

Proponents of open adoption have argued that inclusive arrangements may eliminate questions for the child and reduce uncertainty and stress for all concerned. Those in favour of closed adoption have argued that this enables all concerned to achieve closure and get on with their lives (Fravel et al, 2000). However, for both the fostered and adopted children in this study, it was not so much continuing contact per se that helped them come to terms with belonging to two families, but the nature and quality of that contact, together with the children's perceptions of their birth parents and their lack of a strong desire to be reunited with them. Some children, who had predictable and satisfying contact with birth parents, managed to reconcile a sense of belonging to two families. Others, with more intermittent and problematic contact, did not. Equally, although most of those without any direct contact with birth parents felt reasonably secure in their sense of belonging to substitute families, a few children who had no contact of this kind nevertheless expressed ambivalence about whether they belonged in these families.

Perceptions of belonging may be shifting rather than fixed, as children's perceptions of where they belong may subtly change with the passage of time and as they move from one context to another. New people may enter or leave a child's life, especially when they move to a new family, leading to the possibility of forming new attachments, although previous relationships are likely to have a continuing resonance. Children may become more preoccupied with parents as they grow older, or more concerned about questions of identity and belonging (Gilligan, 2000). The relative foster carers of 15-year-old Maurice, who had lived with them since he was two years old, felt that time had led him to accept his place in their family: 'He sees himself more as our son now.' Although Maurice's account suggested that they were probably right about this, he indicated that he had nevertheless begun to feel more questioning about his place in the family.

Some adolescents, like Maurice, may become increasingly pre-occupied with their birth families, a preoccupation that can involve the fantasy of an idealised parent. Others, after many years living in foster or adoptive families, may, like Naimh, wish to put behind them any sense that they belonged to abusive or neglectful birth parents, although such strategies may be fluid and might change over time.

For some children, however, a sense of genealogical connectedness to the birth family may be continuous, including a sense of connection with one or both birth parents, siblings or grandparents. Many felt a part-icularly strong sense of connectedness to birth siblings (or half-siblings), including those they had never met. A few were very anxious to make contact at some point in the future with younger siblings they had never known.

Belonging was enacted in the everyday interactions and activities of the children's foster or adoptive families. It was the interplay of this routine, everyday behaviour with children's own desires for belonging, and their perceptions of different people in their lives, that gave shape to their understanding of their place in these families. As Morgan has argued, the notion of family 'represents a constructed quality of human inter-action or an active process, rather than a thing-like object of detached social investigation' (Morgan, 1999, p 16). Thus, families are defined more by 'doing family things' than simply by membership of a household or kinship network (Morgan, 1996). The day-to-day practice of 'doing family things' shaped children's lived experience of family life and helped to create, and sustain, their perceptions that they belonged to, and would remain in, their foster or adoptive families.

Summary

Children in long-term foster care

- Some children who had had no direct contact with birth parents for many years lived in foster placements that were quasi-adoptive in nature. Children and carers lived as if the child belonged to the foster family, while nevertheless accepting that they had another, biological, family. These children's primary identification, at this stage in their lives, was with their foster families. Although birth parents were psychologically present for the children, they were physically absent and this appeared to facilitate the children's and carers' ability to live as if they belonged to one another in a relatively unproblematic way. Placement in infancy, for some children, meant that these foster families provided the only home the children had ever known.

- The exclusive nature of these foster placements, where the severity of parental abuse or rejection meant there was no direct contact, appeared to facilitate the children's sense of emotional security and belonging. In these circumstances, however, adoption by carers might have been more appropriate than long-term foster care.

- For another group of children, foster care was inclusive, as they had relatively unproblematic face-to-face contact with birth parents. These children appeared able to reconcile the fact that they, in different senses, belonged to both a birth family and a substitute family. Although there was some ambivalence and anxiety on the part of children or carers, the children appeared able to manage attachments to two families without too much inner conflict, viewing their foster carers just like another family.

- A third group of children in foster care were more obviously troubled by feelings of ambivalence, hurt and anger towards their birth parents. These children had some face-to-face contact with birth parents, but it was usually intermittent. Although settled in their foster placements, their complex feelings about their birth parents led them to feel a more qualified sense of belonging to their foster families. Conflicts of loyalty were not always apparent to their foster carers, some of whom perceived the children as their own and thought the children felt a reciprocal sense of unqualified belonging.

- One child's sense of belonging had become provisional, due to a combination of the recent death of his foster father and the destabilising actions of social services, his birth mother and his carer. These difficulties were reinforced by the fact that this child's attachment disorder and severe behaviour problems made him very difficult to care for.

Children who were adopted

- Children adopted by carers indicated a strong sense of belonging to their adoptive families. Although a few wondered about their birth parents, there was no apparent sense of divided loyalties at this stage in their lives, despite the fact that two were late-placed with these carers. These late-placed children expressed their relief at having achieved the legal security of adoption. The fact that carer–child relationships were already strong before the adoption application was made contributed to the success of these carer adoptions.
- Most of the children adopted by strangers had been placed as infants. For the majority of those interviewed, including two who were late-placed, their primary identification was with their adoptive families. Although birth parents were psychologically present to the children, to varying degrees, none of them had any direct contact with them, although some were inquisitive about birth relatives. These children appeared to feel emotionally secure in their adoptive families.
- In the three families where adoption was under strain, the children had particular difficulties. One young boy had an attachment disorder and severe behavioural problems and two adolescents had learning difficulties. One of these also had a diagnosis of Asperger's syndrome and her carer had found it difficult to bond with her. One of the children felt confused and troubled by the fact that he had two families and struggled both cognitively and emotionally to reconcile the two.

14 Perceptions of permanence

Permanence has been defined as the emotional, physical and legal conditions that afford a child a sense of security, continuity, commitment and identity (Department for Education and Skills, 2004a). In this chapter, we explore how far children and their carers perceived their current living arrangements as constituting a permanent, long-term home for the child. At the very least, did children and carers expect the placement to last until the child reached the age of 18? More than this, did children in long-term placements perceive that the families who cared for them represented a family for life, which would offer emotional and perhaps practical support to them in the longer term? This chapter draws on data from both our survey and our interviews to examine these issues.

A permanent home?

All but two of the adoptive parents surveyed reported that they were unreservedly offering a permanent home to their children and all but one considered that they were offering the child a "family for life". A high proportion of long-term foster carers also anticipated that they would continue to act as quasi-parental figures in the long term. Three-quarters of them considered their home to be the child's permanent home and just under three-quarters felt that they were offering the child a family for life.

We asked the children's adoptive parents/carers about plans for where the child would live until they were 18 years old. All the adoptive parents and the majority of the long-term foster carers who responded expected the children to remain with them at least until they were 18 years old (and possibly longer).

Carers indicated that the legal status of two children was about to change, as one was about to be adopted by his carer and the other was to be placed on a residence order. The majority of children who had experienced unstable care careers appeared to be settled as far as anyone could predict, as 82 per cent of their carers anticipated that the children would remain with them until the age of 18. However, carers were less

Table 14.1
Where carer expected child to live until 18 years old (n = 125)

	Carer adoption (n = 24)	Stranger adoption (n = 33)	Stable foster care (n = 46)	Unstable care (n = 22)
Stay here	24	33	41	18
Change placement	–	–	3	–
Independence at age 16/17	–	–	2	1
Don't know	–	–	–	3

Table 14.2
Whether carer expects child to remain after age 18 (n = 125)

	Carer adoption (n = 24)	Stranger adoption (n = 33)	Stable foster care (n = 46)	Unstable care (n = 22)
Yes	23	33	32	9
Unsure	1	–	11	6
No	–	–	3	7

certain about whether the children in stable foster placements, as well as those who had experienced past instability and were currently in foster or residential placements, would remain there after the age of 18 years.

All of the children adopted by strangers and all but one of those adopted by carers were expected to remain with their adoptive families after they reached the age of 18. However, over one-quarter of the long-term foster carers were unsure about whether the child would remain with their family beyond the age of 18, and in a few cases they thought that they would not. Half of the 17 fostered children in the unstable care group were expected to remain in their current placement into adulthood, but this seemed unlikely for the others.

Perceptions of permanence

The York study of foster care (Sinclair *et al*, 2005c) distinguished between four aspects of permanence:

- Objective permanence – occurring when children have a stable placement that endures until they are 18 and, ideally, beyond this;
- Subjective permanence – occurring when children felt a sense of belonging to their substitute families;
- Uncontested permanence – which would be high if a modus vivendi had been reached between the two families;
- Enacted permanence – occurring where all concerned behaved as if the family was a lasting unit.

That study followed up a broad cross-section of children in foster care and included many children in less settled circumstances than most of those in this study.[70] Although it is difficult to be certain of this prospectively, the children in our study who were adopted, in stable foster care or on residence or special guardianship orders, apparently enjoyed *objective* permanence. Due to differences between the samples for that study and our current one, permanence was *contested* for some children in the earlier study but was no longer an issue, if ever it had been, for the children in ours. The previous chapter touched on the question of enacted permanence, which could enhance a sense of belonging. In the rest of this chapter we explore whether children and carers felt a sense of *subjective* permanence.

Adopted children

Children who were adopted were secure in the knowledge that they could remain with their families long term and this was also the case for the child interviewed who was on a residence order. Indeed, some children placed at an early age were not aware that the permanence of their home might be any different from that for other children, perhaps due to their

---

[70] As explained in our chapter on methodology, the 90 children in our York sample were drawn from the sample for that study.

young age or their learning difficulties. Other children simply assumed that they would stay "forever":

> *No, no, she wasn't aware that she perhaps wasn't ours in the same way that other children were, so I think that to her it was just one day and something that we did and that was it.* (Adoptive parent of Tania)

> *She tells me, 'Well, when I'm grown up, I'm not leaving you.'* (Adoptive parent of Sheila)

> *I don't think he'll ever leave home, he's not intending to ever leave home, he's here for good, he said.* (Adoptive parent of Jordan)

For late-placed children subsequently adopted by their carers, there was a palpable sense of relief that they now had legal permanence:

> *And he's done loads of stories at school about, you know, his, his mum and dad and how happy he is and he's staying here now . . . and that's all he ever wanted. But just, he's got . . . he's got like a, something around him now.* (Adoptive parent of Terry)

Equally, the adoptive parents anticipated that children would remain with them as long as they needed to and that they would be a family for life for them. The only exception was a carer adopter who felt that, due to his adopted son's learning difficulties, he would like him to move to a hostel once he reached adulthood.

Children in stable foster placements

Despite the absence of legal permanence, most of the children in stable foster placements who were interviewed also anticipated that they would stay with their foster families until they reached adulthood and that they would remain closely in touch with them in the long term. They envisaged that they would continue to see their foster carers regularly and that the carers would continue to play a parental role in their lives. Some of the older children anticipated that foster carers would eventually act as grandparents to any children they might have. Children in foster placements that appeared quasi-adoptive in nature, and those who appeared able to emotionally reconcile their relationships with both families in their lives, assumed that they would remain with foster carers until adulthood and continue the relationship with them in the long term. Their carers took the same view.

> *I've got a good head on my shoulders, I think I'll be fine, you know, I've got mum and dad here [referring to foster carers] . . . they'd be like grandparents [to his children], definitely.* (Nathan)

> *As far as I'm concerned, Alex can stay as long as he wants, well forever if he wants, until he sets up a relationship and wants to set his own life in motion, but as far as I'm concerned this is his home, this is his home forever.* (Foster carer of Alex)

Sarah had regular contact with her birth mother and wished to see more of her, but was not sure that she wanted to return to her in the near future. She viewed her foster home as a permanent home that would be available to her as long she wanted:

> *Like, well, I said to my mum [foster carer], I said to her that I will probably like stay here until I've got my life sorted, got money and like a job and everything, and know like how to look after myself and stuff like that. Yeah, I probably would still keep in touch with [carers] 'cos, like, they're just basically my parents to be honest . . . I'd just come back and see mum [foster carer] and everything, and tell her how my life's going and stuff.* (Sarah)

However, in the absence of legal security, even children whose carers' unequivocally told them they were fully part of the family could nevertheless feel some anxiety about their future. Kate's foster carer recounted an incident where her daughter had asked Kate what she wanted to do when she left school, which she interpreted as a question about where she would live:

> *She said 'I don't know what I will do . . . 'Cos I don't know whether [foster carers] will want me to stay with them' and yet we always say*

to her, 'Your home is here, if social services, even if at the end of the day they're paying us an allowance to look after you at the moment.' I said, 'But if that allowance ends it's not going, going to be, ever going to be a case of right now you're going to need to go.' I said, 'Because you're, you're no different to us than our own daughters.' I said, 'As far as we're concerned we love you, you're part of our family, you know, you've been here six years!' (Kate's carer)

Kate appeared to be feeling more confident about this at the time she was interviewed: 'They're not in no hurry, it's just nice, it's like they're not going to chuck me out in any hurry.'

The picture was more mixed for the six children who felt a qualified sense of belonging to their foster families. Maurice assumed he would stay with his relative foster carers forever: 'I just kept telling Auntie Chris I'm staying till I'm 50.' Others were more uncertain about their future. Two carers thought that after the children left school they might eventually move away to live closer to their birth parents, but nevertheless hoped and assumed they would always remain in touch with one another. For Gordon and Rachel, who were fostered by their grandparents, their sense of permanence, in terms of where they would live, was somewhat qualified due their grandparents' time-limited commitment to providing them with a home. Fortunately, their sense of family belonging was uncomplicated so they assumed that their grandparents would always be there to offer support once they had left home. Josie, however, felt some anxiety about her future and this had been unwittingly heightened by her social worker when he raised the question of her long-term home:

I think it's worried Josie over the years because she was asked once about, you know, where can you see yourself living . . . it obviously has worried her I think . . . she's not too sure what's going to happen to her, and she's got that little funny feeling well, you know, 'where am I going to go, am I going to have to leave [foster carers] when I leave school and where am I going to go' and she, she just, you know, we've said to her, 'No, Josie, this is your home, you know, we're not going to kick you out, we won't do that.' (Carer of Josie)

Well-intentioned consultation with children about plans for leaving care may sometimes have an unintended destabilising effect on otherwise settled foster placements. Selwyn and Quinton have argued that, at a time when children need to focus on their GCSEs, offers of leaving care grants and independent accommodation may sometimes have a detrimental effect on the stability of the placement (Selwyn and Quinton, 2004).

Statutory reviews could also be unsettling for children who considered their long-term foster placements as their home. Twelve-year-old Alex, for example, had lived with his foster carers since he was an infant. He remembered no other home and had no contact with his birth family. His carers viewed him as a son and he viewed them as parents. In this context, the fact that the permanency of his placement was mentioned at every review, however reassuringly, appeared rather insensitive:

> *They have a review every six months and that is brought up every time, they tell you that he's in the best place, he's going to stay. When it comes up in every review, yes, they always say yes, Alex is alright where he is, he's staying where he is and that's it.* (Carer of Alex)

Children who experienced unstable care

Unsurprisingly, the children who had previously lived in apparently long-term placements and had since moved on were less likely to perceive their current placements as permanent. Among the seven children interviewed who had histories of unstable care, three had lived in their current placements for two to three years. All three hoped they would remain there, but both they and their carers were uncertain as to whether they would be allowed to do so:

> *I'll live here as long as possible . . . That's if she can cope with me. [laughs] . . . I'd love to still live here.* (Robin, 16 years old)

> *But if social services weren't involved, then I'd probably stay until I was about 19 and then start looking for my own place.* (Jacob, 15 years old)

His foster carer hoped he would be allowed to stay, but was worried about social workers' plans for him:

Yeah, I mean, they probably will push for him to leave at 18, but I was hoping that they might regard him as a bit more needy, 'cos I think he is a more needy child or, you know, a needy young man, that will need a bit more support. And, for instance, if he went in the same place as his brother [a foyer] he would be lost and I don't think he deserves that actually, and I couldn't do that to him, so I wouldn't encourage it at all. (Jacob's foster carer)

Fourteen-year old Kristian had lived with his foster carers for nearly three years and assumed he would remain with them long term. His foster carers thought he would be moved into a flat when he was 18 years old but, like carers of children in stable foster care, nevertheless viewed him as one of the family and expected to stay in touch with him:

But I just see him as a family even when he's 18, 19, and the children will, our children will say that too. (Kristian's foster carer)

Three other children, who had lived in their current placements for a year or less, assumed they would be leaving once they reached the age of 16-18 years and their carers' understanding was also that the placements would be likely to end at that point:

Well my social worker said it's . . . what's it called, when you're here for a while but you don't know how long? . . . Short-term, yeah. Short-term fostering thing, but at the moment I think I'm going to stay until I'm 16 now here 'cos I enjoy it. (Daniel, 13 years old)

Until I'm 16, yeah, 'cos then I'm off in the RAF . . . have a year off, then I'm off to see my family in New Zealand and then I'm coming back and going in the RAF. (Monica, 14 years old)

Well yeah, definitely 16, when he gets to 18 he knows that he's not under social service's jurisdiction anymore and he will want to go home. He's made that quite clear . . . Well, that's the plan in his mind,

I can't say it would be my plan but . . . if that's what Johnny wants then fair enough . . . But until, until he's old enough to make his own decisions and he is out of social services' jurisdiction, you know, I'll look after him, I'll be his little keeper. [laughs] . . . You know, I think he'll still be involved with us. (Foster carer of Johnny, ten years old)

Summary

- Social workers and carers anticipated that all children who were adopted would remain in their current homes until the age of 18. This was also the expectation in relation to most of those in stable foster care and half of those who had experienced unstable care. However, a few children in both these fostered groups were expected to return to their birth parents before then or move to independence at the age of 16 or 17.
- All of the adopted children (and adoptive parents) interviewed assumed that the children would stay with them long term, as did those in quasi-adoptive foster placements. Other children in stable foster care hoped and expected to remain in their foster placements long term and viewed their carers as a family for life, but some were uncertain about what would happen to them in the future.
- Among the children with unstable care careers who were interviewed, responses were predictably mixed. Those who had been in their current placements for two to three years hoped they would be able to stay long term, as did their carers. Those placed for one year or less mostly anticipated that they would move on at 16.

15 **Placement stability and change**

This chapter compares placement stability for children who are adopted or looked after and examines the predictors of placement instability for looked after children.

In order to make a fair comparison of patterns of placement stability in adoption and foster care, we were concerned that our findings should not be biased by the loss to follow-up of 26 children from the original York sample. We therefore made serious efforts to discover what had happened to the placements of this group of children who we were unable to include in our total survey sample (see Appendix 2).

All but one of the 18 missing children, who had been adopted by the time they were last surveyed in 2001, were thought to be still settled in their adoptive homes. Half of the eight children in foster care at that time had since left the care system through adoption or residence orders and one remained in his index placement, but no information was available on the remaining three. In the analysis that follows, we take account of this information on the children missing from our survey sample.

Comparing placement stability in adoption and foster care

Comparing the relative stability of adoptive and long-term foster placements is more complex than it might at first appear. The ending of a foster placement may not always be due to a disruption, as many children may make a planned transition from their initial placement in care (Ward and Skuse, 2001; Sinclair *et al*, 2007). Even after spending three years in a foster placement (as all of those in our sample who remained in care by follow-up had done), a move may be beneficial rather than harmful to a child who is receiving poor-quality care in a placement. So while multiple placement moves are certainly undesirable, some children who make only one or two moves may do so for positive reasons.

It is also difficult to compare like with like, for two reasons. First, children who were in adoptive placements at the time of our survey had, on average, entered these placements at a much younger age than the children who continued to be looked after had entered their index foster placements. Many of those adopted by strangers were under one year old when placed for adoption. Second, for such a comparison to be meaningful, it is important to compare rates of disruption after a similar follow-up period. However, we know that in several cases earlier placements for adoption had disrupted within a few weeks (and in the other cases we do not know how long the children had remained in their adoptive placements before the disruption occurred), whereas in relation to long-term foster care we are measuring the disruption of foster placements that had lasted for three years or more.

With these caveats in mind, we looked more closely at the difference in the stability of adoption and of long-term foster care and at the predictors of instability. Five children had experienced the breakdown of an adoption and six had experienced the breakdown of a placement for adoption. Few details were available on these past adoption breakdowns, but at least four of the children who had been placed for adoption had returned to care within 12 weeks. All but one of the adoption breakdowns had occurred many years earlier, before the children had entered their index foster placements. Eight of these children had since been successfully adopted by new parents. Both of the children who had not been re-adopted had settled in foster care. In total, therefore, 97 children had either been placed for adoption or adopted at some point in their lives and, of these, 11 per cent (11) were reported to have experienced the breakdown of an adoptive placement.

At the time of our survey, 100 of the children in our survey sample were still looked after, of whom 37 (our unstable care group) had left their index foster placements after living in them for three years or more. Less than two-thirds (63) of the children who were still looked after continued to be fostered by their index carers. However, a further 35 children had also remained with their index foster carers, either adopted by them or on residence orders.

These 35 additional children are not included in our figures on stable/unstable care careers because they had left the care system. Nevertheless, their index foster placements had clearly been successful, indeed so successful that their carers had wished to change the legal status of the

Figure 15.1
Stability of index foster placements and adoptive placements (per cent)

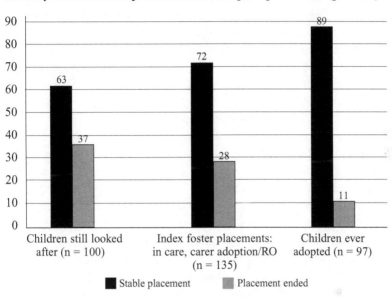

placement. If we include these placements in our calculations, we find that fewer children (28%) had experienced unstable care after spending three or more years in their index foster placements. The remaining 72 per cent had remained settled with their index carers for seven years or more, although not all of them remained in the care system. Figure 15.1 shows the proportion of placements that remained stable; first, for children who were still looked after, second, for those who were still looked after together with those whose index carers had adopted them or taken out residence orders and third, for all children who had ever been placed for adoption.

Compared to the wider population of children who are looked after, our figures are likely to over-represent those who were adopted by their index foster carers, as 39 per cent of the adopted children in our survey sample were adopted by their carers, whereas in England as a whole only 15 per cent of children adopted from care are adopted by their carers (Department for Education and Skills, 2003). For this reason, the true proportion of children within the wider population who remain settled with their current or former long-term foster carers for seven years or more is likely to be lower than the rate of 72 per cent found for our survey sample. Nevertheless, although children who are adopted clearly experience greater stability than those in long-term foster care, the difference in stability rates may be somewhat narrower than it initially appears once those who leave the care system but remain with their foster carers are taken into account.

Following the logic that carer adoptions and residence orders taken by former foster carers could be seen, in a sense, as stability that was the continuation of a period spent in long-term foster care, we compared the stability of stranger adoptions to patterns of stability for all other children in the study. We used multivariate analysis to examine the relative effects of being adopted by strangers, age at last entry to care and SDQ (Strengths and Difficulties Questionnaire) scores for emotional and behavioural difficulties. Both adoption by strangers and age at last entry to care were found to be predictive of whether the children remained in their index placements by follow-up, but SDQ scores were not. However, since 58 per cent of the children adopted by strangers had been placed for adoption before they were one year old, it was difficult to disentangle the relative effects of these two variables to discover whether it was the adoption *per se* or the very early age at which children were placed for adoption that made the difference to placement stability. The children who had been adopted by strangers had a mean age at placement of 2.6 years, compared to a mean age of 4.1 years for children in stable foster care.[71] The children in the unstable care group had entered their index foster placements later still. It is therefore difficult to know whether adoption *per se* provides additional protection from the risk of instability, over and above the benefits of early entry to the placement. As we did not have data either on the age at which children whose adoptions had broken down had been placed with the adoptive families concerned, nor the time period up until disruption, it was difficult to come to firm conclusions about this.

The comments of social workers, managers and fostering teams in our

---

[71] Independent sample t-test significant at p = .012 (n = 137).

interviews and focus groups indicated that, despite their genuine commitment to the child and intention to care for them into adulthood, in some
cases the challenge of caring for children with very difficult behaviour or
attachment problems, sometimes in combination with personal
difficulties in their own lives, could lead long-term carers to return
children to the local authority. The professionals interviewed felt that the
lack of legal parental responsibility sometimes led even long-term foster
carers, when circumstances were extremely difficult, to give up on a child
when perhaps an adoptive parent might have felt a greater sense of
personal obligation to persist. This may well be true for some carers
although, as our chapters on child and carer perceptions of belonging and
permanence showed, foster carers' love for a particular child and commitment to him or her may lead them to persist, even in extremely
difficult circumstances. Perceptions of "parental" obligation and responsibility undoubtedly vary between long-term foster carers but it seems
likely that being fostered rather than adopted contributes to the risk of
disruption, and this is in keeping with our statistical evidence.

Why did some looked after children experience instability?

Among those children in long-term placements who are *not* adopted by
strangers, why do some remain settled with long-term carers while others
experience placement instability? As we have seen, among the children
who had not been adopted by strangers, 72 per cent continued to be
fostered by their index carers, had been adopted by them or were cared for
by their former carers on residence orders. The remaining 28 per cent had
experienced more unstable care, having left their index carers after three
or more years in placement. However, this overall rate masks some local
variation. In one authority, Unitary Authority (East), a significantly higher
proportion of children had experienced unstable care, while in County
(South) a higher proportion of children had remained settled with their
index carers.[72]

---

[72] Chi-square test significant at p = .005. Outer London Borough was omitted from this
calculation as only five of its children had not been adopted by strangers (of whom only
one was still looked after).

Table 15.1
Per cent in each authority remaining with index carer per cent (n = 127)

	With index carer	Left index placement
County (North) *n = 20*	80	20
County (South) *n = 24*	92	8
Unitary authority (East) *n = 24*	42	58
Unitary authority (Midlands) *n = 20*	75	25
Inner London borough *n = 17*	76	24
Unitary authority (North) *n = 22*	64	36

This local variation in stability rates suggests that variations in policy and practice, such as the quality of supervision and permanency planning, may have some impact on children's care careers. Data on the national performance indicator on placement stability indicate that local variation in patterns of stability does indeed exist, although it should be noted that the national indicator takes a different approach to measuring stability to that taken in this study. An analysis of local variation on this stability indicator concluded that higher rates of instability were due to inco-herence across organisations, a lack of leadership, financial instability, and a lack of priority for looked after children, compounded by planning drift, a high rate of looked after children and a lack of active placement support services (Held, 2005). A lack of adequate placement choice with-in authorities has also been linked to placement instability (Triseliotis *et al*, 2000; Held, 2005). There may be variation *within* local authorities too, as children served by teams with high workloads and high levels of unallocated cases are more likely to experience instability (Sinclair *et al*, 2007).

However, although the local variation we found is striking, and is consistent with previous research, we must be cautious in extrapolating from this finding as our *survey sample* was not representative. Equally, although we found a similar pattern for our more representative *census sample*, we cannot be absolutely sure that all of the local authorities provided us with administrative data on *all* children who had been in long-term placements. If some did not, the resulting sampling bias would distort our findings on stability rates between local authorities.

Among the children who had not been adopted by strangers, age at entry to care and scores on the SDQ were the key predictors of placement instability after 2001/02.[73] Mean age at last entry to care was significantly higher for those in our unstable care group (5.3 years) compared to those who had remained settled with their index carers (3.6 years).[74] Those who had entered care later also entered their index placement at an older age than those who remained continuously with their index carers. Many previous studies of foster care and adoption have found that children placed at an older age are more likely to experience placement disruption (Berridge and Cleaver, 1987; Thoburn, 1990; Triseliotis *et al*, 1997; Triseliotis, 2002; Rushton, 2004).

For some, later entry to care may have occurred because their difficulties only emerged, or came to social services' attention, at a later stage in their lives. However, given the national variation in rates of children looked after between local authorities, local policy and practice in relation to thresholds for taking children into care may also have played a part. Greater or lesser decisiveness by local authority gatekeepers and local courts may also have had some influence. These factors may not only influence the age at which children begin their final episodes of care but may also help to explain the possible local variation in placement stability.

In Chapter 9, we compared SDQ scores for emotional and behavioural difficulties for children in different stability groups and found that those with unstable care careers were likely to have higher scores for total difficulties and conduct disorder at the time of our follow-up in 2006. We then compared SDQ scores for our stability groups at three points in time from 1998 to 2006 and found that children who had experienced unstable care careers after 2001 *already* had significantly worse scores on the SDQ in 1998 and 2001, compared to other children whose lives subsequently proved to be more settled.

---

[73] Logistic regression with remained with index carer/unstable care as the dependent variable, significant at p=.05 for age at last entry to care and p = .035 for SDQ score 2006 (n = 88). When SDQ score 2001 was substituted for the 2006 score, this was a highly significant predictor of stability (p = .009) and age at entry was no longer significant. However, the number included in this analysis was small (n = 37).

[74] Independent samples t-test significant at p = .004.

Our analysis of scores on the SDQ and the Expression of Feelings (EFR) measures also indicated that late placement seemed to reduce the chance of improvement both on the SDQ scores and in scores for inhibited attachment. Children who entered care significantly later would have been exposed to adversity within their families for a longer period of time. This may help to explain their higher SDQ scores and associated placement instability, since longer exposure to adversity is known to reduce children's ability to recover from abuse and neglect (Rutter, 2000). We know from previous studies that the risk of placement disruption is higher for children with emotional and behavioural difficulties, as carers may find it hard to cope with children's past experiences and current difficulties. One study found that this was only true for those aged 11 and over (Sinclair et al, 2007) and, consistent with this, another reported a strong association between adolescence, behavioural difficulties and disruption (Ward and Skuse, 2001). The association between behavioural difficulties and placement disruption appears to be particularly strong for older children, like those in our unstable care group.

We have also seen that scores for carer rejection were higher for those with high SDQ scores in 2001, who were predominantly the children in our unstable care group. For the children who had subsequently experienced unstable care, scores for carer rejection (perhaps more accurately described as a relatively less-accepting approach) had been significantly higher in 2001. Their greater disturbance may have made them more difficult to care for and thus have increased the risk of placement disruption. The number of children on whom these data were available was small, however.[75]

Rejection by substitute carers may increase the level of disturbance, or lead to a child being seen as disturbed, irrespective of whether he or she is (Sinclair et al, 2005b). Disturbance and parenting style may interact and, in combination, influence the risk of placement disruption. Quinton and colleagues (1998) followed up children one year after they had been placed for adoption. They found that where children were overactive and

---

[75] One-way Anova significant at p = .002. Mean scores for carer rejection were 6.5 in 2001, compared to 4.5 for stable foster care and 4.15 for adoption (n = 64). However, there were only six children in the unstable care group.

restless, or had been rejected by their birth parents, a less responsive parenting style on the part of adoptive parents was associated with a poorer outcome (in that the placement had either disrupted or was not going well). Where children had low levels of difficulty, parental responsiveness was not a factor, but where children's behaviour had worsened by follow-up, it was. In this study, parental responsiveness was found to be related to placement stability in two ways: through its relationship to the development of children's attachments and by its association with parental resilience.

Certainly, resilience on the part of substitute carers is a necessary quality when caring for children with high levels of disturbance. A large Scottish study reported that many carers find fostering very stressful, particularly when caring for difficult children (Triseliotis et al, 2000). Other studies of foster care have found that some carer-related factors may play a part in placement disruption. In the study by Sinclair and colleagues, for example, disruption was associated with whether carers had experienced previous disruptions, previous allegations of abuse or a high level of distress as a result of caring for children in the past (Sinclair et al, 2005b). Other carer-related factors previously found to be associated with disruption include carer stress and family tensions associated with caring for difficult foster children (Berridge and Cleaver, 1987; Farmer and Moyers, 2008).

Resilience in coping with children who present difficult behaviour may also be undermined by unrelated events in carers' lives, and these too may contribute to the risk of placement disruption. Social worker comments on our questionnaires gave some indication of why previous placements had disrupted, although these data were not comprehensive. Among the 37 children in our unstable care group, three placement disruptions had followed the breakdown of a carer's marriage or the discovery of domestic violence in the foster home, and in one case the grandmother caring for a child had become too ill to continue. Three children in our unstable care group had also experienced a bereavement in their foster family. However, in a further 19 (51%) cases, social workers indicated that previous placements had disrupted as a result of the children's difficult behaviour, which had proved too stressful for their foster carers.

A further source of stress for foster carers is the fear of false allegations of abuse, which are clearly very distressing. One study found that 16 per cent of foster carers had previously experienced false allegations of this kind (Sinclair *et al*, 2005a). Unfortunately, in a small number of cases, such allegations may prove to be true. For ten of the children interviewed (5% of our total sample) there was clear evidence of abuse or neglect by previous foster carers. We did not ask about carer abuse and this evidence emerged unprompted during our interviews, so we do not know whether we discovered the full extent of carer abuse experienced by the children in our study. However, carer abuse was certainly the reason for the disruption of 14 per cent (five) of the index placements of the 37 children in our unstable care group. In a further five cases, children had been moved as a result of allegations against foster carers (though we do not know whether these were ever substantiated) or due to concerns about an unsafe adult in the foster home.

In considering the reasons for the disruption of index foster placements, we found that carer-related reasons (life events, abuse by carers and unsubstantiated allegations of abuse) lay behind the disruption of index placements for 51 per cent (19) of this group. This is substantially higher than the figure of 30 per cent of disruptions that occurred for carer-related reasons (including illness or a change in household composition) found in a study of placement breakdown (Berridge and Cleaver, 1987). However, in that study, as in ours, problems posed by the children contributed to at least half of the disruptions, sometimes in combination with carer-related problems.

Conclusion

Risks to placement stability may arise through the interaction of a combination of factors. It is the process whereby these factors interact, rather than individual factors in themselves, that leads some children to settle in stable placements and others to experience placement disruption. As we have seen, qualities in the child and the carer, including child disturbance and parenting style, carer behaviour and life events, and the strength of the carer's commitment to the child may interact and so increase or diminish the risk of placement disruption. These findings are similar to a US study of carer commitment to foster children, which found that child behaviour was significantly associated with caregiver commitment. However, that study concluded that it was not possible to determine the direction of the association between child behaviour and caregiver commitment (Lindheim and Dozier, 2007). In contrast, another US study of new entrants to care argued that child behaviour problems are the result, and not the cause, of placement instability. That study found that behaviour problems increased for children who experienced placement instability, and that the risk of instability was unrelated to their behaviour problems at entry to care (Rubin *et al*, 2007). The patterns identified by that study may differ from ours because it examined instability only during the first 18 months after entry to care, whereas our study investigated instability for children apparently settled in long-term foster placements. Many placements disrupt in the first year of placement, and the reasons for this may differ from the reasons for disruption for children who, like our unstable care group, have already experienced at least three years stability in their index placements before those placements disrupted. For the children in this study, all of whom had been in long-term care, placement stability appeared to be the result of the two-way interaction of child and carer-related factors.

It is also important to take account of the context in which this process occurs. Foster care does not afford carers parental responsibility, in legal terms, so it is possible that in very stressful circumstances some might give up on children somewhat more readily than adoptive parents (although, as we have seen, in some cases carers' love for the child may lead them to carry on against the odds).

The local authority context may also affect patterns of placement stability. Local thresholds for taking children into care may have influenced social work decisions that resulted in the late placement of children in our unstable care group. Equally, local policy, resources and culture may have shaped the effectiveness of both social work planning and social work responsiveness to emerging difficulties in placements. Social workers in some authorities may take decisive action to "rescue" children, or to plan effectively for them, at an earlier stage than others. Another study has found that within authorities, available placement resources and variations between social work teams in staffing levels may be associated with variations in the extent of placement instability between teams. The degree of support from children's schools and their relative readiness to exclude children may also play a part (Sinclair *et al*, 2007). Local policy, decisions about resources, and local practice cultures may also influence the level and nature of support available to children and carers to prevent disruption. Given the often stressful nature of caring long term for late-placed children, support to children and carers may be needed to ensure placement stability.

Finally, our findings on abuse in care highlight the importance of paying attention to placement quality as well as placement stability. Other research has found that younger children may remain in poor-quality placements, but these may disrupt if children are old enough and have the temperament to influence the ending of an unsatisfactory placement. The quality of a placement may affect stability, but only for children over the age of 11 (Sinclair *et al*, 2007). We know that a small number of children in our study were left for many years in very unsatisfactory placements where they experienced abuse or neglect. Other placements may sometimes prove unsatisfactory for less serious reasons. Although placement stability is clearly of great importance in ensuring children's emotional security, it is essential that professionals remain alert to issues of placement quality too.

Summary

- Nearly all of the children who had been adopted were still in their adoptive placements by follow-up, but 11 per cent of them had experienced adoption breakdown at some point in their lives.
- Long-term foster placements were more likely to disrupt than adoptive placements. However, 72 per cent of children had remained with their index carers, either in foster care, on residence orders or adopted by carers.
- For children who were still with their index carers at follow-up, the key predictors of placement stability were age at entry to care and scores on the SDQ.
- Variations in placement stability were also influenced by the interaction between the level of child disturbance and the carers'

parenting style, in relation to the degree of acceptance or rejection of the child.

- Analysis of qualitative data indicated that both child behaviour and carer-related issues, such as marital breakdown, influenced placement stability. For a small number of children, placements had disrupted due to abuse or neglect by foster carers.
- Placement quality should be viewed as being at least as important as placement stability.

16 Supporting adoption

Local authorities' duties to maintain adoption support services, previously set out in the Adoption Act 1976, were strengthened by the Adoption and Children Act 2002. The 1976 Act had included provision for the payment of adoption allowances only in exceptional circumstances and research in the 1990s revealed wide variations between authorities in the provision of adoption support and payment of allowances (Lowe, 1997). The 2002 Act and associated regulations gave local authorities a general duty to provide adoption support services for children, adopters and birth families before, during and after adoption. These include support to birth families for contact. Universal services, including local education and health authorities and other relevant agencies, were also given a duty to provide post-adoption support.

Authorities have a legal duty to assess children's needs for support but the actual provision of support is discretionary. Local authorities, therefore, do not have a duty to provide support services to individual children and families, even if assessment indicates that they are needed. Although there has been an expansion of support services, adoptive families in difficulty have no entitlement to adoption support.

Rushton and Dance's study (2002) of the development of adoption support services in 120 local authorities found that most reported an increase in the number of children being referred for adoption support. The authorities reported that increasing numbers of children required adoptive placements at an early age because of parental substance misuse or mental health problems, and were concerned about the potential effects of these adversities on children's subsequent development and future needs. They were anxious about the potential demand for adoption support, but found it difficult to estimate what the extent of this demand might be, making it difficult to plan service provision.

Children who have experienced maltreatment, separation from birth families, and possibly multiple placements in care prior to placement for adoption, may have extensive support needs. The challenge to adopters, and to the providers of support services, is therefore considerable. Both children and their adoptive parents may require support, and this is particularly likely to be the case where children are late placed and have had lengthy exposure to adversity. However, a number of studies have found considerable variation in the availability and quality of adoption support services and noted that adopters often had difficulty in persuading professionals of the seriousness of their children's problems and could be dismissive of the concerns of adoptive parents (Quinton *et al*, 1998; Lowe *et al*, 1999; Rushton and Dance, 2002; Selwyn *et al*, 2006).

However, even where high-quality parenting advice is provided to adoptive families, the serious and long-term nature of the children's difficulties can make it difficult to achieve change in the short term. A recent evaluation of a short-term parenting advice service to adopters in the first 18 months of placement found that it was difficult for these services to bring about significant change in psychosocial problems and suggested that children may need a longer period of stable family life before change can be achieved. However, these services raised parenting satisfaction with the adoption which, the researchers argued, might contribute to the longer-term stability and success of the adoption (Rushton and Monck, 2009).

Developing support services

Managers and staff who took part in our focus groups and interviews felt that the provision of funds for the development of adoption support services was one of the most positive aspects of the new policy on adoption. The Government made £70 million of ring-fenced funding available for developing adoption support services over the three years from 2003 to 2006. The authorities in our study used this money to expand staff in their adoption services and develop dedicated adoption support teams. All were agreed that the Government's provision of ring-fenced funds for adoption support had had a big impact and had led to the development, or expansion, of support services. However, two managers expressed some concern as to how the new posts would be funded once the ring-fenced adoption support grant came to an end.

Despite the discretionary nature of provision in this area, managers from the seven local authorities spoke with real enthusiasm about the services they had been developing or commissioning, which were provided directly by local authorities, singly or in consortia. For example, one of the unitary authorities had set up a consortium with two neighbouring authorities and had jointly funded four adoption support posts. Support services were also commissioned from other agencies, such as mental health services, education (supporting children at school) and voluntary agencies, such as After Adoption. Managers were also keen to make good use of universal services to support adoptive families, integrating the services provided by different agencies in the spirit of Every Child Matters. One manager, from a large authority that had set up a centrally managed team of locally based adoption support workers, explained that local primary care trusts had so far been amenable to providing or paying for therapeutic work with children. Some managers were concerned that universal services might not have sufficient understanding of adoption to provide appropriate support. One manager argued that both fostered and adopted children often needed specialist help:

We don't feel confident about universal services picking this up because universal services don't understand the requirements yet . . . We can't afford to let go of those targeted services until we are happy that more mainstream services are ready to pick up these needs.

Some authorities extended their support services to families offering a variety of permanent placements. One manager from a large county explained that his authority felt that decisions about support should be made in relation to a child and family's needs at any point in time, and should not depend solely on the child's legal status. Thus, support was to be provided to kinship carers, or long-term foster carers, for example, as well as to adoptive families. One of our London authorities held a similar view and had set up an adoption support panel that considered the support needs of children and families in relation to both adoption and long-term foster care.

There was some anxiety about the potential demand for services, particularly in view of the cross-border arrangements set out in the Adoption and Children Act 2002. These regulations require that, for families living outside the placing authority, the placing authority retains responsibility for support services only for the first three years after placement. Thereafter, the authority in which the child lives takes over responsibility for assessing the need for support services and has the discretion to provide these services. Two authorities actively engaged in trying to assess the potential demand for adoption support services were finding it particularly difficult to assess the number of adopted children previously placed in their areas by other authorities.

Comparing support services

Earlier research undertaken prior to the 2002 Act showed that adoptive families were often unaware of the support services available (Lowe *et al*, 1999). However, by 2005, the managers interviewed for this study were reporting a huge growth in demand for adoption support services. This was felt to be due to adopters hearing about the new regulations and to local authorities publicising their new support services.

The adoptive parents who completed our survey questionnaires told us about the support services they had received during the past year. We asked similar questions of foster carers and were able to compare the use of services, as shown in Table 16.1.

Most of the adoptive relationships in our sample were long standing, as 98 per cent of the children adopted by strangers and 93 per cent of those adopted by carers had been living with their adoptive parents for five years or more. In the context of these long-established arrangements, the use of adoption support services was high. In total, 46 per cent had received support from either a social worker or an adoption agency during the past year. Nearly one-third of the adoptive parents reported that they had received support from social workers during the past year and just over one-quarter reported receiving support from an adoption agency during the same period. The other parents indicated that support from these sources was 'not applicable', possibly because they did not feel they needed it at this point in the children's lives. When provided, social work support was often highly valued by adoptive parents struggling to cope in difficult circumstances:

Table 16.1
Professional support received during past year per cent (n = 128)

	Adoptive parents (n = 59)	Foster carers (n = 69)
Social worker	31	100
Adoption agency	27	–
GP or paediatrician	51	49
Child psychiatrist	15	13
Clinical child psychologist	14	12
Educational psychologist	27	28
School/teachers	81	83
Education social worker	17	31
Speech therapist	17	12
Short-breaks/respite scheme	8	28

Our social workers are there on the end of the phone whenever we need them. I've rung them up about him and his behaviour, because it was getting to a stage where I was getting fed up of being beaten up. Well, now it's more like he'll grab my hand now for a cool down, rather than . . . so it's not, it's working its way out. So we're understanding, I'm listening to him a bit better and he's listening to me a little bit more, so.

Adoptive parents mentioned various types of support, speaking positively about support provided by social workers and by voluntary agencies such as Adoption UK and After Adoption. A few also mentioned adoption groups. One mentioned that attending an adoption support group was useful because it served as a reference point that gave her a context for understanding her own child's behaviour, but she wished for more support than the group could provide:

You know, certainly at certain ages where, where things are, you know, is it because they're adopted or is this a normal thing? And I suppose, when you go to support groups that's quite good that you can actually air some of this, but it would be nice to have somewhere where you

could tap into and, I don't know whether, whether the child could
perhaps be assessed in some way.

Universal services were working with a substantial minority of adopted children. Schools were reported to provide support in most cases. Over a quarter of the adopted children had seen an educational psychologist in the past year and 17 per cent had seen an education social worker. Support with mental health had also been provided during the past year, as 23 per cent of the adopted children had seen either a child psychiatrist or a clinical child psychologist or both.

Some adopted children were receiving multi-agency support due to their considerable difficulties and the particular problems posed by their behaviour at school:

The Government did bring in more post-adoption, and thank goodness
they did because to take a child with this amount of problems, when
you've not been trained, I mean thank goodness we had a child
before. . . . I got CAMHS involved and they were fantastic. Social
services came in and they were fantastic, but they don't have resources.
The clinical psychologist went in every other week to talk to the staff,
was email-able to the teacher. She was exemplary, and Jane, the social
worker, was fantastic, and then he used to go to see Joe, the clinical
psychologist, once a week, that year. (Adoptive parent of Niall)

However, a problem with the support provided was that it was time limited. Once the intensive support to Niall ended, he was again excluded from school. Where parents did not currently feel the need for support, they nevertheless valued the fact that support services were available. One parent, who had attended an adoption support group in the past, was happy to know that adoption support would be 'there if I need it but not right in your face'.

Some adopters may be reluctant to ask for help, fearing that this would be a sign of failure or because they prefer to struggle on alone. Help-seeking behaviour may be complex and some adopters may not welcome the intrusion of professionals into family life (Selwyn *et al*, 2006; Rushton and Monck, 2009). Although adoptive parents generally valued the provision of support services and many felt they needed them, one carer was concerned that the use of support services would mark her child out as different:

> *No, none at all. Never, we never have and we never wanted it. How can you settle into a family if you've always got, you know, other people popping in? It's not the same, is it? No, I, didn't really want people to interfere 'cos I thought well, you know, I've done this a lot and I know what I'm doing, and yeah, it's fine.*

All of the foster families had received support from a social worker during the past year. Several foster carers were particularly positive about the support they received from their fostering link workers, but others mentioned receiving advice and support from the children's social workers, although satisfaction with the support they provided varied. Otherwise, the use of support services was similar for children who were fostered, apart from the fact that they appeared more likely to have received support from an educational psychologist. The use of services was also similar between fostered children with stable or unstable care careers, other than that respite care services were more commonly used for children in stable foster placements. This was probably due to the higher number of children with disabilities or chronic health problems in the stable foster care group, although not all of the children using respite care services had these difficulties. However, we should not assume that support is always available to fostered children who need it. An assessment of a child's need for support, or clear plan to provide it, may not always be made at the point that a care plan is made, so support from other professionals may not always be forthcoming when needed.

The fact that similar proportions of adopted and fostered children were receiving professional support might provide some encouragement to carers thinking of adopting but worried about a loss of support. However, this survey was conducted at a time when the Government had made ring-fenced money available to develop adoption support services. We are not in a position to know whether local adoption support services have been successfully mainstreamed and have sufficient resources allocated to them now that the adoption support grant is no longer available.

Financial support

The Children Act 1989 provided for the subsequent Adoption Allowance Regulations 1991, which permitted adoption agencies to pay adoption allowances in certain circumstances. In the Adoption and Children Act 2002 and the Adoption Support Services Regulations (2005), it was the Government's intention to overcome the financial obstacles to adoption for children in public care. The new regulations aimed to address disincentives to adoption, such as the loss of fostering allowances for carers wishing to adopt or the inordinate cost of adopting sibling groups. Under these arrangements, local authorities may pay financial support to adopters until the child reaches the age of 18 or ceases their full-time education. This is a discretionary payment and each local authority may make their own decisions about the local threshold for support and the amounts to be paid, so there is likely to be local variation in the readiness with which allowances are paid and the amounts agreed. The Regulations set out a number of specific criteria that allow the payment of one-off sums or allowances, a key change being that foster carers who go on to adopt may now receive an allowance for a transitional period of up to two years after the adoption.

In a significant shift, the Government made more money available through ordinary means-tested benefits and allowances, such as family credit and child tax allowances. Previously, few state benefits or allowances had been available to families who were caring for a child who was not their own (and was not fostered by them), but these rules were relaxed. Adopters and holders of residence orders can now claim other state benefits and allowances as well as the means-tested adoption and residence allowances provided by local authorities. As a result, local authorities' role now is to top up those benefits where necessary, rather than be the sole provider of support. Situating funding for adoption support within this framework of universal benefits mirrors a broader shift to situate adoption support services within a universal service framework.

Managers in our seven local authorities welcomed the significant amount of money that had come with the Act, which had helped them to offer more extensive support to adopted children and their new families. They mentioned offering financial support to help adoptive families make changes to their houses, provide domestic support or help with transport costs, to pay for educational aides for children who did not have a statement of special educational needs and to buy in therapeutic support when local CAMHS services were unable to meet a child's needs. One commented, 'I don't know what we would do if we didn't have that money'.

However, the new regulations were perceived to be extremely complex and managers expressed anxiety about the immediate and long-term financial implications of the new rules and about how best to deal with the inconsistencies in the new financial framework. For example, there was concern about the anomaly that looked after children who become cared for under the special guardianship provisions retain their entitlement to leaving care services, which has considerable financial implications for local authorities, whereas children adopted from care, or who become cared for on residence orders, do not.

Managers were preoccupied with resolving, at local level, the difficulties posed by a number of anomalies in the new regulations. As one of them explained:

> . . . we've got looked after child status that is not means tested and that attracts all the leaving care support, including higher education maintenance . . . We've got residence allowance that ceases on the 18th birthday and there's no facility to pay beyond that . . . We've got staying in the foster placement post-18 and where that's appropriate for the child we support that, but the tax position is different . . . from the 18th birthday they don't attract those [foster care tax allowances] . . . and adoption financial support stops at 21, they could be in the middle of their degree course by then . . . but if they're on special guardianship and aftercare arrangements, they can have it [financial support] to 25, if they're in higher education . . .

There was also a broader concern that decisions about finance should follow decisions about the best permanency plan for the child and not vice versa. As another manager explained:

> The route to the right option could take the child and carers through different legal statuses at different points in time. The permanency

plan has to move with them without coming up against financial hurdles at different points . . . You get all this when you are a looked after child, some of this you lose when you become adopted, or if you move right back into your own extended family without an order, you don't get anything. These are the things we have got to avoid.

Given the complexity of the various requirements of the tax and benefits systems and the new adoption regulations, it was therefore difficult to draft local policies that ensured equity and transparency in support arrangements. These difficulties were reinforced by anomalies and inconsistencies regarding the nature and duration of support for children and carers in various types of permanent placements. So while welcoming the new opportunities for local authorities to provide financial support, managers were concerned about the detailed policy, practice and financial implications of the new arrangements. It is possible that variations in the local solutions found to these difficulties may have had some influence on variations in the use of different types of permanent placement.

We asked carers who completed our survey questionnaires whether they received any financial support to help them look after the children. Foster carers receive a fee and sometimes an additional allowance for caring for children, so naturally all of these indicated that they received financial support. Nearly two-thirds (62%) of the carer adopters and 16 per cent of the stranger adopters reported that they were currently receiving an adoption allowance. Eight per cent were also receiving a disabled living allowance for their child, as were five per cent of foster carers.

Conclusion

The Adoption and Children Act 2002 gave local authorities a duty to make provision for adoption-related services and to assess the needs of children and families, but the actual provision of such services is discretionary. The Act and associated regulations have recognised the distinctive support needs of adoptive families but at the same time require support services to be integrated within mainstream, universal services. Although the adoption support provisions give adoptive families special status in that they 'put adoptive families at the front of the queue for services' (Masson, 2003), adoptive families must nevertheless negotiate their entitlement to receive adoption-related services. Luckock and Hart have pointed to the ambiguity underlying recent policy on this issue, which aims to main-stream adoption support while at the same time raising the profile of adoptive parents as potential users of services. They argue that govern-ment has drawn on two benchmarks in discussion of adoptive family life, "normative" biological parenting and corporate parenting (Luckock and Hart, 2005). Most adoptive parents would wish for "normal" family life yet at the same time some might also wish for the kinds of intensive services that a corporate parent might provide for looked after children who need them. However, while they are entitled to an assessment for support services, they may not be entitled to receive them.

Nevertheless, at a time when ring-fenced money for developing adoption support services was available, local authorities were enthusi-astically developing adoption support provision in collaboration with other statutory or voluntary agencies. Nearly half of the adoptive families in this study were receiving support from social workers or voluntary adoption agencies and a smaller number were receiving support from health and education professionals. Others indicated that adoption support was 'not applicable' (rather than denied to them) at the time of the survey, or that they did not want services because these might undermine their attempts to view themselves as "normal" families.

In contrast, long-term foster carers may expect some support (from social workers, at the very least) by virtue of parenting on behalf of the corporate parent, and the children they care for are entitled to particular attention from other professionals, for example, in education. In practice, looked after children and their foster carers do not always gain access to support at the time they need it, even if they may theoretically have greater entitlement to it than adoptive families. In particular, help from education or mental health services may not be forthcoming (Wade et al, 1998). Like adoptive parents, long-term foster carers may therefore have to negotiate timely access to the services that children need. However, unlike adoptive parents, long-term foster carers have only limited autonomy and must negotiate the division of responsibilities between themselves, as substitute parents, and the local authority as corporate parent. They must therefore provide "normal" parenting to children who they intend to care for into adulthood, but without the full authority to do so. Similarly, social workers of children in long-term foster care may tread a fine line between making a limited withdrawal, to avoid being over-intrusive, yet remaining aware of the potential for stress in the long-term placement of difficult children and hence the need to oversee the placement (Schofield *et al*, 2000).

Summary

- Over 90 per cent of the adopted children had lived with their adoptive parents for over five years. Although the adoptions were long standing, nearly half (46%) of the adoptive parents had received support from social workers or adoption agencies during the previous year. Significant minorities of adopted children had received support from a variety of education and mental health professionals during the previous year.
- The proportion receiving support from these professionals was similar for adopted and fostered children, except that the fostered children were more likely to have seen an education social worker. However, our survey was undertaken during the period when a ring-fenced sum was available to authorities for the development of adoption support services and we do not know whether the same level of provision has been sustained since the ring-fenced funding ended.
- Managers faced a complex task in developing local policies on financial support to children in different circumstances. It was difficult to ensure equity in arrangements for financial support in relation to adoption, special guardianship, residence orders and kinship care.
- Nearly two-thirds (62%) of the carer adopters and 16 per cent of the stranger adopters reported that they were currently receiving an adoption allowance.

17 Conclusion

Shortly after the Labour Government came to power in 1997, there began a period of intense policy activity and legislative reform, which aimed to tackle the social and economic costs of social exclusion. This included a focus both on early intervention to prevent social exclusion and on specific groups at risk of exclusion, including looked after children, who were known to be vulnerable to poor outcomes in adult life (Biehal *et al*, 1995; Wade, 2006). During the 1990s, the rising number of children who remained looked after long term, the quality of care and the outcomes for children who were looked after had all provoked concern. Within a year of Labour coming to power, there was evidence of policy attention both to the quality and outcomes of care and to strategies to promote exit from the care system.

Over the next few years, a series of policy initiatives focused on looked after children, including Quality Protects, Choice Protects, the more wide-ranging Every Child Matters programme and eventually Care Matters. These initiatives were accompanied by a programme of legislative reform including, and of particular relevance to this study, the Adoption and Children Act 2002. This aimed, among other things, to increase the chance that children would leave the care system through adoption.

Against this background of intense policy interest both in increasing adoption and in the outcomes of long-term care, this study compared three types of permanent placement for children: adoption by strangers, adoption by carers and long-term foster care. At the heart of the study lies the key question of how best to meet the needs of children who cannot safely be reunited with their parents. Two further questions follow from this: How can we provide emotional and legal security, a sense of permanence and positive outcomes? And how successful are adoption and long-term foster care, respectively, in providing security and permanence, and in promoting positive outcomes?

To answer these questions, we have explored the different pathways that children follow through, and in some cases out of, care, and the outcomes associated with these pathways. We have considered a range of outcomes, comparing the emotional, behavioural and relationship difficulties of children in each type of placement, their participation and progress in education and the stability of their placements. However, how children feel about their experiences is of equal importance. We have therefore explored how children make sense of being fostered or adopted, their perceptions of belonging and permanence and how they feel about the contact they have with their birth families, if any.

In order to explore these issues we:

- conducted focus groups and interviews with managers, staff and foster carers in the seven local authorities that took part in the study;
- analysed administrative data on our census sample (n = 374);
- conducted a postal survey of the carers and social workers of 196 children in our *survey sample*: these children had all been in foster care in 1998/99 and, three years later, had still been living in the same foster placements (their "index" placements) or had been adopted by strangers or their foster carers;
- analysed historical data collected on 90 of the children in our *survey sample*, who had been previously surveyed in the York studies of foster care conducted five and eight years earlier (Sinclair *et al*, 2005b, 2005c);
- interviewed 37 children and their foster carers or adoptive parents.

Placement stability and exit from care

Our analysis of administrative data on 374 children in our census sample showed that, seven or more years after they entered their index foster placements, 45 per cent of the children in the study had left the care system through adoption (36%), reunification (5%) or residence orders (5%) and 32 per cent were still settled in their long-term foster placements. However, 23 per cent had left their index foster placements after living in them for three or more years and had experienced unstable care careers.

In this report we have focused principally on four groups of children.

The adopted children comprise two groups: those adopted by strangers and those adopted by their former foster carers. The children who were still looked after at the time of our survey also fall into two groups. We call those who had remained in their index foster placements for seven or more years our "stable foster care" group. The other children, who had lived with their index foster carers for at least three years before these placements disrupted, we call our "unstable care" group. At some points, we also consider a fifth small group of children previously placed in long-term foster care, for whom foster carers or relatives had taken out residence orders by the time of our survey.

Comparing emotional, behavioural and educational outcomes

The carers and adoptive parents of the children in our survey completed a measure of the children's emotional, behavioural difficulties, the Strengths and Difficulties Questionnaire (SDQ). Across the sample as a whole, 38 per cent of the children had total scores on the SDQ that indicated clinically significant emotional and behavioural difficulties. The most common difficulties were conduct disorder (37%), hyper-activity (33%) and peer problems (33%). Lower scores on the SDQ, indicating less serious difficulties, were predicted by entry to the current placement at the age of three or under. There was also a weak correlation between high scores for conduct disorder and the total number of placement moves the children had ever experienced.

We found no significant difference between children in long-term foster care and those who had been adopted in the likelihood that they would have significant mental health difficulties, and this is consistent with the findings of other studies (Sinclair *et al*, 2005c; Selwyn *et al*, 2006). However, children who were in our unstable care group had significantly worse scores for emotional and behavioural difficulty than those in stable foster placements. In one sense this is a positive finding, as it shows that many children in foster care may be doing no worse than those who are adopted. On the other hand, our findings show that adopted children may have emotional and behavioural difficulties as severe as those of looked after children, and therefore have similar support needs.

Carers also completed a measure of the children's Expression of Feelings in Relationships (EFR), designed by David Quinton. On this measure, there was again no difference between children in our stable foster care and our adopted group. However, children in our unstable care group had higher total scores on the EFR, indicating greater difficulty in relationships. In particular, they had higher scores for inhibition (or stoicism) compared to the children in settled foster placements or adoptive homes. We found a similar pattern on our measure of developmental progress, originally developed for use on the Looked After Children Assessment and Action Records. Scores on this measure were similar for children who were adopted or in stable foster care, but were significantly worse for children in the unstable care group.

For the sub-sample of 90 children on whom we had collected these measures five and eight years earlier, we found that scores on the SDQ had showed little change over time, although there was improvement for some children and some deterioration for others. On average, scores on the EFR for disinhibited attachment improved and scores for inhibited attachment got worse, in part because the children grew older. Late placement seemed to reduce the chance of improvement on the inhibited attachment, SDQ and developmental progress scores. Every effort should therefore be made to ensure that, as far as possible, children are placed in their final, long-term placement as early as possible.

Sadly, children in the unstable care group were doing worse on these measures, both at the time of our survey and eight years earlier. However, it is positive that on all of these measures the scores of children in long-term foster care were similar to those of children who had been adopted. Nevertheless, for the adopted children and those in stable foster placements, average SDQ scores for total difficulties were nearly four times higher than the average for children in the general population.

We have seen that, on the whole, for most children SDQ scores showed little change over time. This was the case for those who were adopted or who had experienced stable care, as well as those in our unstable care group. The severity of children's emotional and behavioural difficulties may therefore be largely determined by pre-placement adversity early in their lives. This is a disturbing finding, as it suggests that even high-quality parenting may not lead to significant improvements in emotional and behavioural difficulties. Some children, however, did show some improvement (or deterioration) over time.

Late placement appeared to reduce the chance of improvement on the SDQ and the EFR, so carers and parents may find it easier to effect change if children enter their permanent placement as early as possible. Permanency planning therefore needs to be both timely and effective. The difficulty of bringing about improvement in children's emotional and behavioural difficulties also has another important implication, namely that adoptive families, foster carers and the children they care for may need extensive support to address mental health and behavioural difficulties. The Government's new policy of using the SDQ to screen children looked after for one year or more for emotional and behavioural difficulties may help to identify those looked after children who need this support.

However, the lack of change that we found in relation to emotional and behavioural difficulties may possibly be due to the fact that the SDQ was originally designed as a screening measure and not as a measure of change and may not, therefore, be sufficiently sensitive to detect any real changes that might have occurred. More research is therefore needed using a more sensitive instrument specifically designed to measure change. Such a study would benefit from a prospective design, although this would be costly.

Educational participation and progress

Children in stable foster care were doing as well on measures of partici-pation in education and educational progress as those who were adopted. Although they were more likely than the adopted children to display behavioural problems at school and to truant, they were no more likely to be excluded and their scores were similar on our measures of general educational progress. Again, this finding is both positive and negative. For children whose foster placements endure over time, it is encouraging to find that educational outcomes may be no worse, on average, than those for children who are adopted. However, we know that looked after children do significantly worse on measures of educational outcomes, in comparison with the general population. It is therefore discouraging that adopted children were doing no better than those in stable foster placements.

Our unstable care group was doing significantly worse on all measures of participation and progress in education. Compared to the children who were adopted or in stable foster placements, they were more likely to have truanted and also more likely to have been excluded from school in the previous six months, to display behaviour problems at school and to do worse on our measures of educational progress.

However, the strongest predictor of doing badly at school, on a composite measure of participation and progress, was having high scores for emotional and behavioural difficulties on the SDQ. We know from our analysis of the SDQ scores that the unstable care group already had more severe difficulties than others from an early age, so it is likely that their school problems were also long standing. The new policy of using the SDQ to screen children who are looked after for one year or more for emotional and behavioural difficulties may therefore help to identify those in particular need of support to promote their integration and progress at school. Such support should also be available to adopted children who need it.

Perceptions of belonging and permanence

In our interviews with children and their adoptive parents or foster carers, we explored their perceptions of belonging and permanence. Most of the children adopted by strangers had been placed as infants. For the majority of those interviewed, including two who were late placed, their primary identification was with their adoptive families. Although birth parents were psychologically present to the children, to varying degrees, none of them had any direct contact with them, although some were inquisitive about birth relatives. These children appeared to feel emotionally secure in their adoptive families.

Children adopted by carers indicated a strong sense of belonging to their adoptive families. Although a few wondered about their birth parents, there was no apparent sense of divided loyalties at this stage in the children's lives, despite the fact that two were late placed with these carers. These late-placed children expressed their relief at having achieved the legal security of adoption. The fact that carer–child relationships were already strong before the adoption application was made contributed to the success of these carer adoptions.

Most of those settled in long-term foster homes viewed their carers as parental figures and called them Mum and Dad. They felt a strong sense of belonging to their foster families. For a small number of children, who had been placed with these carers in infancy and identified themselves with them more or less exclusively, these foster placements were quasi-adoptive in nature. Placement in infancy, for some children, meant that these foster families had provided the only home they had ever known. The exclusive nature of these foster placements, where the severity of parental abuse or rejection meant there was no direct contact with birth parents, appeared to facilitate the children's sense of emotional security and belonging. In these circumstances, however, adoption by carers might have been more appropriate than long-term foster care.

For another group of children, foster care was inclusive, as they had relatively unproblematic face-to-face contact with birth parents. These children appeared able to reconcile the fact that they, in different senses, belonged to both a birth family and a substitute family. Although there was some ambivalence and anxiety on the part of children or carers, the children appeared able to manage attachments to two families without too much inner conflict, viewing their foster carers 'just like' another family and generally appearing to feel a reasonable sense of emotional security, despite lacking the legal security afforded by adoption.

A third group of children in stable foster care were more obviously troubled by feelings of ambivalence, hurt and anger towards their birth parents. These children had some face-to-face contact with birth parents but this was usually intermittent and sometimes difficult for the children. Although settled in their foster placements, their complex feelings about their birth parents led them to feel a more qualified sense of belonging to their foster families. These conflicts of loyalty were not always apparent to their foster carers, some of whom perceived the children as their own and thought the children felt a reciprocal sense of unqualified belonging.

All of the adopted children interviewed assumed that they would stay with their adoptive families long term, as did those in foster placements that were quasi-adoptive in nature. Most children in stable foster care also hoped and expected to remain in their foster placements long term and viewed their carers as a family for life, but some were uncertain about what would happen to them in the future.

How did placements become permanent?

Half of the long-term foster placements had initially been planned as permanent placements. Initial plans for short- or medium-term placement had changed, as attempts at reunification failed or plans to find alternative permanent placements had not come to fruition. It was unclear, in retrospect, whether children had drifted in care due to a lack of planning, or whether a clear plan had been made for them which had resulted, for some, in a change in the purpose of their existing placement.

A number of long-term foster carers told us that they had offered to care for the children long term because they had grown to love them and often because they wished to protect them from the vagaries of the care system. Carer adopters gave similar reasons for adopting children they had formerly fostered. One-third of the long-term carers were relatives of the children who had chosen to look after the children long term because of the family relationship, either as foster carers or on residence orders.

What influenced decisions about adoption?

Analysis of our survey indicated that children were more likely to be adopted if they had last entered care at a younger age and lived in certain local authorities rather than others. These findings are consistent with evidence from national statistics and the findings of another, much larger, survey (Sinclair et al, 2007). Adoption was also more likely if children had never been placed with relatives and if face-to-face contact with birth parents had been prohibited.

The mean age at last entry to care was 1.5 years for children who had been adopted by strangers. Nearly two-thirds of them had begun their final episode of care before they were one year old and 85 per cent had done so before they were three. Carer adoption offers a chance of adoption to children who enter care later. Those adopted by carers had entered care at 3.1 years on average, although half of them had done so before the age of one. In contrast, children who remained in long-term foster care had begun their last episode of care when older still, at 3.9 years, on average. As a result, they had entered their current placement later, at an average of 4.1 years, compared to 2.6 years for children adopted by strangers and 3.6 years for those adopted by carers.

There may be good reasons why children are not adopted, including the extent of any continuing relationships with birth families and the children's own wishes. Decisions about adoption are informed by the nature of parent–child relationships and the severity of the problems that have led to the child's permanent removal from them, which lay behind decisions to forbid contact. The availability of other relatives to care for the child long term, and the desirability of placing the child with any relatives who might be available, also influenced the likelihood of adoption.

However, decisions about adoption are also influenced by local policy, resources and practice cultures. We found that children living in some local authorities were more likely to be adopted than those living in others. It was also clear from our focus groups and our interviews with local authority managers that views as to who was adoptable varied. Local practice wisdom, for example on the desirability of seeking adoptive placements for older children and the feasibility of doing so, may have a substantial impact on day-to-day social work decisions (Biehal and Sainsbury, 1991). Variations between social work teams may also influence the likelihood of adoption. Other research has found that, other things being equal, teams under pressure due to staff shortages may be less likely to make adoptive placements than those with a higher ratio of staff (Sinclair et al, 2007). Some authorities have reported finding it difficult to manage the tension between the policy of refocusing services to keep families together and a policy drive to increase adoptions from care (Oliver et al, 2001). Decisions on adoption may therefore be determined as much by local policy, resources and practice cultures as by children's needs.

We also asked social workers why the children who were still looked after had not been adopted. One-quarter of them reported that this was because the children had been too old. The most common reason given, in around half the cases of children who were not adopted, was that the child was too settled in foster care. This begs the question of why foster carers did not choose to adopt the child. Carers indicated that this was to some extent due to a fear that they would lose financial and other support from children's services, issues which the Adoption and Children Act 2002 has sought to address. We found that nearly two-thirds of the carer adopters who took part in our survey were receiving an adoption allowance.

In around one-third of cases, social workers reported that children had not been adopted because they were thought to be too bonded to their birth families and in a similar proportion of cases the birth family's opposition was cited. In one in eight cases, social workers reported that the child had not wanted adoption. In cases of this nature, special guardianship might offer a route out of care to children placed with long-term foster carers, in circumstances where both view the arrangement as permanent.

Comparing the stability of long-term foster care and adoption

Long-term foster care is intended to be permanent, but for many children it is not. Among the children who had not been adopted by strangers, 72 per cent remained with their index foster carers seven or more years after they entered their long-term foster placements, either fostered or adopted by them, or cared for on residence orders. However, although 11 per cent of the children had experienced the breakdown of an adoptive placement earlier in their lives, 28 per cent (of those not adopted by strangers) had left their index carers and experienced unstable care. The risk of placement instability was therefore higher for children in long-term foster placements than for those who were adopted.

However, it was difficult to compare like with like, as the adopted children had been significantly younger when they entered their adoptive homes, compared to the children who remained in the care system. A large part of the difference that we found in stability rates is likely to be due to the fact that children who are adopted are often placed in infancy, which reduces their exposure to adversity (although genetic factors may nevertheless affect their future functioning). Long-term foster care is often, though not always, used for children who enter care at a later age and for whom placement outside the care system has not been planned or, if planned, has not been achieved. This study, and others before it, found a strong relationship between age at entry to placement and the risk of disruption, so differences in disruption rates need to be interpreted in the light of differences in age at placement (Berridge and Cleaver, 1987; Thoburn, 1990; Triseliotis, 2002; Rushton, 2004). It is therefore difficult to come to firm conclusions as to whether it is adoption *per se* or the earlier age at which children are adopted that has the greater effect on stability.

Furthermore, and related to their earlier age at placement, the children in our study who were adopted by strangers were significantly younger at the time of our survey than those in our long-term foster care and unstable care groups. A far higher proportion of children in our unstable care group (90%) had reached adolescence by the time of our survey than was the case for those who were in stable foster care (67%), adopted by carers (36%) or adopted by strangers (21%). The placements of older children are known to be more vulnerable to disruption (Berridge and Cleaver, 1987; Sinclair *et al*, 2007), so this too makes it difficult for us to be sure that in comparing disruption rates we are comparing like with like.

What influenced placement stability?

We also investigated the predictors of placement stability in relation to the children who had not been adopted by strangers, comparing children who were still settled with their index carers with those in our unstable care group. We found that age at entry to care and the severity of emotional and behavioural difficulties were the key predictors of stability. Children who had remained settled with their index carers had last entered care significantly younger, at a mean age of 3.6 years, than those in the unstable care group, who had only begun their final episode of care at an average age of 5.3 years.

The severity of the children's emotional and behavioural problems appeared to increase the risk of placement disruption. For a sub-sample of

90 children, we had data collected five and eight years before our survey. Comparing scores on the SDQ over time, we found that the children in our unstable care group had already had significantly worse scores on our measure of emotional and behavioural difficulties (the SDQ) eight years earlier, compared to children who went on to experience stable foster care or be adopted. Although data on the reasons for placement disruption for our survey sample were not comprehensive, social workers reported that, for at least half of the children who had experienced placement disruption, the children's behaviour had contributed to the disruption.

There may also be carer-related reasons for placement disruption, although these may not always be the sole reason for placement breakdown. Five years before our current survey, the index carers of the children whose foster placements subsequently disrupted (our unstable care group) had been rated as less accepting on our measure of carer rejection, compared to the carers of the children who subsequently remained in stable foster placements. Rejection by carers may be prompted, or reinforced, by children's disturbance. It may also increase the level of disturbance. Disturbance and parenting style may interact and, in combination, may influence the risk of placement disruption. Some carers may show greater resilience in coping with children who have serious emotional and behavioural difficulties than others. As our qualitative data showed, some foster carers may continue to care for children in difficult circumstances due to their love for particular children and their commitment to them. Equally, in some authorities, carers may be better supported by social services and other agencies in caring for such children.

In a small number of cases, events in carers' lives, such as marital breakdown or bereavement, also contributed to the disruption of placements. Worryingly, for 14 per cent (five) of the children in our unstable care group, their previous long-term foster placements had ended when evidence of carer abuse or neglect had come to light. However, among the sample as a whole, a total of five per cent (ten) were known to have experienced abuse or neglect by former foster carers. Another five children who were in stable placements at the time of our survey had also experienced abuse or neglect by carers earlier in their lives and a further five had been moved due to allegations against carers, although we do not know whether these were ever substantiated. Clearly this evidence of carer abuse is deeply disturbing. Although we did not have comprehensive data on reasons for the disruption of children's index foster placements, for 40 per cent of the children in our unstable care group, placements had disrupted partly, or entirely, for carer-related reasons (due to carers' life events and substantiated or unsubstantiated allegations of abuse).

It is important to consider risks to placement stability in context and to understand how they operate in combination with one another. The children whose index foster placements had disrupted had higher levels of disturbance, which had been apparent many years earlier and had changed little over time. The children's level of disturbance had possibly been intensified by late separation from birth families, which may in some cases have been a consequence of delay on the part of social workers. These late-placed children already had serious emotional and behavioural difficulties by the time they entered their index foster placements.

However, risk factors such as late placement and high SDQ scores should not be seen as unvarying, independent determinants of outcomes. What is important is the process by which they interact with each other, as well as in combination with other factors in children's and carers' lives over time, that may make both children and carers either more or less resilient in the face of difficulty. As we have seen, disturbance and parenting style may interact, and events in carers' lives may influence their willingness to persist in difficult circumstances.

Child and carer relationship styles may create a downward spiral, as perceived rejection by carers may result in more clingy, demanding behaviour on the part of children and so increase carer stress. However, qualities in the carers and children that led them to become closely attached to one another undoubtedly made a difference to placement stability too. Our qualitative data showed that those long-term foster carers who persisted in caring for children despite their behavioural difficulties often felt a genuine love and a powerful commitment to them. The context of being a foster carer rather than an adoptive parent may also help to shape patterns of placement stability. In the face of considerable stress and difficulty, perceived (and actual) differences in parental responsibility and the absence of a sense of family obligation may lead carers to give up on children somewhat more readily.

There was also some evidence, albeit inconclusive, that the local authority context may help to shape patterns of placement stability. Such variations may be due to variations in local policy, staff and placement resources and practice cultures. It is also possible that the variations in practice between social work teams may also have played a part (Sinclair *et al*, 2007). Particular senior and team managers may have taken a more proactive view in relation to permanency planning than others elsewhere. In some authorities, the focus may be predominantly on protecting children, with less time given to planning, particularly at times of staff shortage or organisational change. Authorities, or teams, with sufficient staff resources may give more attention to supporting foster placements under pressure, while those with more placement resources may be able to match children more successfully with carers. What is important is that where local authorities have higher rates of instability, there is clearly scope for doing something about this. It should be possible to identify what it is about local policy, use of resources and practice at different levels within the agency that contributes to this instability.

Implications for policy and practice

This study has shown that the experience of long-term, stable foster care may be very positive. Although it cannot give them legal security, long-term foster care may provide children with emotional security and a sense of permanence. As Lahti observed long ago, the perception of permanence is key (Lahti, 1982). The problem remains, however, that although long-term foster care can offer permanence, it often fails to do so.

Timely decision making and timely planning for permanence are therefore essential, to enable children to enter their permanent placements as early as possible. As our study and others have found, delay in entry to permanent placements may be caused by delays in planning for children, a lack of adoptive or foster placements, unsuccessful attempts at reunification, a lengthy search for relative carers, and delays resulting from shortages of court time or repeated requests by the court for fresh assessments (Sinclair *et al*, 2005c; Selwyn *et al*, 2006; Ward *et al*, 2006).

Our findings suggest that carer adoption should be encouraged. Carer adoption offered late-placed children a chance of adoption, and hence legal as well as emotional security, which they might not otherwise have had. Carers and children had already formed a strong bond prior to the adoption and some of the children that we interviewed expressed a sense of relief at achieving the legal security of adoption. Nevertheless, despite the lack of legal security, many of the children in stable foster placements seemed to feel emotionally secure in their placements and considered them to be their permanent home. Others in stable foster care felt some ambivalence due to their feelings about their birth families, but most of these were nevertheless settled and happy in their placements.

We also found that, despite being placed at an older age, children in long-term foster placements may nevertheless do as well as adopted children on measures of emotional and behavioural difficulties. They also had similar scores on our measures of participation and progress at school. It is therefore encouraging to find that, in many respects, children in stable, long-term foster placements may do as well as those who are adopted. This is important, as adoption will not be appropriate for all children and not all children wish to be adopted.

At the same time, it is discouraging that adopted children were doing no better than those in stable foster care and that, on average, both groups were more likely to have mental health difficulties than the wider population of children. Even some settled children receiving excellent parenting showed high rates of disturbance, many years after they had entered these placements. For the children in our unstable care group, whose previous long-term foster placements had disrupted after three or more years, emotional and behavioural difficulties were particularly serious and had contributed to placement instability.

Children in all of these groups may therefore have high support needs. The fact that adopted children were doing no better than those in stable foster care indicates that they may need an equivalent level of support with mental health problems and any behavioural or educational diffi-culties. Currently, however, the regulatory framework governing financial assistance and other support and services to adoptive families is overly permissive and, in light of these findings, needs strengthening. Now that the Government's adoption support grant to local authorities has ended, levels of support to adoptive families may be determined as much by the resource decisions of local authorities as by levels of need.

The children in our unstable care group had entered care later, generally had greater emotional, behavioural and relationship difficulties and were less likely to be doing well on our measures of participation and progress at school. They had already had significantly worse scores on the SDQ eight years earlier, compared to children who were subsequently adopted or settled in long-term foster placements. In these circumstances, even high-quality substitute parenting may not necessarily produce substantial change. Evidence from a survey conducted eight years before our current survey indicated that children's former long-term foster carers had been more likely to be rejecting than the foster carers of children in more settled circumstances. Rejection is clearly harmful to children and every effort should be made to interrupt the negative spirals that can occur when difficult behaviour leads to lack of acceptance by carers, which may in turn lead to more difficult behaviour.

The age at which children are taken into care seems to be crucial. For some, late entry to care may have occurred because their difficulties only emerged, or came to social services' attention, at a later stage in their lives. However, it is also likely that local differences in policy and practice affect the nature and effectiveness of permanency planning. The question is: what can be done to improve planning and support for children in authorities that are less likely to place children for adoption, or to ensure stability in foster care? There are some issues over which local policy makers and senior managers may have more control, for example, in the proportion of resources that are devoted to increasing and supporting adoption, or to supporting children and foster carers, and in the mechanisms set up to ensure effective decision making and planning for permanence. Other potential drivers of local authority variation may be harder to address, such as staff shortages, the actions of local courts and local practice cultures.

Rates of children looked after vary between local authorities, and it is likely that local policy and practice in relation to thresholds for taking children into care may also have played a part in shaping the care careers of the children in this study. In authorities with high thresholds for care entry, children may be less likely to be reunified with parents (Dickens *et al*, 2007). Local thresholds may be influenced not only by concern about resources but by the bleak view of the care system evident in the Green Paper *Care Matters* and in much public and professional debate. Although there is clearly much that can be improved in relation to planning and support, these concerns about the quality of care may not necessarily apply to many children in long-term foster care. As this study has shown, children who successfully settle may feel reasonably secure despite being troubled, to varying degrees, by their relationships with their birth families. On most measures, they were doing no worse than adopted children, although still less well than children in the wider community.

Much of the evidence on poor outcomes for looked after children comes from studies of older children leaving care, but research on leaving care has found that children who have been looked after from a younger age in stable placements do relatively well and that it is those who enter as teenagers (and fail to settle) who have particularly poor education and employment outcomes (Dixon *et al*, 2006). Yet this lack of confidence in the quality of care may lead to a philosophy of "last resortism", which may leave some children unprotected or may delay their inevitable entry to care (Packman and Hall, 1998; Biehal, 2005; Masson, 2008). In these circumstances, delaying difficult decisions about entry to care, or delaying decisions about permanency, may mean that children lose their chance of adoption or, if adoption is not appropriate, of stable foster care. Clearly, there is a fine line to tread between offering high-quality support to keep children in their families and not exposing them to serious adversity for periods so lengthy as to substantially increase the risk of serious emotional or physical harm, which clearly has long-term consequences for them. This study has shown, however, that even if permanent adoptive or foster homes are found in which children experience loving and stable care, many children (and their carers or adoptive parents) are likely to need substantial ongoing support if they are to have a chance of realising their full potential. This is what children and their substitute families want. It should also be what local authorities endeavour to provide.

Appendix 1
Recruitment and data collection

Recruiting the survey sample

We had addresses and in many cases telephone numbers for carers and adoptive parents of children in the York sample who returned questionnaires in 2001. At that time, however, we did not raise with them the possibility of taking part in further research. Current contact details were checked with social services staff where possible.

We asked the local authorities to approach all the current adoptive parents/carers of both the York sample and the booster sample with an agreed letter on our behalf, forwarding a survey questionnaire. The covering letter was signed by the local authority and demonstrated that authority's support for the survey. In the event that the questionnaire was sent to an out-of-date address, labels were affixed to the envelopes requesting them to be forwarded, if the correct address was known, or returned to the research team if not. Where the carer did not respond, we asked the relevant agency to forward another letter on our behalf to make sure that a failure to respond meant that they did not wish to take part.

The local authorities also provided us with details of the children's current, or last, social workers. Where no workers with recent knowledge of the child were available, team managers were asked to provide some limited information derived, if possible, from the child's file. For children who had been adopted, we asked the adoption teams which member of staff had last been in contact with the child and their adoptive family. In cases where families had taken part in group activities arranged for adoptive families, had letterbox contact or had requested adoption support, contact was relatively recent, but in other cases social workers could provide little information. As a last resort, we asked the adoption team managers to provide as much information as possible from the child's file, although where this was the case, the returned questionnaires were often sparsely completed.

Our original intention was to use the booster sample to increase the total survey sample in each local authority to 30, with the number of additional children recruited to the booster sample in each authority determined by the number of York sample cases it already had. However, in practice, the number of children available for both the York and booster samples varied across authorities and it was this that ultimately determined the size of the booster sample we eventually sought to recruit from each research site. For example, our Outer London Borough had only three children who met the criteria for the York sample and only 15 who met the criteria for the booster sample, bringing their total to a maximum of 18. We sought to compensate for these recruitment difficulties by recruiting more children to the booster sample from other authorities.

Recruiting the interview sample

In order to maximise the size of our interview sample, it was essential that our recruitment materials were easily accessible to the young people as well as to their parents or carers. We decided to invest resources in the professional production of a full-colour leaflet, together with an audio disc for those who found it easier to listen to the information than read it. We also decided to involve children in similar circumstances to those in our target sample in the design of the materials. Following the model developed for recruiting children to a previous study of adoption, we worked closely with a graphic designer to produce draft information leaflets and consent sheets (Thomas *et al*, 1999). We then asked a voluntary agency which operated a local children's rights service to arrange a meeting with a group of looked after children who attended a weekly drama group that the service had set up. We offered to give gift vouchers to the children to thank them for their assistance and to provide food and drinks. Following discussion with their group's facilitator, the children agreed that we could attend one of their regular meetings to consult them about our recruitment materials.

We took drafts of our information and consent leaflets along to the meeting. The information leaflet was in a question-and-answer format. After an initial warm-up activity led by the group's usual facilitator, who was present throughout, the children initially dressed up as "foster carers" and "children", with the "foster carers" asking the questions in the leaflet and the "children" reading out each answer. The children rapidly decided that they all wanted to ask all the questions and to read out all the answers too. With much hilarity, a discussion followed, which was very productive. The young people were quite critical of some aspects of the draft and we encouraged them to make suggestions for improvements to the wording, colour scheme, text and layout. Among other suggestions, they insisted on the inclusion of cartoon figures, advised us on appropriate colour schemes for leaflets aimed either at boys or girls and also insisted that the offer of a £10 voucher be more obviously displayed. The look of the final versions of the leaflet was quite different to the draft and very much improved.

Following this meeting both the wording and the graphic design were revised. We eventually produced separate leaflets for boys and for girls, which were visually different although the wording was identical. These A4, colourful leaflets had four sides and, on the back page, included a photograph of the two researchers, which the children had chosen. A CD was recorded, which used the same conversational format as the leaflet, modified to suit the medium, and the questions were asked by a young person who was willing to be recorded. The audio disc and its cover were professionally produced by a local community media studio. A simpler leaflet and a consent sheet were also designed for the children's carers. Packs were posted to the carers who had provided their names and addresses. An accompanying letter requested the carers to pass the children's pack to their child and to discuss the information with them. The information packs contained:

- a covering letter to parent/carer
- an information leaflet for parent/carer
- a consent form for parents/carers (unless child was over 16)
- a pack for the young person, containing:
  − a colour leaflet (separate boy and girl versions)
  − an audio CD with cover to match the leaflet
  − a consent form for the young person.

Interviews with children

Initial drafts of our interview schedules for the interviews with children were much improved following consultation with our research advisory group and academic colleagues outside the group, including John Triseliotis and Beth Neil. Interviews with children and parents/carers were semi-structured and both covered similar topics. The children's interview was divided into seven sections:

- *About you*: This included a warm-up activity, in which children were provided with felt-tips and paper and asked to draw a poster showing what they liked doing. Interviewers chatted with them as they did this and prompted them, if necessary, with questions about their day-to-day lives at home, at school and in their leisure time. They were also invited to say how their friends might describe them and how they would describe themselves.
- *About this family*: This section included questions that explored their relationships with carers and others in the home and their sense of belonging.
- *Adoption: what you know about it*: This section was covered with the adopted children, using an adapted version of Brodzinsky's Children's Understanding of Adoption schedule and play people (Brodzinsky *et al*, 1984b).
- *About your story*: Children were invited to tell us why they thought they had come to live in this family, what explanations had been given to them about this and what they thought about the decisions that had been made about where they should live.
- *About the people in your life*: We used a sheet of paper on which was printed a series of colourful concentric circles. The central one was marked "really love" then, moving outwards, they were marked "love", "like", "don't like" and "really unhappy with". They were asked to choose play people to represent their friends and decide where to place them on the map. They were then asked to do this using the figures to represent members of their foster/adoptive family and, finally, they were asked if they wished to choose figures representing their birth parents and siblings and place these on the map. If

necessary, interviewers prompted them to explain why they had placed people where they had.

- *About the contact you have with people*: This included questions about who they were in contact with, if anyone, the type of contact, and a number of prompts about how they felt about this contact.
- *About the future*: This included questions about where they might live when they were "grown up" and their understanding of when this might occur, and an exploration of whether they viewed their foster/adoptive family as a family for life.

Interviewers adapted the style of the questions as appropriate to the age and intellectual capacity of the children, although, surprisingly, even the teenagers proved quite happy to take part in the activities involving play people. As might be expected, older children and teenagers were often more forthcoming than children of eight or nine years, and therefore required fewer prompts, but nevertheless the interview worked well with the majority of younger children.

Appendix 2
Sample attrition for the York sample

Children lost to follow-up in 2006

We identified 116 children eligible for inclusion in the York sample, according to the criteria set out in Chapter 4. Table A2.1 shows their placements in 2001 and 2006.

Table A2.1
Children in 2001 survey: placement status in 2006 (n = 116)

2001 placement	n	2006 placement	
Adopted	73	Adopted	55
		• by carer 16	
		• by stranger 39	
		Not in 2006 survey	*18*
Fostered	43	Carer adoption	1
		Stable foster care	15
		Unstable care	8
		Residence order	9
		Returned home	2
		Not in 2006 survey	*8*

We were unable to include 26 of these children in our 2006 survey. In seven cases, local authorities no longer had contact details for the children (usually because they had been placed for adoption in another local authority) and in four other cases, they refused to forward our questionnaire because the placement was known to be under stress. Sadly, one adoptive parent informed us that their child had recently died. In another 14 cases, neither the carer nor the social worker returned a questionnaire.

Through contacts with local authority staff and by examining the local authorities' administrative data, we managed to discover the current circumstances of many of the missing children. The majority (18) had been adopted by 2001 and the remaining eight children had been in foster care at that time. We managed to identify the current placement of five of the fostered children, but no information was available on the remaining three.

In order to discover how many adoptions had endured, we sought information from local authorities on the adopted children we were unable to include in our survey. Social services were able to provide information on five of the 18 missing adopted children. They knew for certain that three of these children were still living with their adoptive parents, that one child had recently died and that another adoption was known to have broken down.

We made every effort to find out what had happened to the 13 missing adopted children who remained. We discovered that none of these children were looked after by the local authorities that had placed them for adoption. Where they had been placed for adoption in a different local authority, we contacted social services there, who confirmed that the children had not entered their care. Although we do not know for certain, we think it is likely that these 13 adoptions had endured. The adoption teams that had placed them for adoption told us it was their policy to inform birth parents if any adoptive placements broke down and they felt

Table A2.2
Children in York sample lost to follow-up in 2006 (n = 26)

Placement in 2001	Placement in 2006	Number
Foster care (n = 8)	Foster care	1
	Adopted by stranger	1
	Adopted by carer	1
	Residence order	2
	No information available	3
Adopted (n = 18)	Still adopted	3
	Child died	1
	Disrupted	1
	Adoption thought to be continuing	13

confident they would have heard if any breakdowns had occurred. The fact that no information about an adoption breakdown was recorded in relation to these 13 children suggests that these placements were likely to be ongoing, although we cannot be absolutely certain.

Children missing from the 2006 survey: analysis of change on SDQ

It was important to check whether the results of our analysis of change over time on the Strengths and Difficulties Questionnaire (SDQ – our measure of mental health difficulties), presented in Chapter 9, were biased in any way by the loss of some children from the sample by the time of our 2006 follow-up. A key issue was whether, as a group, the children lost to follow-up might be more, or less, likely to have positive outcomes in 2006 than those we were able to include in our survey. As far as we knew, only one of the 18 missing adopted children had experienced an adoption breakdown, so the breakdown rate was somewhat smaller for this group (5%) than for the adopted children included in the 2006 survey (13%).

First, we examined whether the children for whom we had SDQ scores in both 2001 and 2006 were representative of all children in the same placement groups in our total survey sample. Table A2.3 compares the scores for children in the York sample included in the analysis of change on the SDQ to scores for the total survey sample.

For every group, mean scores were lower (better) for the sub-groups included in the change analysis compared to the same group in the total

Table A2.3
Mean SDQ scores 2006

Placement type in 2006	Total in survey sample Mean SDQ score (n) (n = 103)	Included in change analysis Mean SDQ score (n) (n = 54)
Carer adoption	12.68 (n = 22)	12.07 (n = 14)
Stranger adoption	11.68 (n = 34)	10.96 (n = 30)
Stable foster care	13.43 (n = 47)	10.8 (n = 10)

survey sample. However, this difference was more marked for the children in stable foster care, so the sub-group included in the change analysis may have had somewhat less serious emotional and behavioural difficulties, on average, than the total group of children in stable foster care in our full survey sample.

We then considered whether the children lost to follow-up were those with greater/lesser mental health difficulties than those whom we were able to include in our analysis of change on the SDQ. Mean scores for total difficulties on the SDQ (in 2001) were available for only 16 of the children lost to follow up. As Table A2.4 shows, scores on the SDQ were significantly lower (i.e. better) for the ten adopted children lost to follow-up than for those we were able to include in the 2006 survey, so the group we followed up had more serious emotional and behavioural difficulties, on average, than those we did not. However, we found a similar pattern for children who had been fostered in 2001, although the difference between the two fostered groups was not significant, as shown in Table A2.4.[76]

Table A2.4
Mean SDQ scores (2001) for those in or missing from 2006 survey

	In 2006 survey (n)	Not in 2006 survey (n)	Sig. p
In foster care in 2001 (n = 32)	15.49 (26)	12.29 (6)	.545 (ns)
Adopted by 2001 (n = 66)	11.04 (56)	6.73 (10)	.011

Had we been able to include the missing adopted children in our York sample in our 2006 survey, who comprised roughly one-fifth of the potential sample, the mean SDQ scores for the adopted group would have improved to some extent. However, roughly one-fifth of the fostered children were also lost to follow-up, and this group of missing children similarly had lower mean scores in 2001 than the fostered children who were included in our 2006 survey. Although this difference in scores

---

[76] Mann Whitney-U tests.

between the two groups of fostered children was smaller than that between the groups of adopted children, and was not significant, the pattern was nevertheless similar to that for the adopted children. For both groups, it was the children with less serious difficulties (in 2001) who were lost to follow-up. Had all the missing children been included in the 2006 survey, our comparison of change in SDQ scores for the two groups may therefore have come to broadly similar conclusions.

Finally, we considered whether the results of our analysis of change on the SDQ were influenced by the fact that the carer adoption group included a higher proportion of children with disabilities than the other groups and, as we saw in Chapter 8, children with disabilities are likely to have higher (worse) scores on the SDQ compared to children not reported to be disabled. Nine disabled children who had been adopted were included in the change analysis, six of whom had been adopted by carers. These accounted for 20 per cent of all adopted children in this analysis. However, 30 per cent (three) of those children in the stable foster care group who were included in the change analysis were also disabled, so it seems unlikely that disability would have had a major impact on the results of this analysis.

To sum up, we compared children missing from our change analysis to those included in it in three ways. First, we compared the sub-group of children included in our analysis of change on SDQ to those in the total survey sample for whom SDQ scores were available. This comparison showed that the fostered children included in our analysis of change on the SDQ had somewhat lower SDQ scores in 2006 than the total group of long-term fostered children in our survey sample. On average, they appeared to have less severe difficulties and may not, therefore, have been representative of all children in the sample who experienced stable foster care. Second, we compared the SDQ scores for 2001 for children included in our change analysis to those for children lost to follow-up. This analysis showed that those included in the change analysis had had more severe difficulties in 2001 than those lost to follow-up, but this was true for similar proportions of the adopted and the fostered children. Our findings on change over time for the adopted and fostered groups did not, therefore, appear to be biased as a result of sample attrition. Third, we considered whether there was a higher proportion of disabled children in the adopted group, which may have raised the mean SDQ score for this group, but found a similar proportion of disabled children in the fostered group.

References

Allen N. (2003) *Making Sense of the New Adoption Law*, Lyme Regis: Russell House Publishing

Ball C. (2005) 'The Adoption and Children Act 2002. A critical examination', *Adoption & Fostering*, 29:2, pp 6–17

Barth R. P. and Berry M. (1988) *Adoption and Disruption: Rates, Risks and Responses*, New York: Aldine de Gruyter

Beek M. and Schofield G. (2004) *Providing a Secure Base in Long-term Foster Care*, London: BAAF

Berridge D. and Cleaver H. (1987) *Foster Home Breakdown*, Oxford: Blackwell

Berridge D. (2007) 'Theory and explanation in child welfare: education and looked after children', *Child & Family Social Work*, 12, pp 1–10

Berridge D. and Saunders H. (2009) 'The Education of Fostered and Adopted Children', in Schofield G. and Simmonds J. (eds.) *The Child Placement Handbook. Research, Policy and Practice*, London: BAAF, pp 327–44

Berry M., Dylla D., Barth R. P. and Needell B. (1998) 'The role of open adoption in the adjustment of adopted children and their families', *Children and Youth Services Review*, 20:1/2, pp 151–71

Biehal N. and Sainsbury E. (1991) 'From values to rights in social work', *British Journal of Social Work*, 21, pp 245–57

Biehal N., Clayden J., Stein M. and Wade J. (1995) *Moving On. Young people and leaving care schemes*, London: HMSO

Biehal N. (2005) *Working with Adolescents. Supporting Families, Preventing Breakdown*, London: BAAF

Biehal N. (2006) *Reuniting looked after children with their families*, London: National Children's Bureau

Biehal N. (2007) 'Reuniting children with their families: reconsidering the evidence on timing, contact and outcomes', *British Journal of Social Work*, 37:5, pp 807–23

Bohman M. and Sigvardsson S. (1980) 'A prospective, longitudinal study of children registered for adoption', *Acta Psychiat. Sound*, 61, pp 339–55

Bone M. and Meltzer M. (1989) *OPCS Survey of disability in Great Britain: Report 3 – Prevalence of disability among children*, London: HMSO

Bowlby J. (1979) *The making and breaking of affectional bands*, London: Tavistock Publications

Brodzinsky D. M., Schechter D., Braff A. M. and Singer L. M. (1984a) 'Psychological and academic adjustment in adopted children', *Journal of Consulting and Clinical Psychology*, 52, pp 582–90

Brodzinsky D. M., Singer L. M. and Braff A. M. (1984b) 'Children's understanding of adoption', *Child Development*, 55:3, pp 869–78

Brodzinsky D. M. (1993) 'Long-term outcomes in adoption', *The Future of Children*, 3:1, Spring 1993, pp 154–66

Brodzinsky D. M. (2006) 'Family structural openness and communication openness as predictors in the adjustment of adopted children', *Adoption Quarterly*, 9:4

Carroll J. S., Olsen C. D. and Buckmiller N. (2007) 'Family boundary ambiguity: a 30 year review of theory, research and measurement', *Family Relations*, 56, pp 210–30

Cleaver H. (2000) *Fostering family contact*, London: The Stationery Office

Dance C. and Ruston A. (2005) 'Predictors of outcome for unrelated adoptive placements made during middle childhood', *Child and Family Social Work*, 10:4, pp 269–80

Department for Children, Schools and Families (2009a) *DCSF: Children Looked After in England (including adoption and care leavers) year ending 31 March 2009*, National Statistics/DCSF, London.

Department for Children, Schools and Families (2009b) *Outcome Indicators for Children Looked After. Twelve Months to September 2008 – England*, London: Department for Children, Schools and Families

Department for Education and Skills (2003) *Statistics of education: children adopted from care in England 2002–2003*, London: DfES

Department for Education and Skills (2004a) *Every Child Matters: Change for Children*, London: DfES

Department for Education and Skills (2004b) *Draft Regulations and Guidance for consultation: Care Planning and Special Guardianship*, London: DfES

Department for Education and Skills (2005) *Special guardianship guidance: Children Act 1989: The special guardianship regulations 2005*, London: Department for Education and Skills

Department for Education and Skills (2006) *Care Matters: Transforming the lives of children and young people in care*, London: Department for Education and Skills

Department for Education and Skills (2007a) *Care Matters: Time for change*, London: Department for Education and Skills

Department for Education and Skills (2007b) *Children looked after by local authorities year ending 31 March 2006*, London: Department for Education and Skills

Department of Health (1993) *Adoption: the future, Cm 2288*, London: HMSO

Department of Health (1995) *Child Protection. Messages from the Research*, London: HMSO

Department of Health (1998) *Adoption: Achieving the right balance (LAC 98 (20))*, London: DfES

Department of Health (2000) *Adoption: A new approach, White Paper, Cm 5017*, London: HMSO

Department of Health (2001a) *Children looked after by local authorities year ending 31 March 2000 England*, London: Department of Health

Department of Health (2001b) *National Adoption Standards for England*, London: Department of Health

Department of Health (2002) *Children Looked After by Local Authorities Year Ending 31 March 2001, England. Commentary*, vol. www.dcsf.gov.uk/rsgateway/DB/VOL/v000509/clacommentary.pdf, London: Department of Health

Department of Health and Social Security (1985) *Social Work Decisions in Child Care*, London: HMSO

Department of Health and Welsh Office (1992) *A Review of Adoption Law: Report to Ministers of an interdepartmental working group*, London: DH

Dickens J., Howell D., Thoburn J. and Schofield G. (2007) 'Children starting to be looked after by local authorities in England: an analysis of inter-authority variation and case centred decision making', *British Journal of Social Work*, 37:17

Dixon J., Wade J., Byford S., Weatherly H. and Lee J. (2006) 'Young people leaving care: a study of costs and outcomes', Report to the DfES, Social Work Research & Development Unit, York: University of York

Dixon J. (2007) 'Obstacles to participation in education, employment and training for young people leaving care', *Social Work & Social Services Review*, 13:2, pp 18–34

Family Rights Group (1986) *Promoting Links: Keeping Families and Children in Touch*, London: Family Rights Group

Farmer E. and Moyers S. (2008) *Kinship care: fostering effective family and friends placements*, London: Jessica Kingsley Publishers

Fox Harding L. M. (1991) *Perspectives in Child Care Policy*, London: Longmans

Franzen E. and Vinnerlung B. (2006) 'Foster children as young adults: many motherless, fatherless and orphaned. A Swedish national chort study', *Child and Family Social Work*, 11:3, pp 254–63

Fratter J., Rowe J., Sapsford D. and Thoburn J. (1991) *Permanent family placement: a decade of experience*, London: BAAF

Fravel D. L., McRoy R. G. and Grotevant H. D. (2000) 'Birthmother perceptions of the psychologically present adopted child: adoption openness and boundary ambiguity', *Family Relations*, 49, pp 425–33

Frazer L. and Selwyn J. (2005) 'Why are we waiting? The demography of adoption for children of black, Asian and black mixed parentage in England', *Child and Family Social Work*, 10:2, pp 135–48

George V. (1970) *Foster care: theory and practice*, London: Routledge and Kegan Paul

Gibbons J., Gallagher B., Bell C. and Gordon D. (1995) *Development after physical abuse in early childhood: a follow-up study of children on protection registers*, London: HMSO

Gilligan R. (2000) 'The importance of listening to the child in foster care', in Kelly G. and Gilligan R. (eds) *Issues in Foster Care: Policy, Practice and Research*, Jessica Kingsley Publishers

Goldstein J., Freud A. and Solnit A. (1973) *Beyond the Best Interests of the Child*, New York: Free Press

Goodman R. (1997) 'The Strengths and Difficulties Questionnaire: A Research Note', *Journal of Child Psychology and Psychiatry*, 38:5, pp 581–86

Gordon D., Parker R. and Loughran F. (2000) *Disabled Children In Britain: A re-analysis of the OPCS Disability Survey*, London: The Stationery Office

Harwin J., Owen M., Locke R. and Forrester D. (2003) *Making Care Orders Work. A study of care plans and their implementation*, London: The Stationery Office

Held J. (2005) *Qualitative Study: 'The Placement Stability of Looked after Children'*, London: Department for Education and Skills

HM Government (2010) *The Children Act 1989 Guidance and Regulations. Volume 2: Care Planning, Placement and Case Review*, London: Department for Childrens, Schools and Families

HM Government/Communities and Local Government (2008) *National Indicators for Local Authorities and local Authority Partnerships. Handbook of Definitions Annex 2: Children and Young People*, London: HM Government/ Communities and Local Government

Holman B. (1975) 'The place of fostering in in social work', *British Journal of Social Work*, 5:1, pp 3–29

Howe D. (1998) *Patterns of adoption*, Oxford: Blackwell Science

Howe D. and Feast J. (2000) *Adoption, search and reunion: the long-term experience of adopted adults*, London: The Children's Society

Ivaldi G. (2000) *Surveying Adoption. A Comprehensive Analysis of Local Authority Adoptions*, London: BAAF

Jackson S. and Martin P. (1998) 'Surviving the care system: education and resilience', *Journal of Adolescence*, 21, pp 569–83

Jackson S. (2002) 'Promoting stability and continuity in care away from home', in McNeish D. *et al* (eds) *What works for children?*, Buckingham: Open University Press

Kadushin A. (1970) *Adopting Older Children*, New York: Columbia University Press

Kohler J., Grotevant H. D. and McRoy R. G. (2002) 'Adopted adolescents' preoccupation with adoption: the impact on adoptive family relationships', *Journal of Marriage and family*, 64, pp 93–104

Lahti J. (1982) 'A follow-up study of foster children in permanent placements', *Social Service Review*, pp 556–71

Lewis J. (2004) 'Adoption: the nature of policy shifts in England and Wales 1972–2002', *International Journal of Law, Policy and Family*, 18, pp 235–55

Lindheim O. and Dozier M. (2007) 'Caregiver commitment to foster children: the role of child behaviour', *Child Abuse and Neglect*, 31, pp 361–74

Lowe N. (1997) 'The changing face of adoption', *Child and Family Law Quarterly*, 9:4

Lowe N., Murch M., Borkowski M., Weaver A., Beckford V. and Thomas C. (1999) *Supporting adoption. Reframing the approach*, London: BAAF

Lowe N., Murch M., Bader K., Borkowski M., Copner R., Lisles C. *et al* (2002) *The Plan for the Child. Adoption or long-term fostering*, London: BAAF

Luckock B. and Hart A. (2005) 'Adoptive family life and adoption support: policy ambivalence and the development of effective services', *Child and Family Social Work*, 10:2, pp 125–34

Macaskill C. (2002) *Safe Contact? Children in Permanent Placement and Contact with Their Relatives*, Lyme Regis: Russell House Publishing

Maluccio A. and Fein E. (1983) 'Permanency planning: a redefinition', *Child Welfare*, 62:3, pp 195–201

Masson J. (2003) 'The impact of the Adoption and Children Act 2002. Part 2. The provision of services for children and families', *Family Law*, 33, pp 644–49

Masson J. (2008) 'The state as parent: the reluctant parent? The problems of parents of last resort', *Journal of Law and Society*, 35:1, pp 52–74

McSherry D., Larkin E., Fargas M., Kelly G., Robinson C., Macdonald G., *et al* (2008) *From Care to Where? A Care Pathways and Outcomes Report for Practitioners*, Belfast: Institute of Child Care Research, Queen's University Belfast

Meltzer H., Gatward R., Goodman R. and Ford T. (2000) *The Mental Health of Children and Adolescents in Great Britain*, London: The Stationery Office

Meltzer M., Gatward R., Corbin T., Goodman R. and Ford T. (2003) *The Mental Health of Young People Looked After by Local Authorities in England*, London: The Stationery Office

Morgan D. H. J. (1996) *Family Connections*, Cambridge: Polity Press

Morgan D. H. J. (1999) 'Risk and family practices', in Silva E. B. and Smart C. (eds) *The New Family?*, London: Sage

Munro E. and Ward H. (2008) 'Balancing parents' and very young children's rights in care proceedings: decision-making in the context of the Human Rights Act 1998', *Child and Family Social Work*, 13:2, pp 227–34

Neil E., Beek M. and Schofield G. (2003) 'Thinking about and managing contact in permanent placements: the differences and similarities between adoptive parents and foster carers', *Journal of Clinical Child Psychology and Psychiatry*, 8:3, pp 401–18

Neil E. and Howe D. (eds) (2004) 'The "Contact after Adoption Study": Face-to-face contact, in *Contact in Adoption and Permanent Foster Care: Research, theory and practice*, London: BAAF

Office for National Statistics (2007) *Social Trends 37*, Basingstoke: Palgrave Macmillan

Office for National Statistics (2008) *Social Trends 38*, Basingstoke: Palgrave Macmillan

Oliver C., Owen C., Statham J. and Moss P. (2001) *Figures and Facts. Local Authority Variation on Indicators Concerning Child Protection and Children Looked After*, London: Institute of Education

Owen M. (1999) *Novices, old hands and professionals: adoption by single people*, London: BAAF

Packman J. and Jordan B. (1991) 'The Children Act: looking forward, looking back', *British Journal of Social Work*, 21, 1991, pp 315–27

Packman J. and Hall C. (1998) *From Care to Accommodation*, London: The Stationery Office

Parker R. (1966) *Decisions in Child Care*, London: Allen and Unwin

Pemberton C. (2010) 'Care referral highs "here to stay", *Community Care*, 21 January 2010

Phillips R. D. (2007) 'The need for information on how the attachment difficulties of adopted and looked after children affect their schooling', *Adoption & Fostering*, 31:3, pp 28–38

PIU (2000) *The Prime Minister's Review of Adoption*, London: Cabinet Office

Quinton D., Rushton A., Dance C. and Mayes D. (1997) 'Contact between children placed away from home and their birth parents: research issues and evidence', *Clinical Child Psychology and Psychiatry*, 2:3, pp 393–1045

Quinton D., Rushton A., Dance C. and Mayes D. (1998) *Joining New Families: a Study of Adoption and Fostering in Middle Childhood*, Chichester: Wiley

Rowe J. and Lambert L. (1973) *Children Who Wait*, London: Association of British Adoption and Fostering Agencies

Rowe J., Cain H., Hundleby M. and and Keane A. (1984) *Long Term Foster Care*, London: Batsford/BAAF

Rowe J., Hundleby M. and Garnett L. (1989) *Child Care Now*, London: Batsford/ BAAF

Rowlands J. and Statham J. (2009) 'Numbers of children looked after in England: a historical analysis', *Child and Family Social Work*, 14:1, pp 79–89

Rubin D., O'Reilly A., Luan X. and Localio A. (2007) 'The impact of placement stability on behavioural well-being for children in foster care', *Pediatrics*, 119, pp 336–44

Rushton A., Treseder J. and Quinton D. (1988) *New parents for older children*, London: BAAF

Rushton A. and Minnis H. (1997) 'Annotation: Transracial family placements', *Journal of Clinical Child Psychology and Psychiatry*, 38, pp 147–59

Rushton A. and Dance C. (2002) *Adoption Support Services for Families in Difficulty. A Literature Review and UK Survey*, London: BAAF

Rushton A. (2004) 'A scoping and scanning review of research on the adoption of children placed from public care', *Clinical Child Psychology and Psychiatry*, 9:1, pp 89–106

Rushton A. and Monck E. (2009) *Enhancing Adoptive Parenting. A test of effectiveness*, London: BAAF

Rutter M. (2000) 'Children in substitute care: some conceptual considerations and research implications', *Children and Youth Services Review*, 22:9/10, pp 685–703

Samuels G. (2009) 'Ambiguous loss of home: the experience of familial (im)permanence among young adults with foster care backgrounds', *Children and Youth Services Review*, 31, pp 1229–39

Schofield G., Beek M., Sargent K. and Thoburn J. (2000) *Growing up in Foster Care*, London: British Agencies for Adoption and Fostering

Schofield G., Thoburn J., Howell D. and Dickens J. (2007) 'The search for stability and permanence. Modelling the pathways of long-stay looked after children', *British Journal of Social Work*, 37, p 14

Schofield G., Ward E., Warman A., Simmonds J. and Butler J. (2008) *Permanence in Foster Care: A Study of Care Planning and Practice in England and Wales*, London: BAAF

Schofield G. (2009) 'Permanence in foster care', in Schofield G. and Simmonds J. (eds.) *The Child Placement Handbook. Research, Policy and Practice*, London: BAAF

Seglow J., Pringle M. K. and Wedge P. (1972) *Growing up adopted*, Windsor: NFER

Sellick C. and Thoburn J. (1996) *What works in family placement?*, Barkingside: Barnardos

Selwyn J. and Quinton D. (2004) 'Stability, permanence, outcomes and support. Foster care and adoption compared', *Adoption & Fostering*, 28:4, p 10

Selwyn J., Sturgess W., Quinton D. and Baxter C. (2006) *Costs and Outcomes of Non-Infant Adoptions*, London: BAAF

Selwyn J. and Wijedasa D. (2009) 'The placement of looked after minority ethnic children', in Schofield G. and Simmonds J. (eds) *The Child Placement Handbook. Research, Policy and Practice*, London: BAAF

Shaw C. (1998) *Remember my messages*, London: Who Cares? Trust

Sinclair I., Gibbs I. and Wilson K. (2005a) *Foster carers. Why They Stay and Why They Leave*

Sinclair I., Wilson K. and Gibbs I. (2005b) *Foster Placements. Why They Succeed and Why They Fail*, London: Jessica Kingsley Publishers

Sinclair I., Baker C., Wilson K. and Gibbs I. (2005c) *Foster Children. Where They Go and How They Get On*, London: Jessica Kingsley Publishers

Sinclair I., Baker C., Lee J. and Gibbs I. (2007) *The Pursuit of Permanence A Study of the English Care System*, London: Jessica Kingsley Publishers

Social Services Inspectorate (2000) *Adopting Changes. Survey and Inspection of Local Councils' Adoption Services*, London: Department of Health

Tarren-Sweeney M. (2007) 'Retrospective and concurrent predictors of the mental health of children in care', *Children and Youth Services Review*, 30, pp 1–25

Thoburn J., Murdoch A. and O'Brien A. (1986) *Permanence in Child Care*, Oxford: Basil Blackwell

Thoburn J. (1990) *Success and failure in permanent family placements*, Aldershot: Avebury

Thoburn J., Norford L. and Rashid S. (2000) *Permanent family placement for children of minority ethnic origin*, London: Jessica Kingsley Publishers

Thoburn J. (2002) *Adoption and permanence for children who cannot live safely with birth parents or relatives*, Quality Protects Research Briefing 5, Department of Health: Making Research Count, Research in Practice

Thoburn J. (2005) 'Stability through adoption for children in care', in Axford N., *et al* (eds) *A Festschrift for Roger Bullock. Forty Years of Research, Policy and Practice in Children's Services*, Chichester: John Wiley & Sons

Thomas C., Beckford V., Murch M. and Lowe N. (1999) *Adopted children speaking*, London: BAAF

Treasury/DfES (2007) *Policy Review on Children and Young People. Discussion paper*, HM Treasury

Triseliotis J. (1990) *Foster Care Outcomes. Research Highlight*, London: National Children's Bureau

Triseliotis J., Shireman, J. and Hundleby, M. (1997) *Adoption: theory, policy and practice*, London: Cassell

Triseliotis J., Borland M. and Hill M. (2000) *Delivering Foster Care*, London: BAAF

Triseliotis J. (2002) 'Long-term fostering or adoption? The evidence examined', *Child and Family Social Work*, 7:1, pp 23–34

van den Dries L., Juffer F., van IJzendoorn M. and Bakermans-Kranenburg M. (2009) 'Fostering security? A meta-analysis of attachment in adopted children', *Children and Youth Services Review*, 31, pp 410–21

Wade J., Biehal N., Clayden J. and Stein M. (1998) *Going Missing: Young People Absent from Care*, Chichester: Wiley

Wade J. (2006) 'Support for young people leaving care in the UK', in McAuley C., *et al* (eds) *Enhancing the wellbeing of children and families through effective interventions – UK and USA evidence for practice*, London: Jessica Kingsley Publishers, pp 228–39

Wade J., Dixon J. and Richards A. (2010) *Special Guardianship in Practice*, London: BAAF

Ward H. (1995) *Looking After Children: Research into Practice*, London: HMSO

Ward H. and Skuse T. (2001) 'Performance targets and stability of placements for children long looked after away from home', *Children and Society*, 15:5, pp 333–46

Ward H., Munro E. R. and Dearden C. (2006) *Babies and Young Children in Care*, London: Jessica Kingsley Publishers

Williams J. (2004) 'Social work, liberty and law', *British Journal of Social Work*, 34, pp 27–52

Wright L., Flynn C. and Welch W. (2007) 'Adolescent adoption and the birth family', *Journal of Public Child Welfare*, 1:1, pp 35–63

Index

Compiled by Elisabeth Pickard